The PORTABLE POETRY WORKSHOP

JACK MYERS

Australia Canada Mexico Singapore Spain United Kingdom United States

The Portable Poetry Workshop
Jack Myers

Publisher: *Michael Rosenberg*
Development Editors: *Marita Sermolins* and *Kristin Swanson*
Production Manager: *Michael Burggren*
Director of Marketing: *Lisa Kimball*
Marketing Manager: *Katrina Byrd*
Manufacturing Manager: *Marcia Locke*
Compositor, Text Designer: *Shepherd, Inc.*
Cover Art: *Werner Hoeflich, Untitled (AquaStripe), 1998, oil on canvas.*
Cover Designer: *Circa 86, Inc.*
Printer: *Transcontinental*

Printed in Canada.
1 2 3 4 5 6 7 8 9 10 07 06 05 04

For more information, contact Wadsworth, 25 Thomson Place, Boston, Massachusetts 02210 USA, or you can visit our Internet site at http://www.wadsworth.com

ISBN: 0-155-06002-3

Library of Congress Cataloging-in-Publication Data

Myers, Jack Elliott,
The portable poetry workshop : a field guide to poetic technique / by Jack Myers.
p. cm.
Includes index.
ISBN 0-15-506002-3
1. Poetry--Authorship. 2. Poetics. I. Title.

PN1059.A9M94 2003
808.1--dc21

2003044989

Contents

Preface

The Portable Poetry Workshop is a book for poets who are interested in the writing workshop method. Here they will find a useful guide for generating content, trying out contemporary techniques, understanding modern conventions, considering certain "craft moves," and generally firming up their own personal aesthetic for the composing and revising of their work. The focus on *technique,* whose study and application will not in the least demystify or puncture the beauty and exhilarating effects of poetry, serves the poet in the same way that any tool might help a builder to create more effectively. In fact, the etymology of the word *technique,* itself, pertains to *making.*

This book is not meant to replace or compete with an individual teacher's perspectives or the preferences that he or she brings to a workshop; it is merely meant as a craft checklist and guide for the working poet. This book does not focus on the basic devices of poetry per se (such as symbol, metaphor, synecdoche, metonymy, traditional fixed forms, meter, and rhyme schemes, etc.), all of which are rightfully time-honored tools taught the world over in literature courses and textbooks. There's no need for yet another book on that. So this book has compiled workshop methods, strategies, techniques, perspectives, and terminology meant to provide practical, hands-on suggestions for the shaping and reshaping of content and form as they derive from the transforming interplay among experience, memory, and imagination. It's what you would expect a well-trained, working poet-teacher would offer to a college workshop. Many of the terms in the book have been informally coined in the colloquial style of workshop parlance to facilitate reference and description; others are traditional terms.

The basic aim of a workshop is to inculcate in students—through questions, discussion, and critique—a format and a procedure for anticipating the many different points of view offered by workshop members. In time this process becomes internalized as a paradigm or forum that poets can refer to in the solitary work of the imagination. Simply put, the aim of this book is the aim of any poetry workshop: to make writers better and more objective readers of their own work and to accelerate their artistic growth through a developmental process.

The book begins with a discussion of imagination, creativity, and consciousness; moves on to consider ways to technically generate and connect content; proceeds to exemplify the three other main structural aspects of a poem (opening, closure, title); goes on to examine specifics of free verse form and technique; considers effective aspects of style in terms of over-writing and under-writing; offers an array of types of poems; and ends with some practical considerations. But the reader is welcome to dip into the book peripatetically to read at will about lineation; imagery; sonics; cinematic techniques; syntax; characterization; lateral, horizontal, and vertical tensions; thematic, argumentative, and natural shapes; logic; juxtaposition; narrative elements; and a host of technical moves within these larger categories. Generously salted into each section are comments, discussion, exercises, and examples by poets who show skill in the topic under discussion. So, the book can be read as (1) a discussion of craft and theory issues; (2) a reference work on technique; and (3) an anthology of poems.* Also, words that appear in boldface (for example, **metaphor**) are briefly defined in the Glossary at the back of the book.

It should be noted that the context of the technique being discussed determines the function of a device and how it is viewed, although there could well be additional ways in which the technique functions. Oftentimes a technique or device, such as a simile, may be viewed as an example of a kind of transition, but that same construction in other contexts of usage could also be an example of substitution, or a way to extend or elaborate content. As another example, an address to a specific person might be considered for the discussion of an apostrophe, or it could also fall under the category of supplying texture and detail.

Jack Myers

*Due to the sometimes prohibitive cost of reprinting some poems, I have resorted to using some poems twice for different examples of technique and style; in other cases, I have merely cited the authors and titles of poems in the hope that the reader might then locate and read these works. In other cases, the examples without attribution are my own.

REVIEWERS

Paul Allen, Jr.
College of Charleston

Ben Bennani
Truman State University

Mark Christensen
Bemidji State University

Michael Colonnese
Methodist College

Jonathan Holden
Kansas State University

Getting Started

The very aim of art—to fix the ineffable—is a paradoxical, impossible, and yet sacred task. Its impulse is probably no different from the same urge that birds have to sing or animals have to grunt, squeal, cluck, or bleat: the urge to manifest the inner. And the nature of poetry itself, beyond language and the art's elaborate history of conventions, is all about process, shaping whatever we are trying to sculpt from inchoate fog that allows us to feel what it is to be human. Mark Strand, in an article in the *New York Times Book Review,* referred to this opaque and antediluvian quality in saying:

> Poetry is language at its most beguiling and seductive while it is, at the same time, elusive, seeming to mock one's desire for reduction, for plain and available order. It is not just that various meanings are preferable to a single dominant meaning. It may be that something beyond meaning is being communicated, something that originated not with the poet but in the first dim light of language, in some period of beforeness.
>
> Therefore, reading poetry often seems like searching for the unknown, for something that lies at the heart of experience but cannot be pointed out or described without being altered or diminished, something that nevertheless can be contained so that it is not so terrifying. It is not knowledge that poetry contains, at least not as I conceive knowledge; rather it is some occasion for belief, some reason for assent, some avowal of being. It is not knowledge because it is never revealed. It is mysterious or opaque, and even as it invites the reader, it wards off the reader.

And yet, despite this mysterious and evasive arena at the very center of the project we call art, something larger than and beyond us calls us to it and, in the act of creativity, something profound in us is satisfied. Strand says:

> Without poetry we would have either silence or banality, the former leaving us to our own inadequate devices for experiencing illumination, the latter cheapening with generalization what we wished to have for ourselves alone, turning our experience into impoverishment, our sense of ourselves into embarrassment.

So, keeping the more spiritual and arcane mission of art in mind, we necessarily turn from the sublime to the practical, to the practice and work of poetry, the craft in the art, which we must learn and relearn for that moment when whatever's beyond what can be practiced aligns itself with our skill. There is, of course, in the art of poetry a highly technical legacy accumulated through its historically long lineage. The terminology of the craft, which probably contains more technical terms than any other art, rivals those found in the domain of a science. So, a cautionary word or two about the ultimate and relative value of technique *vis à vis* art seems to be in order. In an interview this editor conducted with the poet W. S. Merwin, which appeared in the *Southwest Review* in 1982, Merwin said:

> In an age when time and technique encroach hourly, or appear to, on the source itself of poetry, it seems as though what is needed for any particular nebulous hope that may become a poem is not a manipulable, more or less predictably recurring pattern, but an unduplicatable resonance, something that would be like an echo except that is repeating no sound.

Which brings us to getting started.

There's nothing more daunting than feeling the impulse to write, yet not having any subject while facing the blank page. So, either consciously or through unconscious habit, poets have developed a slew of approaches, stances, exercises, rituals, and techniques intended to soften and make comfortable this moment of encounter and to avoid stultification. The poet William Carlos Williams had a kind of workmanlike, "Just do it!" attitude toward writing: basically, he said that a writer is one who writes. Take anything flat, a piece of paper, a shingle, and just put pen to it. One hundred eighty degrees away, William Stafford had a much softer and sympathetic attitude toward the creative process. Each morning he'd get up, and with the spirit of a child's wondering, he'd adopt a welcoming and entertaining attitude toward whatever might unexpectedly arise from his memory and imagination. If a poem came from that, fine; if it didn't, fine. Here are more specific and practical ideas to getting started and sustaining writing.

Sacred space. A poet must consistently put aside a block of time during the day that is reserved solely for reading and/or writing, or quite possibly, for just daydreaming and musing. This time-as-space is sacrosanct, inviolate. Let nothing intrude upon it. Under this self-imposed mandate, the poet will be invulnerable to any impingement on writing: a phone call, some leftover housework, errands, friends, and families' needs. You must keep in mind that no one in the world cares if you write a poem. Most people don't want to be bothered about it when you do produce something. This may sound harsh and cynical, but just test it: stand on any busy corner anywhere in the country and, in one hand, have for sale the poems you've written; in the other, for the same price, have for sale a "gimme cap" with the words *poets make heroic couplets.* See which makes money first and fastest. It is the poet, first and last, who has to make sure there's a time and place in which to write; only then will people take the inviolability of that time as seriously as the poet does.

Reading. The quickest and most effective means to ease one's way into writing is to read—preferably others' poetry. It is a generally accepted rule of thumb among poets that 40% of learning to write well is composed of reading. Why is this? Because poetry writing requires a special kind of "ear" and stereoscopic, "double vision," one which William Stafford called "squinting," in which a simultaneous confluence of literal and figurative levels of meaning occurs, and unlocks in you an inner "zone" to poetry writing. Reading poetry, or any good, imaginative literature, quickly establishes you in that rarified aesthetic place. It is to writing what the sun is to the wilderness. And this holds as true for beginning the writing of a specific poem as it does for a poet's overall, long-term poetic development. It takes no more than an hour a day of writing to produce a substantial body of work over the years. And this is made easier, more enjoyable, and richer by adding a small, 15 minute reading component to the writing session.

Imitation. A close second to reading in order to stimulate writing is to exercise and challenge one's skill through imitation, by trying to write in the manner of or in outright tracing of another's poet's style. It's the best way to absorb technique and to make it a conscious, accessible poetic tool that can be reached for whenever needed. Just about every poet you will read has some technique to offer, and the best way to discover that, to see it and make it your own, is by trying to write in the style of the poet you're reading. If you model your exercise-poem after the same syntax and sentence structure, the same frequency and kinds of images and **figurative** language, the same stanzaic structure, you will quickly get inside the style of another poet. Imitating Wallace Stevens' work can teach you how to use images to express abstract, philosophical themes effectively; imitating the poetry of Sharon Olds, with her use of the personal anecdote and narrative, will show you how to move easily from the personal to the universal; imitating Charles Simic's work will highlight and develop the use of images that have resonance and dimensionality, their own inner lives. Every serious student of art—in painting, dance, music, sculpture—passes through a *mandatory* imitation stage that teaches the student how to technically accomplish certain illusions. These influences become the shoulders he or she will stand on to become accomplished. Why should poetry, which, yes, comes from the heart, and, yes, which doesn't require the learning of a new medium (but which has a longer history than any of the other arts, and which has literally thousands of technical terms) be any different? Especially when the art requires control of denotative meaning.

Feeling. Feeling is opposed to "knowing." Theodore Roethke said "We go by feeling, what is there to know?" Your intellect is involved in poetry writing, but, as psycholinguists have discovered, thinking comes from and comes after feeling. If there were no feelings, no instinct, no unbidden emergence of memory and imagination, there would be nothing to think about. The point is that the majority of poems are written from intense feeling, so there's no better place to work from than whatever you might feel strongly about at the moment. Of course, feeling strongly per se doesn't have much to do with writing poetry well—a scream or gasp is not a poem—but if one is interested in writing poetry, it's a primary place to work from.

Freewriting. Just as visual artists sometimes lead their minds out of the rut of habitual thinking and seeing by drawing with their "inferior" hand, so poets often loosen up their set, rational, daily modes of thinking with the practice of "freewriting," writing automatically without thought of or reflection back upon whatever it is they are writing. What this writing might mean, where it comes from, and whether its spelling and grammar are correct or not do not matter. The one rule is that there are no rules except to keep going in order to loosen the strictures of convention and habit. The **surrealists** invented a chance game of poetry called *Cadavre Exquis* ("The Exquisite Corpse") in which each of a number of poets would fill in prescribed grammatical units in a line without having seen any previous lines, a practice that almost always led to novel results. The idea was to reach a new and very different kind of consciousness: "to burn consciousness to the bone," as André Breton said. The point is not so much of paying attention to what gets written as getting beyond the banal and unimaginative quality of normal rationality so that the enormous hypofield of the unconscious becomes engaged.

Journal writing. The literary journal is also a time-honored writer's tradition. Keep in mind that this is a totally free personal space—as free as dreaming is—within which anything goes. You can buy anything from a fancy leather journal with a brass lock to a loose-leaf notebook; what goes into it may be meticulously thought out or scribbled down in a wild and messy hand. Each journal writer sets his or her own style and standards and content. The journal might contain nightly dreams, drawings and doodles, snatches of phrasing, reactions to things read, questions about craft, daily events, ever-changing relationships, specific images, figures of speech, references, a list of favorite foods—anything that might be fodder for a poem or literary thinking. The function of a journal is to keep the poet's attention trained on the aesthetic domain within. And years later, the journal will be a valuable record that tracks your poetic development.

Illustrated below are the concentric circles of daily, long-term, lifelong, and the universal, archetypal domains of interest in which we reside. We must enter into and create an interplay among them if poetry writing is to produce rich and lasting results. In order to write importantly, our minds must perforate the circle of our ordinary, daily concerns, and enter into the realms of the more resonant inner spaces of human beliefs, experience, feelings, and values.

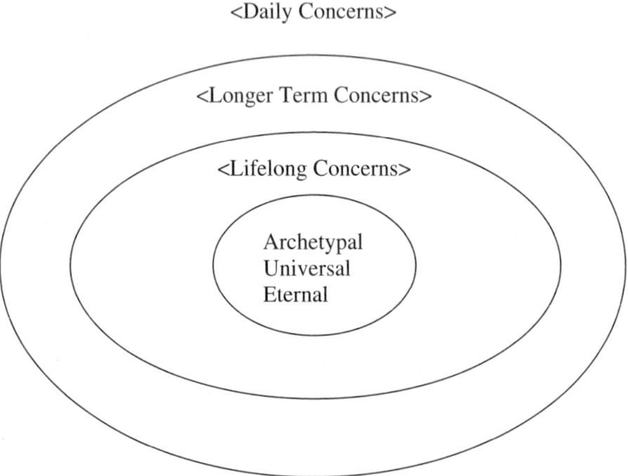

Reading, imitation, feeling, free writing, and locating and exploring one's feelings in a journal are all methods by which it's possible to layer and unite these concentric levels of living and meaning.

CHAPTER

1

General Considerations

CREATIVITY AND CONSCIOUSNESS

Origins

What are the origins of creativity? To theorize on this question, it might be easiest if we were to take a very distant, outside perspective, say that of an alien visitor from another galaxy. In studying the basis for human life, you would quickly see that nature itself loves to create. No matter what level of organic and inorganic existence you might look at, you would see the processes of evolution and devolution at work. The table of elements shows a very orderly evolution from simple to complex molecular structures—inorganic matter evolves into organic matter, which devolves back to inorganic matter and energy. In the hierarchies of biology, you'd see one-celled entities evolve into multi-celled plants, and then the panoply of animal forms of which man is the crowning achievement. On the human plane, in the realm of consciousness, something miraculous happens: man is able to investigate and contemplate his own origins. As Carl Sagan is famous for saying, "We are the stars reaching out to contemplate ourselves." This is literally true. Built into us is a kind of "hyper-impulse," an unconscious push always to transcend our present state of consciousness while staying rooted in our instincts and animal nature. This is the impulse that predisposes us to want to create, to compete, to hone our skills, and to evolve higher by trying to achieve the more difficult. Our brain, the organ that translates our experience of the world into consciousness, according to studies done at the National Institutes of Health, displays three distinct hierarchical stages that recapitulate our evolution (the triune brain theory): the hindbrain, the midbrain, and the forebrain, with each part assigned more or less pyramidally arranged powers, from basic reptilian instinctual responses of aggression, security, and defense, to a mammalian sense of community, to the human projective powers of abstraction and imagination. There is a constant, dynamic, and simultaneous interaction among the parts of the brain whose very function is to make connections within a chaos of activity, and whose impulse is to organize these connections into the orderly formations characteristic of creativity.

How It Functions

Memory and present experience form the floor from which the imagination is able to make its leaps. The creative process seems to work best when we are relaxed and receptive, which brings to mind Wordsworth's definition of poetry:

> the spontaneous overflow of powerful feelings; it takes its origin from emotion recollected in tranquility: the emotion is contemplated till by a species of reaction the tranquility gradually disappears, and an emotion, kindred to that which was before the subject of contemplation, is gradually produced, and does itself actually exist in the mind. In this mood successful composition generally begins. . . .

This state of receptivity that forms the atmosphere for creativity seems to be galvanized into action, many times on the unconscious level, by the power of suggestion triggered by our associations and powers of deduction. The subconscious takes whatever particular information is sent to it by our normal powers of self-awareness and dips that finite piece of information into a bath of generic types. For instance, if you see a bird, the unconscious will take that suggested cue and evoke the category of flight or maybe symbols representing freedom or flow. That, in turn (or possibly simultaneously) reacts with memory, which might offer up specific instances of other bird-related experiences. Then the chain reaction and interchange between memory and imagination, guided by rational and poetic logic, kicks in. The linkage in the chain reaction seems to work as metaphor and simile do, through substitutions, identities, proximity, and/or a comparison of similar and dissimilar things. For instance, if we were to meet someone and take an immediate liking or disliking to that person without quite knowing why, we can assume that memory or intuition in our unconscious has sent suggestive cues about that person's appearance, attitude, manners, or means of expression. That unconscious reaction or untranslated, unconscious knowledge then forms itself into feeling that, when worked on by the conscious mind, translates into our reaction. For poets, the point is that by paying attention to these unconscious signals we become aware of the experience in terms of meaning; we become conscious of what the unconscious is "saying."

Interaction Between Consciousness and Unconsciousness

If there is a first rule in developing self-awareness while in the throes of the creative process, it is to train yourself to watch your unconscious at work, to develop more acutely your mind's ability to observe and track its own workings. This uncanny human power of the mind's ability to watch itself think is called **apperception.** Typically, the unconscious state maintains a receptive mode; the conscious state is typically in an active mode. On the conscious level of experience, the mind's main task is, through observation and attention, to perform the analytical function of discrimination, a process that, opposite to the deductive mode of the unconscious, works inductively. Through the senses, it takes finite material from the world and thinks rationally about that information; in other words, it observes, analyzes, categorizes, and names whatever streams out of the unconscious. For the creative process to work well there has to be an ongoing harmony between these conscious and unconscious levels of awareness. Trying to force associations or meanings merely by way of rational logic cuts off layers of **resonance** and the spirit of creativity. On the other hand, merely writing automatically from an unimpeded stream of consciousness may produce interestingly bizarre and fascinatingly serendipitous material, but it's often disorganized and meaningless.

So while the unconscious may perceive very acutely, with the directness and simplicity of a child, it doesn't also understand the cultural, historical, ethical, or practical context of what it's receiving. This is why its messages in imagery are inscrutable, because it is "uncivilized" and it has no alternative but to combine and synthesize its content from its limited knowledge of what it knows. The unconscious isn't "wrong," it's just limited. There has to be a negotiation and translation between conscious and unconscious thought if the products of creativity are to have meaning, especially to others. Another point worth mentioning is the distinction between the mind's two different currencies of awareness: the unconscious, stemming from the hindbrain, thinks by way of images; the consciousness thinks in verbal language and **figures of speech.** This is why it is often difficult to understand dreams; we are trying to decode images from the primitive, symbolic part of the brain into an understanding through language in the higher evolved forebrain.

Unconscious Operations

Let's look at the unconscious operations of imagination, fantasy, and association. There's an important distinction between the characters of imagination and fantasy, or what Samuel Coleridge called "fancy." The process of fantasizing seems to be the purer, more basic, more other worldly operation of the two. Imagination capitalizes upon fantasy's powers of pure evocation and adds a rational, conscious, directing aspect to it. It is imagination that has a sense of responsibility in bringing order and meaning to fantasy. While imagination keeps from going dry by checking in with intuition and fantasy, it produces meaning by maintaining a balance between the way things are and the fantastical way they are not.

Most art operates by way of the associative mode of thinking, through juxtaposition, substitution, identity, similarity, and dissimilarity, which seem to be more basic operations than rational, syllogistic reasoning. Associative thinking makes the fastest connections it can from its unconscious sea of archetypes. This routing can be done by rote memory, habits of thinking, association, or it can come up with entirely original results through its own process of deductive logic.

Here is an illustration of how the unconscious and consciousness work together. Suppose we are observing water dripping in a sink. Inductively, through the particulars coming in from our observations, our consciousness sends down to our unconscious that image of dripping water into its storehouse of memories and archetypes. Our unconscious then deduces from those observations general categories associated with water or things that drip. Then, memory and imagination in our unconscious will form a new particular or combination of particulars from the information and send that back to the conscious level at which point, if we pay attention, we will become aware that an association on the unconscious level has taken place. Below is an illustration of how our mind processes the image of the sink dripping.

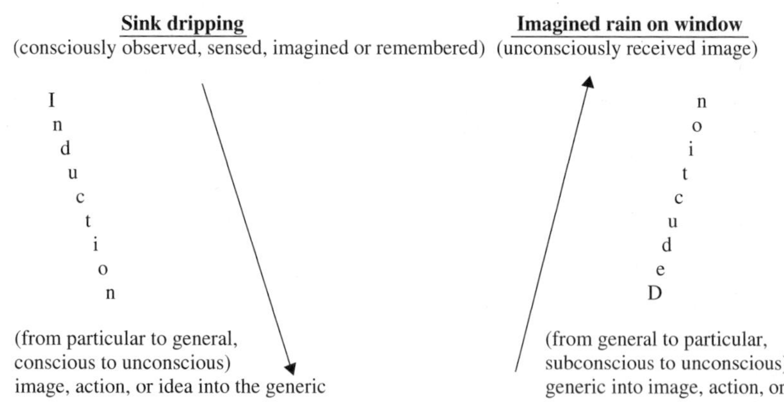

CREATIVITY AND CONSCIOUSNESS EXERCISE

1. Observe an image closely and then track not just what you thought of the image but the paths your thought took.
2. Now put two different images together and perform the same task.
3. Read a lyrical passage of poetry, and as the poem's drama is heightening, stop and see if you can fill in what's about to come next. Then see if you can analyze the interplay among knowledge, your experience, memory, intuition, feeling, and the conventions of language and lyric poetry.

The process of leaping from an image to an idea, such as from observing a light to hitting upon the idea of goodness, seems to work by using the hardwired paths of rote memory that are established either by learned experience, by associating a cluster of experience memories, or by tapping into intuition.

MENTAL PREPARATION

Writer's Block

Usually a solid piece of advice that seems to work when experiencing **writer's block** is to say, "Relax, lower your standards, just play." We may be too preoccupied with matters that won't allow us to relax, in which case we are getting in our own way and are blocking the way to creativity. At other times, it may be a matter of our simply *not seeing,* of not being able to truly focus on and pay quality attention to the life going on in and around us. Of course, there are those who maintain that there is no such "thing" as writer's block, that its occurrence is merely a psychological ploy or projection that writers set up as a kind of unconscious excuse, escape hatch, or blaming device. And all of these explanations are true, whether they're imposed by us or by something outside of us. People do experience, for whatever reason, writer's block. A bouquet of cut flowers might still truly be flowers, but they are cut off from their source, what nourished them, and any possibility of growth.

Is there a way to will one's self into the "zone," that unconscious state of being where creative thought and action seem to flow so effortlessly because somehow we are able to be open to and in tune with what we wish to create? There are probably as many rituals and superstitions about how to attain the zone as there are writers blocked from it. But most artists and athletes agree that it seems to come and go on its own. Perhaps we can smooth the way a bit to encourage this place or visit from the muse. Here's a little magical story that just might address what's behind writer's block:

> Once there was a thriving village in India that had recently experienced years and years of drought. It seemed nothing could be done to change this. Out of frustration and anger the people began arguing and warring with one another. It was then in desperation that the Village Elder, at his wits' end, called in a holy man who, it was rumored, could make rain. Soon the Rain Maker arrived. He said that if the town built a little hut for him a mile outside of town and if the villagers would sit in their huts quietly for three days, in three days it would rain. This agreed, the Rain Maker retired to his hut and sat on his meditation mat and quieted his mind. A day passed, and soon

a bird began to sing, for the bird sensed someone calm was listening. Other birds joined in. The Rain Maker heard a nearby brook, could smell it. He welcomed that smell in. He felt the heat of the sun and sent his joy at the world back out at the world. He imagined the village people when they were once happy and healthy and prosperous and cooperative. He envisioned the love they had for their children and animals and crops. He created these feelings and sent them back out to the people. He kept meditating and sensing, allowing whatever came to his mind to pass through it freely, of its will. Soon the peace that emanated from his hut widened out and soaked into the nearby vicinity, and everything around him began to relax and come back into balance. By the end of the second day, his peaceful state had reached the village, and people began to feel hopeful, cheery, the wind picked up a bit, and soon there were wisps of clouds. On the third day, the clouds drifted together, first as ravelling silver scarves, then as high cottony banks that began to darken and get dense. Later that day it rained. The people came out of their huts and rejoiced. "How magical!" exclaimed the Village Elder, "You are truly wondrous, you are the Rain Maker, you have made it rain!" The little holy man shot a sidelong glance at the Village Elder and said, "How stupid! I did not make it rain. I have no such power. No one can make rain. I simply calmed myself, and that claimed the inquietude of your village, and that brought a balance and harmony back here so the wind could return and blow back the clouds, and the clouds bring rain."

(Anonymous Indian Foktale)

While we cannot "make rain," we can learn how to create the right conditions to "make it rain." Think about what the pronoun "it" stands for in that sentence.

We're Almost Never Not Creative . . .

. . . even when we're asleep. The capacity to be creative is an innate power we exercise without thinking, especially and most freely when we're young. Our power of creativity is like that. Have you ever heard of a carpenter calling up the boss and saying "I have carpenter's block today, I can't come in"? They have energy and skills through which their creativity is applied and they go to work. The capacity is always there, expressing itself in a million forms and so-called "uncreative" activities throughout the day: how you toss something in the garbage can, making up a list of groceries by thinking of what you'd like to eat, creating the curvilincar form of an everyday conversation. It's not creativity that's vanished when we experience writer's block. The block is made up of the things we place in its way and keep compacting until it's so solid we'd need a full-body massage and a week of doing nothing so our brain could drain its tensions.

But to be fair, I must admit there is something very real about the problem of writer's block. You can't just say, as some critics have, that it's just psychological and dismiss it. That's like diminishing the destructive effects of neuroses by saying it's just something psychological.

Stepping Outside the Mirror

A good way to assess why you might be experiencing writer's block would be to apply the same analysis that Jungian therapy does in interpreting the images and the feelings within and of a dream. We naturally tend to be fully and deeply submerged within the matrix of our lives. We are living them and don't think to step outside of them to view them as someone else might. We tend not to look at life phenomenologically, in terms of the curious and interesting set of tensions and directions that make up the event we're living. So what I am suggesting here is to approach your writer's block by looking outside of what you think you know at the specifics within the quality of your time-frame when you're experiencing writer's block.

Just as writers mature, become better, and raise the bar of their last best efforts by becoming better readers of their own work, so too there's no reason why we can't understand and do something about being stuck in writer's block. See if you aren't overwhelmed with everyday-life details, pressured for deadlines, undergoing some strong emotional, relationship or life changes, or asking too much of your writing instead of just playing around inside the activity. These attitudes of accomplishment and many other pressing "real life" problems are what tend to create the detritus of blockage. Try trading in "doing" for "being" until you're at home in "doing within being" and "being within doing" again. Then you'll begin to get beyond seeing in a merely literal, monoscopic way.

Seeing Stereoscopically

How can we get beyond seeing literally? Let's examine what goes into that state of perception. First, there is *focusing our attention on the literal,* the springboard of all art. It is good to see tautologically—seeing that a thing is different from every other thing—but unless that's our goal, and we enjoy our two-dimensional, monoscopic *weltanshaung,* we begin to set up stereoscopic inner vision by connecting the given to what's not there. This requires, secondly, *the act of empathy,* the ability to fully connect to and become one with what we're seeing. That is what our emotions are for, which is why, incidentally, we call them "feelings," the ability to literally put ourselves into what we're perceiving. (Of course, while empathy helps us feel what other people feel, perhaps it only tells us how we would feel if we were them.) Feelings are what invisibly connect us to the world—an intricate, inner, and higher set of the body's external five senses. If you have experienced something somebody is telling you about, and you do it without empathy, then it's just a boring abstract exercise. So, now we've obtained the object and connected our feelings to it. Next, there is an even higher function that needs to come into play. That's the third operation, *the figure-making function of the imagination* that will compare, contrast, identify with, substitute for, or juxtapose what we're perceiving with what we've already experienced in life. Then, it seems to me there are there are two last steps. Fourth is the formation of *an implication, comment, or implied statement* that begins forming itself up from the alchemical combining of our physical, emotional, and imaginative processes, from the characteristics of what we're perceiving and how we feel about it and whatever metaphorical or symbolic transformation we run it through. Last, we begin the inchoate process of bringing to bear on this new perception a host of other, unpredicted, associated objects, actions, events, and thoughts so that a *new aesthetic order of structured thinking* takes place. At any given time, all of this may take place in a logically linear, disjunctive, or unconsciously intuitive manner. In any case, the object of perception has not objectively changed. It is still literally what it is. But we have changed by having transformed our way of perceiving it. (And I use the word "perceive" advisedly since it means "to see through something.") If you are experiencing writer's block, then one or more of these functions isn't in play.

MENTAL PREPARATION: WRITER'S BLOCK EXERCISE

When you are experiencing writer's block, try this little writing exercise:

1. **Attention on the characteristics of the literal**
   Think of a special object you have in your room, on your person, or that you miss because it's at home, and write down the object's characteristics: its size, color, shape, weight, function, or lack thereof.
2. **Feeling**
   Now fuse your feelings to this object, imbue it with what feelings it evokes in you, and briefly write about why it's so special to you.
3. **Figure-making**
   Experience your feelings for this object; associate with it what it reminds you of or what comes to mind. Use a trope such as a simile, metaphor, symbol, or anecdote.
4. **Implication**
   Now, raising the object to the level of something you believe in, write about how you have determined you may or may not live your life from now on.

THE DISCOVERY MODE

Apperception

This is the predominant mode of creative composition among most writers in literary genres today. It is an exploratory way of composing works that calls upon conscious, unconscious, intuitive, and serendipitously "received" lines, general moves and directions, ideas, images, plot developments, and other elements of a poem. Its more recent origins can be traced from John Keats' concept of **negative capability,** the ability to hold one's self in "uncertainies" in order to discover something new about the subject at hand, to the nineteenth-century writings of Samuel Coleridge's *Biographia Literaria,* which called for envisioning an organic form of composition based more on the model of how a living thing grows, rather than any preset and superimposed authorial concept or idea about a subject. Coleridge said that the working of the imagination during the creative process is simply fantasy with a sense of responsibility and directedness. More recently, Denise Levertov, brilliantly furthering Coleridges' *Poetics,* linked content (what is said) to form (how it is said) in terms of its being one simultaneous act stemming from some intuited Platonic idea of a higher form ("organic poetry . . . is a *method of apperception*"; "form is never more than a *revelation* of content"). Poets such as Robert Creeley, Charles Olson, and Robert Duncan have continued to refine this method of organically apprehending the sensed and ultimate form of a poem.

Maybe the Three Stooges, by way of E.M. Forster, defined the **discovery mode** best, when one of them said: "How do I know what I'm going to say until I've said it!?" Richard Hugo makes a solid distinction between academic seekers of knowledge and those involved in purely creative pursuits: "Scholars look for final truths they will never find. Creative writers concern themselves with possibilities that are always there to the receptive." Of course, the element of discovery in creative writing doesn't quite happen by merely uttering something. The theory behind the discovery mode is, as Robert Frost aphoristically said, "No surprise for the writer, no surprise for the reader." But what sort of operations go on in developing this discovery, this surprise? Aside from the complex interplay of conscious and unconscious activity, the human mind has the extraordinary ability to watch itself perceiving while it is perceiving. This capability, called **apperception,** is the mind's ability to watch and record what it is perceiving while it is creating, thinking, and dreaming. In fact, you might recall that when we dream there's always a detached, apperceiving observer in the dream (a part of us) watching ourselves dream, and evaluating and judging what's going on. It is this function of apperception that allows us to trace from what levels of consciousness creative material arrives, and what specific tendencies, resistances, reactions, and "personality" our mind displays.

But what lies behind the receiving and tracing of these perceptions? What do we "go by" when we're judging whether a poem is on track or not? There does seem to be something we are going by, some inner paradigmatic measurement or sensed form that tells us, as in the children's game of "Hot and Cold," when we are hitting or missing what we are trying to create. In Denise Levertov's famous essay, "Some Notes on Organic Form," she explains her idea of there being an idealized, possibly archetypal Platonic order of forms that an experience impresses upon us. First we go through it and then we re-imagine it. This in-patterning of the forces and tensions and **inscape** of an experience is what we are "going by" when we use the discovery mode during the creative process. And, just as in areas of higher math and physics and in matters of the spirit, when we are in the midst of trying to define *a thing,* it inevitably turns out to be *a process;* it is the place in art where *what* we are talking about is a matter of *how* we are talking about it, which is the nexus of the interrelationship between form and content. This is the territory where the investigation of what we sense turns into the discovery of what we think and feel. This mode of writing is quite distinctly at variance with the way that scholars approach the study of poetry. Richard Hugo comments: "One of my reluctant conclusions is that the Ph.D. system tends to train people to teach literature as if it is some grand mysterious system that has little or nothing to do with human existence. . . . such a system attracts its fair share of people who are eager to place knowledge between themselves and their lives."

Fixed Form and Free Verse "Intensions"

The difference between externally imposed fixed-form verse and internally controlled free verse is in what occurs within the mind while writing in these two forms. The following visual illustrations, purposefully chosen for their nonverbal medium, are meant to demonstrate, with the cooperation of the reader, the direction that the mind goes in order to access, retrieve, and create form for both externally and internally derived form.

1. Take a piece of paper and quickly draw an abstract, schematic representation of a tree. After you've done this, think about where your mind went to access the image (See **apperception** on p. 9). Your schematic would probably look something like the diagram to the right.

   Trace back to where your imagination or memory went in order to access this image or form. Most likely it dove into the pool of generic, archetypal, Platonic images of "tree" we all collectively contain, probably how you drew as a child. In other words, your mind went to a received, given, or fixed form.

2. Now take another piece of paper and draw a more realistic tree, one that looks more like a tree you'd see every day. It might look something like this.

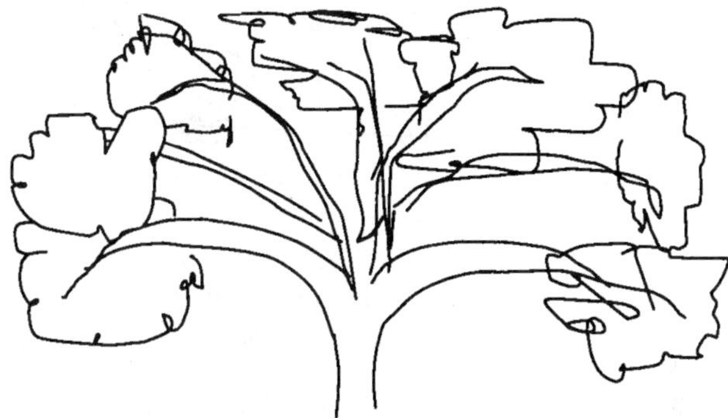

Notice that in order for you to have drawn this image, you would have had to access both the schematic archetypal shape of "tree," and then, by way of memory, imagination, or actually looking at a tree, you would have to had drawn a tree that now has been shaped by circumstance (soil conditions, wind and weather, genetic type, etc.). In other words, your original Platonic or archetypal form has now been changed by your memory or your imagining a special set circumstances or experiences that this tree has undergone. It has a more plastic look that has been shaped by forces within and outside of it. It is a less objective and more specific form than the drawing of your first image. You have subjectively added something of yourself to your first schematic image by allowing your mind to more deeply explore your past or present experience. The original Platonic image has been ghosted over by your and your tree's experience.

3. Now, last, take another piece of paper and imagine a tree whose image or form looks like who you feel you are. Let it represent your sense of your individual character, where you are emotionally, psychologically, and spiritually in life. Let that sense of yourself be the main guide in the drawing of this tree. Be as creative as you like. The following is an example of one person's idea of this self-tree.

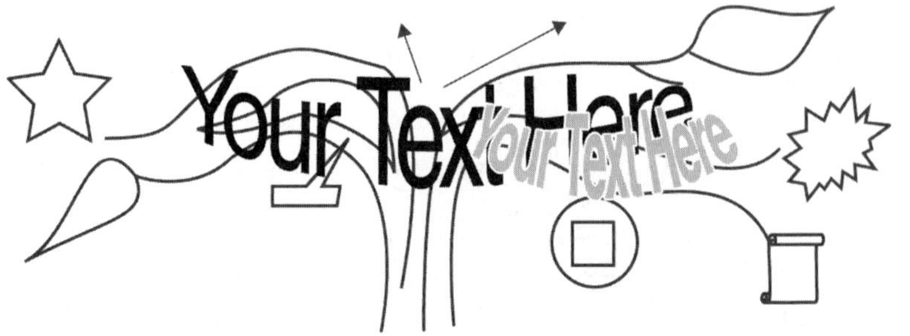

In order to draw this last image you would have had to use the **discovery mode;** that is, you would have had to submerge your mind in your subjective feelings and ideas of who you think you are until what at first seemed like a "thing" or gestalt-like entity turned into a process, the **discovery mode.** In other words, you would have had to throw yourself into a mild state of uncertainty with few external guides (see **negative capabilty,** p. 9) in order to create a form that has been guided by, organically connected to, and reflective of your subjective sense of yourself. This **discovery mode** is the primary method of writing free verse. This is not to say that writing in fixed forms does not contain the same organic process within its method; only that fixed forms work off a given exterior fixed form. Of course, your third image of a tree will have some sense of your original schematic tree, and an implied set of conventions, just as fixed forms do (the sense of "tree-ness," of anchoring and branching out, etc.), but its primary attributes will be derived from and organically connected to your sense of your individual style, of who you are (see **organic composition,** p. 10).

Not Knowing

CHAOS THEORY The nineteenth and twentieth centuries traded in static and relatively predictable Newtonian world views in favor of a more unknowable, constantly shifting *weltanschauung* based on process, uncertainty, and the element of chance. Therefore the metaphor of gambling seems an appropriate model to look at in terms of illustrating a simple example of chaos theory. In the Pachinko game, a small ball trickles through a number of nail-like obstacles and, as in roulette, randomly lands in one of the many available slots at the bottom. An initial impulse in the form of a plunger propels the ball up a chute to the top of the machine where with the help of gravity and inertia it will fall down between rows of pins. Suppose we put bumpers along the path at mathematically precise points, but a few of the bumpers have several micrometers less elasticity than some of the others; then we put in a few holes into which the ball could drop and then reappear at one of several other places. If it reappears at a special place, the reward is that you can shoot it again.

We could go on and on adding new uniform and irregular elements to this very simple example of controlled chaos—including how the player might try to affect the roll of the ball by banging the machine—and add to our consideration causal factors outside the rules, such as dust particles or grease on the board, or malfunctioning parts, or city blackouts and earthquakes.

Now, in the infinitely more complex, self-correcting, and unpredictable creative process, it seems absurd to think that we can or should try to control its limitless variations, such as:

- our own free will;
- creativity's leaping associational paths;
- the permutating, connotative, and denotative levels of meanings in words;
- the subtle logical interaction among linear and non-linear groups of words;
- the universal and particularized mix of images;
- advanced formal training in one's art and medium;
- one's matrix of cultural preferences, biases and ignorances, and personal and cultural myths;
- the universal and archetypal characteristics of gender, age, and psychology;
- our degree of awareness of the levels of consciousness operating within us;
- the context of the styles of the age we live in;
- the locale in which we were born;
- the place in which we now choose to live, down to whether or not the phone rings while we're writing.

If all of the known micro- and macro-universe—from the behavior of atoms to the works of nature to the formation of galaxies—works according to this principle of order coming from chaos, how naïve it is for us to think that we know more about what we are doing in the creative process than what we don't know. As Richard Hugo casually remarked, "Knowing can be a limiting thing."

CHAOS IS NATURE'S MEDIUM FOR CREATIVITY. The secret of artists and other creative people throughout the millennia—whether they are conscious of it or not—is that they know how to collaborate with chaos. Yet, oftentimes it is the very presence of chaos and confusion that leads to fear of failure, that instills resistance in us at the very beginning of the creative process. The most oft-cited characteristic of creative people (aside from popularly being thought of as being slightly crazy) is their ability to remain open during the rain of uncertainty, to embrace the difficult states of paradox, opposition, and ambiguity that are the gateways of opportunity.

There are as many entrances into chaos as there are kinds of people entering it. But there is only one way out, and that is the "con-fusion" of disparities. That's why every time we make a new poem or story it seems as difficult to do as it did the first time. Mass production of the same thing is easy because it's endlessly reproducible. Once immersed in chaos, as we give ourselves over to it by being open, a strange and exhilarating thing occurs: we lose our self-consciousness of what we are doing, of the time and place we are in, and we become one with the flow. It feels as if things are streaming, as if we ourselves are streaming, and all our being is flowing. Then a new development occurs: we have a growing sense that something is beginning to be shaped. We sense that what we are doing is shaping itself as we partner with it in shaping it. We have gone so far into the particular that we emerge onto the level of the universal, and we are empowered to say an old thing in a new way.

If artists had one wish that could be granted, they'd wish to be able to summon up the creative process, the magical "zone," at will, to have a dependable closed system guaranteed by some particular ritual or time or place or access to some trigger to that special consciousness. But that is not the nature of creativity. If were told to write a poem or story in the next 15 minutes, we'd feel a natural resistance to doing it. On the other hand, if we were asked to compete in the next 15 minutes at something we can already do well, that wouldn't be hard to do. This is because competition is based upon the known, upon repetition, consistency, and systemization, which are anathema to the quirky creative spirit whose only repetition is to throw itself into what it doesn't know and what it hasn't yet done. In the 1970s, the poet Donald Hall depicted his now-infamous cartoon of creative writing students in workshops across America as all producing the "MacPoem," the one-page, publishable, predictable "Workshop Poem." I think he was saying that if you think writing poetry is like making a hamburger, that there's some specific method to be learned and repeated over and over again, you're in the wrong business. Like everything else in creation, we too have been thrown into and live in uncertainty and indeterminacy. There is no one, safe answer or secret to writing. Searching for such an answer would be like the bee, the flower, or the apple asking the gardener what the secret to truth and beauty is. The gardener is the last one to know these mysteries. All he knows is that he loves what he's doing.

A good teacher can tell you with practical, technical precision what is and what isn't going on in a poem you've written—what it is, and how and what it might be made better. But he or she can no more explain the creative process than a gynecologist can explain love.

INSIDE CHAOS Within systems of chaos, such as rushing water, wind, and the geological formations of irregular terrain, there is something called "the strange attractor effect." It is akin to that vaguely sensed stage in the creative process where we feel something is beginning to shape itself. Chaotic background is the feeding ground for the emergence of regular, self-forming, coherent patterning. The firing of neurons in our brain provides a rich and high level of neural chaos that is the birthplace of self-organized thoughts and perceptions.

In terms of who we are, if we could trace the conditions under which the last thousand couples of our ancestors met, and the difference in who they were, which eventually resulted in us, we would have to conclude that the complex and exponential combinations of happenstance simply amount to chaos. Well, at least we know who *we* are. Or do we? When I say "I," I think I have a solid, unquestioning, simple sense of the entity called "I." But I am, in fact, not a thing but a process that is in flux in any direction and on any level of existence that I care to look. And it is exactly because of this diversity and nature's method of chance operations that things evolve into new and strengthened formations.

Complexity and Simplicity

Every organic and inorganic process couples the inverse operations of building simplicity-within-complexity-within-simplicity, and the opposite structure of complexity-within-simplicity-within-complexity. Small simple units called fractals aggregate and build into natural, infinitely complex structures that mirror the macro-level of nature. I remember visiting a friend in Pasadena, California, and noticing an irregular crack in his wall which he explained had been caused by a recent earthquake. Upon flying out of L.A., I looked down and saw that the local mountain range had the same shape as the crack in my friend's wall. The complex can become simple, and the simple can become complex. Within the neural chaos of our brain, which has been aptly described as "a connecting organ," we form an abstract gestalt of our experience and personality and thereby implant in ourselves an internal sense of order. And by that imposition of an abstract "self," we re-confirm that gestalt by attracting whatever is in and around us to conform to what and who we think we are, as if a flame thought itself a moth. This seems to be how the creative process works, too. After an initial period of confusion and chaos and being immersed in what we do not know, a vague gestalt within the creative act of composing forms and acts in effect as the composition's brain, if you will, developing, ordering, and transcending the very materials that brought it into being. This interaction of order and irrationality, of dispersion and coalescence, produces infinite combinations of possibilities. In other words, complexity and simplicity are not things, but ephemeral results of an interaction of these processes within other larger and smaller processes, within other larger and smaller processes, etc.

It has not gone unnoticed that, ironically, art aims to fix this flux into the stasis of perfection. But how we as artists interact with our creativity—whether we try to control it, resist its depths, or simply go with it—is the definition of our attitude toward it which, in turn, determines the nature of its results, the poem you make or the story you tell.

THE DISCOVERY MODE: "19 QUESTIONS" EXERCISE

Here's a loaded game of "19 Questions" that, it is hoped, will allow you to open yourself up to wonder and an uneasy alliance between knowing and not knowing.

1. To experience the difference between knowledge and the process of knowing, answer the following questions: What is your name? Where do you come from? What is the difference between knowing your name and where you live, and your having to make up a more fitting name for yourself and the place you feel you come from? Can you feel knowledge giving way to uncertainty and uncertainty beginning to tell its creative story?
2. Make an image or metaphor for what it feels like when you sit down to write. Are you a child told to stay in? Do you feel like the poor miller's daughter in Rumpelstiltskin who had to make gold from straw? Make a new image or metaphor that would make you happier. What changes in character did you make between your original persona and your revised persona?
3. Where do you think that your "creativity" resides—in your head, your intellect, your ego, your unconscious, your heart, your soul, or your body?
4. Under what conditions have you experienced the joy of deep personal learning and insight? How does your understanding of and relationship to discipline fit into this? What would your personification of discipline look like? In this image, are you in service to it, or is it in service to you?
5. What is the difference between how you usually see the world and how you see the world when you're feeling creative? To what do you attribute the difference between these two states?
6. If the power in a work of art doesn't lie in what it says (since paraphrase is not art), and if the effect and achievement of all the arts (literature, film, dance, painting, sculpture, etc.) and their styles are really interchangeable, then what common, irreducible quality resides in all these attempts? Now reverse your perspective: How can you go about accessing that quality for your own art? Aren't the interacting forces and tensions of similarity, opposites, dissonance, dissimilarity, and paradox in art an attempt to mirror the formations of nature?

7. Which do you generally think of as being larger: what you know about the things I am asking about you and art, or what you do not know about yourself and these things? Proportionately speaking, how big is one and how little is the other?
8. Who produces the best literature: someone with an extensive vocabulary who tries to know as much about the world as possible, or someone with just an average vocabulary who merely sits in his or her own room and writes from his head?
9. What do you think is the qualitative relationship of experience to creativity? How is the experience of creativity different in quality than that of normal, daily experience?
10. Which do you think is more powerful, one of Georgia O'Keefe's paintings of flowers or the Vietnam War memorial wall? What makes this so?
11. Which is worth more in the currency of art—the capturing of a fleeting, ineffable moment or the expression of an eternal truth?
12. Do you find the old adage "Write what you know" confusing and frustrating, or satisfying and comfortable? Exactly what does "what you know" mean? Where does your knowledge begin and where does it end?
13. If you are able to answer these questions fairly well, does that mean you are more creative than someone who is having trouble answering them?
14. Would it be fairly easy for you to write a creative piece on what you were thinking and feeling when you bought your first bottle of perfume for your mother or someone else? What does the specificity of this situation and experience suggest about the supposed blank page, writer's block, and the tabula rasa that begins the creative act?
15. Do you normally view being in the state of "not knowing" as a static and empty place, something negative that has to be reversed or filled in; or do you find it to be a place of high energy and activity, full of a sense of potential and opportunity?
16. What is your right hand touching right now? Name it. Now erase the name you just used and turn what you're feeling into a process by describing what your hand is feeling.
17. Now, how were you able to tell what your hand was feeling? Was it through an absolute level of knowledge like a "known" fact, or did your mind move down into your hand to feel what it was feeling?

Or did your mind stay in your head while your hand told your brain what it felt?

18. And last, if I were to give you a near-impossible knot to untangle, and if I told you that you had the rest of your life to untangle this knot, and that whatever you desire—wealth, power, beauty, fame, or peace of mind—would be yours if you could untangle it, would your reaction to my challenge be different if you knew that whatever I was promising wasn't true? Would it benefit you the most to know if what I promised were true, or untrue, or to simply be in uncertainty as to whether it were true or not? Which has truer and more meaningful value for you, the untangled knot, or the process of untangling it?
19. What is it in you that makes you think the things I promised are not true?

ASSOCIATIONAL LOGIC

This form of logic is an intuitive mode of reasoning, operating differently from the more conscious, ratiocinative, formal types of logic, in which the mind associates one image, idea, event, or word with another. It is the kind of thinking that dreaming uses as logic when our mind moves from one thing to another through an unconscious process of **juxtaposition:** things are associated through their proximity in time, space, feeling, quality, or convention. Since this is generally the type of mental process we use when we create a **trope** (such as a metaphor, simile, symbol, and forms of **metonymy** and **synecdoche**), we must use the operations of logic that underlie such figures of language: equivalency, parallelism, substitution, similarity, dissimilarity, shared domain, sequence, archetypes, and paradigms. Although most creativity depends upon the associational mode of thinking, very little is understood about how it actually works because very little is known about the inner terrain of our consciousness. But we recognize associational logic when we experience its wild signature, a movement of the mind that the poet Robert Bly has termed **leaping,** the signature of "dragon smoke" left behind, "a long floating leap at the center of the work," left in much the same way as electrons in atoms (whose actual physical positions are indeterminate) leave behind individually colored tracer marks that indicate where they have been. This leaping occurs when the mind shoots from one level or part of the psyche to another: from conscious to unconscious, from rational to archetypal, from reality to fantasy, from sensing to feeling to thinking. Frederick Nietzsche, in referring to our love for and dependence upon rational, cause-and-effect types of logic said: "The alleged instinct for causality is nothing more than the fear of the unusual."

Although we can locate the employment of a leap in a poem, we cannot know for certain whether or not a poet has actually experienced spontaneous leaping during the composition of the poem because deletions of content during the revision process can create the illusion of its semblance and wipe out traces of rational logic. Sylvia Plath's early drafts of her poems are revealing in this regard since in her final versions what seem like very wild, unexpected, lightning-like strikes among associated images have often been developed by her having deleted logical and rational steps in subsequent drafts of her poems (see pp. 282–285). In other words, poets can create the effect of leaping in the associational mode, consciously employ it as a technique, by wiping out some of the intervening rationally derived steps in a work. For instance, what follows seems like a leap but it was really developed quite logically and consciously:

(RATIONAL LOGIC)	The bird that alighted on the chimney is flapping it wings as if it's frustrated, which makes it look as if it it's trying to lift the house.
(LEAPING LOGIC)	Frustration, that bird trying to lift a house . . .

Bly theorizes that the intuitive, associative mode in writing came to locate itself outside of European culture after the eighteenth century, because, he maintains, the West was much more interested in developing more masculine, rationalistic, and practical forms of logic, the result of which was a tradition of a more linear, rational style of poetry. Instead of leaping or flying, European poets in the eighteenth century opted for what Bly calls, in keeping with his metaphors of movement, "plodding" or, at best, "hopping." Of course, all that changed with the nineteenth and twentieth centuries' explosive advent of **dada, surrealism,** readymades, found art, chance art, and more.

What follows, for illustrative purposes, are some specific examples of associations (highlighted in boldface) categorized by the type of logical operation each example seems to exhibit.

Association via Similarity

The bridge's iron mesh chases **pockets of shadow**
and pale through **blinds** shuttering the corner window

to mark this man, this woman, the young **eclipse**
their naked bodies make—**black, white, white,**
black, the dying fall of light . . .

(Lynda Hull, "Love Song during Riot with Many Voices")

Association via Dissimilarity

Tender, semi-
articulate **flickers**
of your

presence, all
those years
past
(Robert Creeley, "For My Mother: Genevieve Jules Creeley")

Association via Equivalency

And the last bus
Comes letting **dark**
Umbrellas out-—
Black flowers, black flowers.
(Donald Justice, "Bus Stop")

Association via Substitution

In the example poem that follows, the speaker substitutes the bleak winter landscape with the cheery faces he drew while looking out the window. In later life, the latter came to be associated with the former.

When as a child I looked out on
wintry whiteness day after day.
I drew little happy faces on the frosted glass
which is what I see now
whenever there's nothing to see.

Association via Shared Domain

In the example that follows, there's a three-rung **laddering** of associations between sadness, sleep, and wrinkled clothes, which share the common attributes of a lack of freshness, energy, and vitality.

Sadness must sleep in its clothes,
it feels so **wrinkled, soiled, and creased.**

Association via Parallelism

In the following scene a copperhead snake is hunting down a small rodent, and Linda Gregg parallels the copperhead and its prey with her feelings:

The soft thing moving.
He does not see the moving. He is busy coaxing
and dreaming and **feeling the softness moving in him.**
The inside of him feels like another world.
He takes the soft thing and coaxes it
away from **his small knowing.** He would turn and follow,
hunt it deep within **the dark hall of his fading knowing**
but he cannot. He knows that.
That he cannot go deep within his body for the finding
of the knowing. So he slows and lets go. And finds
with his eyes a moving. A small moving that he knows.
(Linda Gregg, "The Copperhead")

Association via Paradigm

As if the sky could no longer hold its color,
that pale blue light sifts down onto the water
like talcum onto a tabletop, or like the fine powder
of memory settling again in the mind in that hour
toward sleep, in that season toward autumn
when the trees begin to fill with a sorrowing air.
(Sherod Santos, "The Evening Light along the Sound")

Association via metonymy

In the following passage, Alberto Rios' description of morning is the result of collapsing the taste of apples and black coffee into a figure of **metonymy.**

and his **mornings** became **apples**
and black coffee out of one cup.
(Alberto Rios, "In the Woman Arms of the Ground")

Association via Archetype

All things come to an end, and the phenomenon of endings is an archetype, a universal and commonly experienced paradigm in human consciousness. The following passage from Robert Bly lists a series of different things that come to an end.

Those great **sweeps of snow that stop** suddenly six feet from the house . . .
Thoughts that go so far.
The boy gets out of high school and reads no more books;
the son stops calling home.
The mother puts down her rolling pin and makes no more bread.

> **And the wife** looks at her husband one night at a party, and **loves him no more.**
> **The energy leaves the wine,** and **the minister falls leaving the church.**
>
> * * *
>
> **And the man in the black coat turns,** and goes back down the hill.
> No one knows why he came, or why he turned away, and **did not climb the hill.**
>
> (Robert Bly, "The Man in the Black Coat Turns")

Association via Time and Space

In Timothy Seibles' passage below, his speaker places the moon he's looking at into different times and places.

> **Above me the moon** looks like a nickel
> in a murky-little creek. This
> is **the same moon that saw me at twelve,**
> without a single bill to pay, zinging
> soup can tops into the dark—I called them
> flying saucers. This is **the same**
> **white light that touched dinosaurs, that**
> **found the first people trying for fire.**
>
> (Tim Seibles, "Trying For Fire")

ASSOCIATING FROM THE SENSES EXERCISE

The following exercise is called **clustering.** It uses the five basic physical senses as conduits to describe in a figurative way what something seems to be to the poet. It uses associational, "off-the-top-of-your head" chains of thinking. Here is an example of clustering sensual associations around the emotion of fear. Try your own practice word or concept.

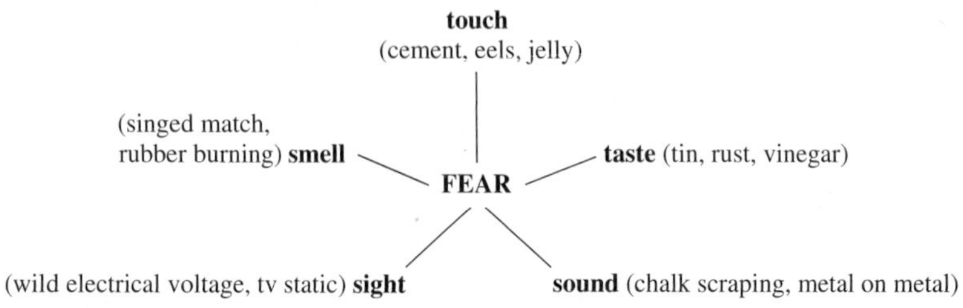

CHAPTER

2

Generating Content

After going through the initial stages of drafting a poem when, as in the start of a painting, it has been "sketched out," usually there will be a need for an **additive revision** in which the poet might ground or **anchor** certain references or content to elaborate, extend, or abstract the poem or link it to other levels, perspectives, and angles of thought, gesture, imagery, or portraiture. Possibly, the poem's **time frames** of past, present, and future need to be ordered differently, maybe one within the other, or one superimposed over another, to create interesting, associative links in time. Or, as often happens, the poet might go about **packing the poem** with images, phrasings, or elements of plot that echo, parallel, or correspond to other images, phrasings, and **plot points.**

TECHNIQUES FOR GENERATING CONTENT

The major problem in creative writing is *creating writing.* This can be seen in terms of how most student poems suffer from being underdeveloped and under-imagined. It may seem either self-evident or possibly strange to say that the content of a poem comes from itself, but when we find ourselves stuck somewhere in the composition process, the best way to create more material is to look back closely at what we have already written and to find ways to elaborate on this previous content. Generating interesting and organically functional content that furthers the original impulse and intention of the poem can be more or less artificially stimulated by choosing from among a variety of technical **moves** that are available to the poet. Here is a technical list that is useful in generating and extending the content of a poem-in-progress.

1. **Adding a figurative comparison or contrast,** such as a metaphor, simile, or symbol.

   (ORIGINAL) He ate an apple.
   (REVISED) He ate an apple
   the size of a man's heart.

2. **Supplying a literal, concrete action or image** (that is either real or imagined).

   (ORIGINAL) The days were cool and dry.

   (REVISED) The days were cool and dry.
   Each morning the dried dew left
   a transparent paisley print of its celebrations
   on the glass-top patio table.

3. **Adding an elaboration, extension, or distinction** to an idea or proposition.

   (ORIGINAL) Computers had sped up modern life.

   (REVISED) Computers had sped up modern life so much
   that the human nervous system was indistinguishable
   from computer microcircuitry.

4. **Adding an idea, meditative moment, or proposition** to an image or plot element.

   (ORIGINAL) He ate soup so politely.

   (REVISED) He ate soup so politely
   you'd have thought something in him
   had given up on life.

5. **Adding a description** to open up a statement or image.

   (ORIGINAL) She seemed to be a pleasant woman.

   (REVISED) She seemed to be a pleasant woman
   although her white uniform, lack of
   jewelry, and white, soft-soled shoes
   made her presence seem menacing.

6. **Adding plot elements** to a **dramatic situation.**

   (ORIGINAL) He had this habit
   of taking off his glasses,
   then sighing.

   (REVISED) He had this habit
   of taking off his glasses,
   looking up through them,
   scanning the sky for a spot,
   and then sighing.

7. **Adding characterization** (by using analogy) to an action or character.

   (ORIGINAL) She was tall, lovely, and well-dressed.

   (REVISED) She was tall, lovely, and well-dressed
   and had that same distant look
   models in fashion magazines had.

8. **Adding word play or musical effects** to a line of thought, image, or action.

(ORIGINAL) When the sick child sat up
he said "I see you!"

(REVISED) When the sick child sat up
he said, "I see you!"
and the doctor couldn't help
but think of the abbreviated letters
of the **I**ntensive **C**are **U**nit.

9. **Supplying dialogue** for a character or situation.

(ORIGINAL) When he was in first grade,
he lightly touched the back of the neck
of the girl sitting in front of him,
the one who never noticed him.

(REVISED) When he was in first grade,
he lightly touched the back of the neck
of the girl sitting in front of him,
the one who never noticed him,
and he asked, "How do you feel?"

10. **Adding specificity** to general description.

(ORIGINAL) The middle of the week at school
moved slowly by.

(REVISED) Tuesday, Wednesday, and Thursday
at school moved by as slowly as
the time-lapse film on sausage making
we had to watch.

Generally speaking, these techniques for creatively and artistically manipulating content will effect a move of the content in either a vertical direction, in which aspects of the theme or thesis of the poem is affected, or in a horizontal direction, in which the level of the content remains stable, but the scope and dimensionality of the poem is increased. At this stage, which focuses on a kind of detailing and filling out, its by-product will be to, again, immerse the poet in the exploratory nature of the creative process, in which imaginative and rational processes on the conscious and unconscious levels of thought will change the content of the poem by adding to, subtracting from, or transforming it in some way.

In the following sections on generating and connecting content, a number of the ways to accomplish this may overlap or even seem redundant. But each technique has been isolated to clearly highlight its particular character and function. For example, while a general move to extend or elaborate content may be termed an **extension** or **elaboration,** that general move might also function as a **segué** or form of **laddering,** or **substitution.**

The Extension

An **extension** in workshop parlance is a way of furthering something toward a more specific definition, description, condition, or level of the poem through, usually, the use of associative logic. For instance, in the dramatic situation below a woman talks about her boyfriend jilting her.

I hated the way you dumped me.

By using an extension, we can characterize both how the woman was jilted and how she felt about it.

I hated the way you dumped me
with all the aplomb of taking out the trash.

Or we could use a **simile,** a simple and effective means of moving from a general to a more specific context of the speaker's feelings. (Most similes use "like" or "as" to indicate their indirect comparisons, but, for more colloquial ease, we could use substitutions such as "in the way," or "as surely as.") The comparison below underlines the amount and quality of disregard the speaker feels her boyfriend demonstrated in the way he broke things off.

I hated the way you dumped me
like laundry down a chute.

Another device or technique for creating an extension is to use the **telescoped metaphor.** This multiple figure consists of a series of metaphors in which one metaphor transforms into a second metaphor, and the second metaphor into a third, etc. If, for instance, we wanted to horizontally stretch the connotative references in the way someone looked at the speaker below, we could use a series of telescoping metaphors.

	When you looked at me
	you looked as if your mind were
(METAPHOR #1)	**crumpling an old laundry list**
	of excuses and denials
(METAPHOR #2)	**that turned into a picket sign protesting**
(METAPHOR #3)	**the Great Depression**
(METAPHOR #4)	**some meteor made of Atlantis.**

In terms of changing levels of reference, watch the extension Tony Hoagland gets out of the opening of his poem "One Season." He extends the opening dramatic situation's action from the personal to the cultural to the biological level.

	That was the summer my best friend
(PERSONAL LEVEL)	called me a faggot on the telephone,
	hung up, and vanished from the earth,

(CULTURAL LEVEL) **a normal occurrence in this country**
where **we change our lives**
with the swiftness and hysterical finality
(BIOLOGICAL LEVEL) **of dividing cells.**
(Tony Hoagland, "One Season")

THE JUMP CUT EXTENSION In the following passage from Alberto Rios' "Madre Sofia," there is an **extension** that causes a reversal in camera angles: from a shot of the gypsy fortuneteller, Madre Sofia, to the young boy whose palm is being read and who is afraid of her rumored powers.

she smelled of smoke, cigarettes,
but a diamond smoke, somehow; **I inhaled**
sparkles, I could feel them, throat, stomach.
(Alberto Rios, "Madre Sofia")

Keep in mind that an extension may also double as a **segue** (see p. 70), a simultaneous change in the focus, subject, or level of the poem; or, structurally, it may also be a **scooter technique** (see below).

THE SCOOTER TECHNIQUE This is a form of extension that uses parallel syntactical phrases—the way that a child kicks the ground to keep a scooter moving—in order to transform the poem's content. A simple example from Ruth Stone's "Turn Your Eyes Away" is her series of similes that describe what the speaker's husband looked like after he hanged himself.

The gendarme came
to tell me **you had hung yourself**
on the door of a rented room
like an overcoat
like a bathrobe
hung from a hook
(Ruth Stone, "Turn Your Eyes Away")

A more complex form of the scooter technique can be found in Gerald Stern's poem "What It Is Like," in which he describes double exterior physical aspects and double interior emotional aspects of a scene.

I will have to tell you what it is like
(EXTERIOR DESCRIPTION) **since I was the one lying on my back**
with my arms in the air and a blanket up to my
chin, since **I was the one on a mattress**
(INTERIOR DESCRIPTION) **and the one trying to make up my mind**
whether it was an early heaven just being there
or whether it was another bitter vertigo.
(Gerald Stern, "What It Is Like")

Laddering

This technique extends concrete (or physical) terms through a number of steps (or rungs) to more general or abstract levels. Of course, the direction of the **laddering** can also be reversed so that the material moves in a downward direction from abstract to concrete. An example of laddering would look something like this:

	You left this life without a second thought,
(CONCRETE)	with all the aplomb of **shutting off a light,**
(GENERAL)	as if it were always **night, and night darkened**
(ABSTRACT)	**into your blackout of my name.**

Wallace Stevens used this move twice in astoundingly brilliant ways in his poem "No Sop, No Possum, No Taters": once, in the stanzas that humanize the cornstalks, and again in the image of snow falling that gets likened to the story of the Fall of Man in the Bible.

In this bleak air the broken stalks
1 Have arms without hands. They have trunks

Without legs or, for that, without heads.
They have heads in which a captive cry

Is merely the moving of a tongue.
2 Snow sparkles like eyesight falling to earth,

like seeing fallen brightly away
(Wallace Stevens, "No Possum, No Sop, No Taters")

TECHNIQUES FOR GENERATING CONTENT: EXTENSION EXERCISE

Write a brief, three- or four-line opening **dramatic situation,** and then add an extension using the following.

1. three lines of commentary, each of which takes the situation to a new level or domain of reference (as in Hoagland's "One Season")
2. a jump cut–associated image or TROPE that expresses the speaker's reaction (as in the example from Rios' "Madre Sofia")
3. two lines using the scooter technique to supply a series of appositions (telescoping forms of an image, as in the passage from Stone's "Turn Your Eyes Away")
4. two parallel and equivalent interior images for the external dramatic situation (as in Stern's "What It Is Like")

TECHNIQUES FOR ELABORATING CONTENT

An **elaboration** is a widening and filling out of an argument or image through the use of tropes, enriched restatement, repetition, and variations. Here are a variety of devices and methods by which a poem can be elaborated.

THE CONCEIT A **conceit** is an imagistic (concrete or abstract) form of elaboration. The Latin orator Cicero considered this device of enlargement "one of the highest distinctions of eloquence." Watch how effective Lynn Emanuel is in elaborating and manipulating her conceit of lover-as-automobile in this passage from "On Waking after Dreaming of Raoul."

If Freud was right and dreams of falling are
dreams of having fallen then you must have been
the beautiful declivity of that hill, Raoul,
the speed was so seductive and the brakes so
unreliable, and so intricate and abstract
that when I touched them they squeaked like a jar lid
coming loose and I was embarrassed, but not sad,
at being the one flat wheel that bumped down the hill
in an unsteady gulp of denial—oh no oh no oh no—
until I woke up chilly, damp, my breath unsteady.
(Lynn Emanuel, "On Waking after Dreaming of Raoul")

Emanuel's conceit begins with the speaker's having "fallen" in love with Raoul. Then that falling becomes the downslope for the speaker-as-runaway-car. Further elaborations that contribute to the formation of the conceit include the unreliable brakes (lack of will power) and a flat tire (her imbalance).

SIMULTANEITY Another technique that's effective but is more commonly found in music, film, and art, as opposed to the more linear form of poetry, is **simultaneity,** the producing of the effect of two or more things occurring at the same time or in the same place or from two points of view.

For instance, if we wanted to create two things happening at once, similar to a split-screen image or double exposure in film, we could write something like this.

The soldier hunkering down in the tropical shower
thought of his wife back in the States
taking her morning shower

Jorie Graham, in her **dramatic lyric** (a generic form of the **dramatic monologue**) "Salmon," employs what the French call a *trompe l'oeil* (trick of the eye) in the use of her **syntax** when she purposely misplaces the verb *run* in her sentence, which seems to make the fish she's watching on TV swim right through her motel room in Nebraska.

I watched them once, at dusk, on television, run
in our motel room halfway through
Nebraska
(Jorie Graham, "Salmon")

INNER CORRESPONDENCES This term refers to images, statements, elements of syntax and grammar, and rhetorical structures and **tropes** that reflect and correspond in some way to other content in the poem. The **correspondences** in the poem's content can be in the form of repetitions, variations, or enhancements that create forces of attraction, tension, and cohesion to help give the poem a sense of depth, fullness, shapeliness, and self-suffiency. It is similar to, but more elaborate than, a **leitmotif** in music, in which variations of a previous part of the score surface at appropriate intervals throughout the composition.

The poem with inner correspondences is particularly aesthetically satisfying, because it is a self-contained emblematic system of words that reinforces its meaning by echoing nuances back and forth. This kind of poem is like a house of mirrors whose reflections delimit, intensify, and deepen thematic concerns. The fullness that is achieved by this method of composition can be brought about through the use of almost any poetic device: image, metaphor, symbol, dialogue, structure, or plot. Behind the surface of this technique is a kind of layered vision, the currency of art, through which the writer perceives things on multiple, simultaneous levels. Flannery O'Connor, addressing fiction writers, termed this quality of perception "anagogical vision," a double or triple kind of layered seeing that runs through all the arts, that allows the writer to perceive different levels of reality in an image or situation.

The difference between a literal and an anagogical or literary version of perception can be illustrated in the following examples.

(LITERAL) He ate an apple.

Here there is no attempt to extend the action beyond the narrow, literal interpretation. Without an elaborating context, the sentence contains no resonance, no outspreading meaning, no thematic depth. But if we add a simple comparison to the sentence, we obtain a vivid reflection on the character, subject, and theme of the would-be poem.

(ANAGOGICAL) He ate an apple the size of a man's heart.

Suddenly there are ramifications in meaning to the man's action, a plot begins to develop, the situation becomes dramatic, and the reader's anticipation is increased. By pairing the word *apple* with *heart,* the writer has begun to create an **emblem** of images that controls the direction of the poem, deepens its significance, and outlines its boundaries. Poetically, this simple pairing of objects opens the poem to wide imagistic and metaphorical possibilities.

It's important to remember that this "technique" is actually derived from the way the writer sees, feels, or imagines that something has happened. It's a way of looking at the world in which complex ideas converge from different perspectives toward a unified focal point. The anagogical technique as a tool in itself can become simply a dry exercise in language manipulation if it doesn't originate from the impact of real experience. Its authority lies in the truth of its inner connections and reflections, and how closely the poem follows the invisible pathways set up by the associations.

Let's look at some of the ways by which poems with inner reflections have been written.

SLANT IMAGERY Just as words can be rhymed, images can be rhymed, too. Like **perfect rhyme,** two rhyming images can evoke a static *quality,* or as in **slant rhymes,** they can create the illusion of process or progression. Here are three slant images: *chandelier, constellation, fireflies.* While the three have the obvious association of light between them, there is also a three-fold transformational process occurring as we move from image to image: from manufactured to natural objects, from inorganic to organic images, and from static to active images. This is the kind of buried or implied plot development that links disparate elements into a complex, self-defining system. They reflect back and forth on each other and act as stepping stones in the plot or theme.

Morton Marcus' poem "Tuba" is built on **slant imagery.** Fitting its thematic movement, the images slant rhyme in an upward direction, conforming to the central character's experience of transcendence from an obese and earthy human into an airy spirit.

Tuba

a flaming tuba
blazes on the boulevard

the flames are wings
and the tuba rises

above the city and up
through the sunlight

a brass kite
sailing to the clouds

harrumping like an uncle
tying his shoelace

who has sprouted wings
that sear through his back

and who finds
he is no longer sitting

by the side of the bed
but flying, flying

over bridges and shops
still doubled over

still tightening the laces
while he wheezes and grunts

all along he had known
this would happen

had been waiting
for the day

when he would be flying
waving to the crowds

smiling and nodding
to his astonished friends

but not this way
not bent over

pulling at his shoelace
harrumping harrumping

as he disappears
into the mouth of the sun
(Morton Marcus, "Tuba")

The uncle's epiphany is prepared and executed by five images and a verb: flaming tuba, flames as wings, a brass kite, harrumping (like a tuba), and the image of the mouth of the sun. The whole story of his enlightenment is contained in the slant imagery and its accompanying levels of meaning. The first point of focus is "a flaming tuba," which contains the idea of fire, the clumsy, bass sounds of the tuba, and the image of brass. The rays of sunlight blasting against the tuba are then transformed into wings, implying the imminence of flight. This idea is furthered by the image of the tuba as "a brass kite." As the tuba rises, it harrumps, and at this point the complex of images comes to rest in the image of the uncle. From the preparing images, we see the uncle as fat, sad, and bald. Because the images come to be contained by the uncle, the poem concentrates on his transformation. He now dominates the hierarchy of slant images and his actions reflect their qualities (shiny, round, evanescent). The last image of the poem, "the mouth of the sun," circles back to slant imagery with the blazing of the tuba and enters a more highly evolved counterpart to that image ("the mouth of the sun") where he will reside happily ever after, burned to pure and airy essence.

STORY WITHIN A STORY A variation of the **objective correlative** (see p. 50) is the play-within-a-play convention. It has the concentric structure of a play in which another play occurs. The inner play or story reflects back upon the drama of the outer play and, as is usual in **dramatic irony,** often the main characters are unaware that they are witnessing an analogy to their own lives. In Larry Ellis' poem, "Dyslexic," the dramatic situation is that of child whose dyslexic reading and speech disability goes either undetected or ignored. The speaker is humiliated by being forced to read aloud a **monologue** before his classmates. Ironically, the student coincidentally "happens" to be reading the passage that opens Charles Dickens' *David Copperfield,* a dramatic monologue that both reflects the student's dilemma and his inner thoughts.

Dyslexic

A chalkboard faced teacher used
to point at my hidden eyes behind
a straight backed blond head of rope.
Catching my eyes she shouts, Read!
aloud first page, . . . *David*
Copperfield. I shake and cough aloud,
everyone stares. Their eyes pierce
my skull and laugh at my twisted
tongue holding words in dying
knots. (Strength!) But they laugh
and push sweat from wheelbarrows out
my eyes dripping and freezing on the page
reflecting the pointer from teacher's
hand tapping on a desk shouting,
"Read!"

Whether I shall turn out
to be the he-
ro in my life o
r whether that statio-
n shall be held by som-
eone else (This) these pages m ust tell
"Stop! Too slow!"
She grabbed my shirt. Her
eyes stopped mine from blinking.
A puddle lay beneath my desk and
the kids still laught spit
balls in my back, like knives.

My nose forced to press against
a cold brick wall. The teacher's
ridicule and the laughing class,
rolled down the crevices between
the layers of brick, like bowling-
balls crashing into my face. Again
and again.
"Read! . . . . Why can't you
READ?"
(Larry Ellis, "Dyslexic")

Correspondence to the Setting

Sometimes the physical setting of a poem acts as a metaphor for the theme. Richard Hugo coined the phrase "the **triggering town,**" a term for a device in the form of a setting or locale that's meant to act both as a springboard into the poem and as a metaphor for the speaker's state of mind. In his poem, "Degrees of Gray in Phillipsburg," the economic and physical collapse of a once prosperous silver-mining town stands for the speaker's spiritual emptiness and his sense of defeat. As the town's setting reflects the speaker, the speaker also reflects the psychology of the town in lines such as, "The principal supporting business now/is rage." Other minor elements, such as the car he drives and the jailed prisoner who has forgotten his crime, also function as **correspondences.**

Degrees of Gray in Phillipsburg

You might come here Sunday on a whim.
Say your life broke down. The last good kiss
you had was years ago. You walk these streets
laid out by the insane, past hotels
that didn't last, bars that did, the tortured try
of local drivers to accelerate their lives.
Only churches are kept up. The jail
turned 70 this year. The only prisoner
is always in, not knowing what he's done.

The principal supporting business now
is rage. Hatred of the various grays
the mountain sends, hatred of the mill,
The Silver Bill repeal, the best liked girls
who leave each year for Butte. One good
restaurant and bars can't wipe the boredom out.
The 1907 boom, eight going silver mines,
a dance floor built on springs—

all memory resolves itself in gaze,
in panoramic green you know the cattle eat
or two stacks high above the town,
two dead kilns, the huge mill in collapse
for fifty years that won't fall finally down.

Isn't this your life? That ancient kiss
still burning out your eyes? Isn't this defeat
so accurate, the church bell simply seems
a pure announcement: ring and no one comes?
Don't empty houses ring? Are magnesium
and scorn sufficient to support a town,
not just Phillipsburg, but towns
of towering blondes, good jazz and booze
the world will never let you have
until the town you came from dies inside?

Say no to yourself. The old man, twenty
when the jail was built, still laughs
although his lips collapse. Someday soon,
he says, I'll go to sleep and not wake up.
You tell him no. You're talking to yourself.
The car that brought you here still runs.
The money you buy lunch with,
no matter where it's mined, is silver
and the girl who serves you food
is slender and her red hair lights the wall.

(Richard Hugo, "Degrees of Gray in Phillipsburg")

METAPHORICAL CORRESPONDENCE One of the logical operations behind making metaphors includes **identity** in the form of similarity or dissimilarity. Setting up a metaphorical identity with another character and his activities and then filling out the remainder of the poem with echoing correspondences can be almost a mathematical exercise in logic, although we're speaking of qualitative rather than quantitative concepts. William Stafford's poem "Moles" compares the moles' way of life with the speaker's. Both the animals' and the human's quality of life, along with their environments, are compared and help form the system of metaphorical correspondences in the poem.

Moles

Every day that their sky droops down,
they shrug before it can harden
and root for life, rumpling along
toward the green part of the garden.

Every day the moles' dirt sky
sags upon their shoulders,
and mine too sags on many a day,
pinned by heavy boulders.

We get tired, the moles and I,
toiling down our burrows.
They shrug dirt along their way,
and I rumple on through sorrows.
(William Stafford, "Moles")

SYMBOLIC CORRESPONDENCE Where metaphor compares something usually unknown and general (the literal term) to something known and specific (the figurative term), as in "Her *mouth* was a *rose,*" a symbol accrues its meaning by absorbing implications from its surrounding context until it comes to stand for an abstract quality that is larger than the sum of its contextual parts. For instance, depending upon its local context, a mountain might be made into a symbol for strength, piety, inspiration, or obstacles. The following stanza is from Allison Hunter's poem "Trophy," which defines a tense mother-daughter relationship. While the daughter is off horseback riding, experiencing the kind of new-found freedom and adventure she associates with becoming an adult, the mother stays at home communing with trophies that are literal representations of her daughter and symbols of her departure from the mother.

The rooms clean by noon, you dusted
the trophies on my desk, each one a portrait
of my posture, miles away: horse welded to rider.
The silver trembled as your cloth rubbed it alive.
(Allison Hunter, "Trophy")

While we might at first think that the trophies stand for the daughter's achievements that her mother is proud of, in the context of the full poem we come to understand that the trophies are symbols of the daughter's alienation from her mother, who finds it easier to clean house than relate to her daughter.

Diagram of Correspondences

In Tony Hoagland's poem, "One Season," there are a host of inner correspondences that show up in the form of images, tropes, parallel phrasing, and plot elements (indicated in boldface and connected by lines in the graphic on the next page.

That was the summer my best friend
called me a **faggot** on the telephone,
hung up, and **vanished from the earth**,

a normal occurrence in this **country**
where we change our lives
with the **swiftness and hysterical finality**

of **dividing cells. That month**
the rain refused to fall,
and **fire engines** streaked back and forth crosstown

toward **smoke-filled residential zones**
where people stood around outside, drank beer,
and watched their neighbors' houses burn.

It was a bad time to be affected
by nearly anything,
especially anything as dangerous

as **loving a man**, if you happened to be
a man yourself, **ashamed** and **unable to explain**
how your feelings **could be torn apart**

by something **ritual** and understated
as **friendship between males**.
Probably I talked too loud

and thought an extra minute
before I crossed my legs; probably
I chose a girl I didn't care about

and took her everywhere,
knowing **I would dump her in the fall**
as **part of the evening score**,

part of practicing the scorn
it was clear I was going to need
to get across this planet

of violent emotional addition
and subtraction. Looking back, I can see
that I came through

in the spastic, fugitive half–alive manner
of **accident survivors. Fuck anyone**
who says I could have done it

differently. Though now **I find myself**
returning to the scene
as if the **pain** I fled

were **the only place that I had left to go**;
as if in my love, whatever kind it was , or is,
were still trapped beneath the **wreckage**

of **that year**,
and I was one of those angry **firemen**
having to go back into the **burning house**;
climbing a ladder

through the **heavy smoke and acrid smell**
of my own feelings,
as if they were the only
goddamn thing worth living for.

Listed according to their separate domains, the correspondences would appear like this:

Imagery	Tropes	Phrasing	Plot Elements
fire engines	dividing cells	That was the summer	watched . . . houses burn
smoke-filled . . . zones	emotional addition and substraction	faggot	loving a man
crossed my legs	evening the score	That month	chose a girl . . . I didn't care about
accident survivors	Fuck anyone	nearly anything	dump her in the fall
firemen	wreckage	especially anything	evening the score fall
	heavy smoke and acrid smell of my own feelings	that year	practicing the scorn
		that year	friendship between men
		as if	I find myself
		as if	
		as if	

The Emblem

This is the visual equivalent to a paraphrase. It is composed of a small constellation of inner correspondences from a poem, usually the images, and named after the symbolic images found on a medieval shield. It's a conceptual tool, much like the concept of **theme,** that writers and critics use to hold an abbreviated mental picture of the poem's figurative content. If we were to create an emblem of Tony Hoagland's poem "One Season" (p. 37) it might include the images of fire, a gawky adolescent, and the haunting presence of two male friends. These are the main images that symbolically outline the forces and tensions in the poem. Conceiving of a poem's emblem is a handy way of weighing and balancing its content so as to gain a sense of whether it is unified, coherent, and complete.

The Flashback and Flashforward

These common literary and cinematic devices act as windows onto past or future experiences that come to bear on and affect a present situation in the poem. Oftentimes the degree of intensity of a speaker's attitude or reaction to a situation has to do with past baggage or what is at risk in the future.

In Sharon Olds' poem "The Quest," a **flashback** to important emotional baggage of parental abuse from the speaker's past impinges on the present and triggers her maternal instincts. Here are lines from the middle of the poem, where the speaker is walking through the city on her quest to try to single out people whose faces have the look of evil (flashback in boldface):

as I walk home I
look in face after face for it, I
see the dark beauty, the rage, the
grown-up children of the city she walks as a
child, a raw target. I cannot
see a soul who would do it, I clutch the
jar of juice like a cold heart,
remembering the time my parents tied me to a chair and
would not feed me and I looked up
into their beautiful faces, my stomach a
bright mace, my wrists like birds the
shrike has hung by the throat from barbed wire, I
gazed as deeply as I could into their eyes
and all I saw was goodness, I could not get past it.

(Sharon Olds, "The Quest")

A **flashforward** can be seen in W. S. Merwin's poem "For the Anniversary of My Death" in which he says with strange accuracy how each year, without knowing it, he passes the date of his death (as if it were an annual birthday). Then he goes to lyrically posit the freedom he will experience after his death.

TECHNIQUES FOR ELABORATING CONTENT: ELABORATION EXERCISE

Write an opening line or two, or even just an image, and then try using the following techniques to amplify what you have written.

1. **The conceit:** Add a metaphor to your opening line and then embellish upon that metaphor so that its characteristics are filled out like filigree (see Lynn Emanuel's "On Waking after Dreaming of Raoul," p. 29).
2. **Simultaneity:** Write in a situation, scene, or image that is occurring at the same time (though not necessarily in the same place) as your opening lines are occurring (see examples, p. 29).
3. **Inner correspondences:** After your opening lines, salt in repetitions, variations, or enhancements of the most significant images, tropes, or actions from your opening lines (see p. 30).
4. **Slant imagery:** After your opening lines, set down a series of associated images or tropes that have similar, though slightly varied, characteristics and attributes of your opening content (see Marcus' "Tuba," pp. 31–32).
5. **Story within a story:** After your opening lines, segue to an anecdote or small story from another time and place that somehow parallels, deepens, and throws light upon the meaning of the opening lines (see Ellis' "Dyslexic," pp. 33–34).
6. **Correspondence in setting:** Start out indirectly writing a poem about your state of being by describing, with a selective eye, details from an urban, suburban, or rural place, so that the images you choose are representative of your inner emotional, psychological, or spiritual state (see Hugo's "Degrees of Gray in Phillipsburg," pp. 34–35).
7. **Metaphorical or symbolic correspondence:** Choose an animal or metaphor that most closely resembles your current state of well-being. Then select some actions or characteristics of the animal, its quality of life, or images of its habitation that feel appropriate and use them to indirectly address your situation (see pp. 35–36).
8. **Flashback and flashforward:** After your opening few lines, use a scene from the past or from the future to exemplify some relationship to what you are writing about in the present (see p. 38).

HORIZONTAL AND VERTICAL CONTENT

A simple method for distinguishing the kinds and functions of content in a poem is to imagine the content of a poem in the shape of a cross, intersecting horizontal and vertical lines. Each direction functions as a complement to the other. The horizontal direction contains the genre or rhetorical mode of the poem (e.g., narration, description, argument, exposition, etc.). The vertical line, which indicates the formation of a theme and thesis, contains (1) the static forces of aesthetic order inherent in a work of art, and (2) the active logical processes that are integral to the formation of its theme (see diagram on p. 42).

The Horizontal Plane of Content

The **horizontal content** of a poem is generally composed of material that describes, defines, narrates, argues, explains, or acts as imagistic or rhetorical decoration. A schematic of the kinds of content on the horizontal plane in poetry—how a poem gets told—would look like this:

Description – Argumentation – Definition – Characterization – Exposition – Narration

The Vertical Plane of Content

The **vertical content** of a poem is composed of two main parts: (1) aesthetic forces of internal order that make a poem hold together and complete its inner shape, and (2) cognitive operations of rational and associative logic that select, transform, and galvanize a poem's theme. In the following diagram, these vertical operations are split into the above two aspects.

Internal Forces of Order	Cognitive/Logical Processes
Tension	**Recognition**
Balance	**Discrimination**
Correspondences	**Classification**
Coherence	**Integration**
Completeness	**Transformation**
Unity	**Understanding**

The left side of the vertical line lists those forces that help create and maintain a sense of internal order in a work of art.

1. **Tension:** elements of a poem that are held together through similarities, dissimilarities, logic, references, and actions
2. **Balance:** the contents of a poem that correspond to or in some way echo, mirror, or enhance one another
3. **Correspondences:** discrete aspects of similarity in sonics, form, imagery, plot, logic, rhetoric, and trope
4. **Coherence:** the overall power of attraction formed by associations in logic, domains of imagery, formal and syntactical effects, sonics, and **location** of the poet's consciousness
5. **Completeness:** the exact amount of form and content that makes the experience of a poem feel aesthetically and logically complete
6. **Unity:** those elements of domain and thematic movement in a poem that go to create an overall sense of oneness

The right side of the vertical line lists the basic cognitive, logical operations that are essential to translating an experience into a work of art.

1. **Recognition:** At first, we must recognize something special about a situation, feeling, or experience in order for us to moved to write.
2. **Discrimination:** Then we go about trying to discern or discriminate what it is that's special about the experience.
3. **Classification:** After we discriminate among the plethora of data, we begin to classify the material we've selected out of the mass of data.
4. **Integration:** The next step is an integration and coordination of the material we've classified.
5. **Transformation:** At this point, the collected data reaches critical mass and we are able to transform what we have perceived.
6. **Understanding:** Ultimately, what we have perceived reaches a heretofore unrealized level of understanding, epiphany, or resolution.

It's worth noting that the same cognitive processes we use in decoding our experience in the world are the same cognitive processes we use when we first read a poem.

Tracking the amounts and design qualities of balance and form between horizontal and vertical aspects of a poem helps determine, during composition, revision, or critical analysis, the working interrelationship between the two. They may be present in equal amounts in a poem, overbalanced toward one or the other, or one may be present only to be "in service" to the other. The appropriate relationship and balance between the two aspects can only be determined by the poem's focus, strategy, intention, and goals. Following is a diagram showing how the two planes intersect.

Aspects of Horizontal and Vertical Content

Internal forces of order		**Cognitive/Logical processes**
Tension	T	**Recognition**
	H	
	E	
Balance	M	**Discrimination**
	A	
	T	
Correspondences	I	**Classification**
	C	
GENRES OF		HORIZONTAL CONTENT
Description–Argumentation–Definition		*Characterization–Exposition–Narration*
	F	
Coherence	O	**Intergration**
	R	
	M	
Completeness	A	**Transformance**
	T	
	I	
Unity	O	**Understanding**
	N	

Types of Horizontal Content

NARRATION AND DESCRIPTION In the following poem by Morton Marcus, the narrative and its accompanying description form the horizontal direction of the poem, while the last line forms the vertical, thematic content.

The Moment for Which There Is No Name

On the sixteenth floor of one of the tall old buildings in the north end of the city, the windows of a vacant apartment look out over the bay. The apartment is empty, the floors and walls bare. There is only a chalked circle on the living room floor. The circles traces the spot where an armchair once stood, an armchair in which an old man regularly sat watching the smokestacks come and go in the harbor in the same way he had watched the swaying forests of masts when he was boy, years before he became a bookkeeper for one of the city's three tool and die works.

The circle was drawn by the old man's grandson, while the child's parents were supervising the movers.

Tomorrow the new occupants will arrive, and preparatory to moving in they will clean the apartment. In the course of their cleaning, they will erase the chalk.

That is the moment for which there is no name.

(Morton Marcus, "The Moment for Which There Is No Name")

EXPOSITION David St. John, through a series of carefully slant rhymed and parallel, selected images, explains the unsolvable, paradoxical relationship in the way that as the scale of what we know lengthens, it continually buries deeper what we do not know. The poem acts as an expanded, imagistic syllogism, using a color scale, to explain these tensions.

I Know

I know the moon is troubling;

Its pale eloquence is always such a meddling,
Intrusive lie. I know the pearl sheen of the sheets
Remains the screen I'll draw against the night;

I know all of those silences invented for me approximate
Those real silences I cannot lose to daylight . . .
I know the orchid smell of your skin

The way I know the blackened path to the marina,
When gathering clouds obscure the summer moon—
Just as I know the chambered heart where I begin.

I know too the lacquered jewel box, its obsidian patina;
The sexual trumpeting of the diving, sweeping loons . . .
I know the slow combinations of the night, & the glow

Of fireflies, deepening the shadows of all I do not know.

(David St. John, "I Know")

TONE In "Man in a Window" by Ralph Angel, it is the speaker's attitude toward the world, his nervous **tone** (created by repetitions of phrasing, disjunctive thinking, idiosyncrasies of colloquial speech, and interspersed, penetrating insights) that gradually accrue into the poem's theme of mistrust and identity. In this example, where the theme is revealed by the horizontal aspect of tone, tone also functions as the poem's vertical content (see pp. 46–48 for more on horizontal content acting as vertical content).

Man in a Window

I don't know man trust is a precious thing
a kind of humility Offer it to a snake and get repaid with
humiliation

Luckily friends rally to my spiritual defense
I think they're reminding me

I mean it's important to me it's
important to me so I leave my fate to fate and come back
I come back home We need so much less always always
and what's important is always ours

I mean I want to dedicate my life to those who keep going just to
see how it isn't ending

I don't know
Another average day
Got up putzed around 'til noon
took a shower and second-guessed myself and
all those people all those people passing through my
my days and nights and all those people and
and you just can't stay with it you know what I mean
You can't can't stay with it Things happen
Things happen Doubt sets in Doubt sets in and
I took a shower about noon you know and I shaved and
thought about not shaving but I
shaved I took a shower and had a lot of work to do but I
I didn't want to do it I was second-guessing myself that's when
doubt got involved

I struck up a
rapport with doubt I didn't do any work and so
and so I said to myself I said well
maybe I should talk about something but I didn't learn
anything

I couldn't talk about anything there was
lots of distraction today
A beautiful day Lots of distraction It had to do with
all these people all these too-many people
passing through my days and nights But I
don't get to hear about ideas anymore know what I mean
Just for the hell of it Talking about ideas
Takes the mind one step further
further than what it already knows Doesn't
need to affirm itself It's one step beyond affirming itself

Vulnerable in a way that doesn't threaten
even weak people Those nice-guy routines
They come up to you
because they know how to be a nice guy
(Ralph Angel, "Man in a Window")

DIALOGUE Some poems composed solely of characters speaking to one another substitute dialogue for description and plot so that the speech of the poems' characters act as horizontal and/or vertical content. Denis Johnson's poem "Travelling" features inane exchanges of repetitive small talk in daily life in a barbershop as the content of the poem.

Types of Vertical Content

Throughout the following stanzas by Naomi Shihab Nye, there are statements, metaphors, symbols, rhetorical questions, and anecdotal fables that explicitly, figuratively, or through **nuance** plumb in one way or another the theme of humanity's interconnectedness (in boldface).

With the Greeks

When you dance Greek-style,
you wave a handkerchief,
the foot stomps, **a necklace of islands**
rises in the blood.
Moving through days,
the shadow of this circle
stays with you.
Outline of a wheeling fish
that says **you are less alone**
than you think.

At the grill, shrimp curl perfectly
on sticks. A sleek woman with a bow-tie
strokes her husband's hand.
What have we in common?
Grandmother spooning honey-puffs
smiles at anyone. Here child, eat,
fortify yourself for the journey
between homes.

Floating heart, who knows
which hand is on which arm?
Whether any story begins or ends
where we say it does,
or goes on like a circle,
common sea between stones and lamps.
In the villages of Greece
windows light up like eyes.
Children carry things in baskets,
a basket sits on the floor.

I heard of an orchard where statues grew up
between the roots of trees. Stones were men,
one trunk had feet. I heard of an island
where snails rose out of the dirt
and saved the people, who were starving.

Tonight there is no ocean
that does not sing. Even sorrow
which we have felt and felt again
in all our lands, had hands.
(Naomi Shihab Nye, "With the Greeks")

Horizontal as Vertical Content

A complication of this simple intersection in functions of content quite often occurs when what nominally might be considered horizontal content (description, argumentation, narration, exposition, etc.) also serves as vertical content that promotes and galvanizes the theme. A poem such as Robert Pinsky's "Shirt" enumerates parts, machines, workers, tasks, and people. Complex social, political, and historical factors behind the making of a simple shirt coalesce into the poem's thesis, of how there is an epic human story and unbelievable complexity involved in the evolution of simple, basic objects, if we would but look.

THE NARRATOR AGENT When actions, images, or tropes in a poem do the work of describing, explaining, or narrating—in other words, act as commentary on behalf of the narrator—then that action, image, or trope is termed a **narrator agent**. As a device it is a very subtle use of indirect statement that is effective because it is part of the poem's **aesthetic surface** and feels less didactic than the narrator, who directly and explicitly comes right out and explains or states his or her point.

In Kate Daniels' poem "Christmas Party," she expertly selects and exploits the rich psychological and emotional possibilities of the images in her setting in order to show how uncomfortable the upper-class speaker of the poem is feeling as she hears a report about war atrocities from the expatriate, Leonel. The boldface font indicates actions, metaphors, and imagery that act as **narrator agents.**

Here, as Leonel speaks in his calm, sore voice,
I feel my hand holding my glass of scotch,
the tiny scratch of ice against the sides,
hear wood burning and falling through the grate,
smell the sweetish smell of applewood, the ghost of fruit.
Next to me, a hand with rings reaches
into a silver bowl of tangerines and walnuts
and comes out full. The luxurious wool
of my trousers bothers me. I feel part
of a long chain of something rich and useless.
(Kate Daniels, "Christmas Party")

In the passage below from Mark Halliday's "Reality U.S.A.," instead of explicitly saying that his main character really has no idea of what reality or "the American Experience" is, and that the examples his character chooses as being illustrative of nitty-gritty reality are actually cliched, quite unreal, and more fodder for his fantasies, he "explains" these ideas by allowing us into his character's inner thoughts. In these lines his character quite ironically and humorously picks out an image on a billboard as an example of reality, and then goes on extrapolating the realities he thinks he's missing.

What about real life?
The woman in the light-blue skirt
on the cigarette billboard has such big thighs!
What is it about thighs? Smooth and weighty,
weighty and smooth: you can tell there's really
something *there.* And to think that
the woman must really exist, it's a photo after all
not a painting, she's somewhere in America—
and to think that some guy gets to lay down
on her and her thighs . . . She's a model,
she probably lives in New York, New York baffles me
I know I could never find her there—but

listen, her sister lives in Baltimore,
hanging out sheets to dry from the balcony
of a light-blue house, lifting her arms—
reality.
(Mark Halliday, "Reality U.S.A.")

His character then goes on to fantasize more cliches and complications about what he thinks is the American Experience.

One final example of the **narrator agent** can be seen in the literal/symbolic description with which Yusef Komunyakaa weaves together both his setting and the "brutality" of a father/son relationship.

We lingered in the quiet brutality
Of voltage meters & pipe threaders,
Lost between sentences . . . the heartless
Gleam of a two-pound wedge
On the concrete floor
(Yusef Komunyakaa, "My Father's Loveletters")

Notice Komumyakaa's subtle serialized use of juxtaposition in "pipe threaders/ "Lost between sentences . . . /the heartless"; and the highly selected, resonant objects he's chosen from his scene: voltage meters, pipe threaders, a wedge, a concrete floor.

HORIZONTAL AND VERTICAL CONTENT EXERCISE

1. **Horizontal correspondence:** After your opening few lines, use description, narration, analysis, process, argument, exposition, or an **extended metaphor** to widen and elaborate the scope of your subject, scene, characters, or action (see pp. 42–43).
2. **Vertical correspondence:** Take a poem you have already written, or a poem by someone else, and practice adding details, images, dialogue, tropes, and/or anecdotes that nuance and indirectly pressure toward the surface the theme of the poem (see pp. 44–46).
3. **Horizontal as vertical content:** Use what would normally be horizontal content (description, narration, exposition, or argument) as vertically directed content by having it develop into the thesis of the poem (see pp. 46–48).

LATERAL AND DIGRESSIVE MOVES

The **lateral move** and the **digressive move** are two very common and similar subtypes that move as **horizontal content** and act to bring to light or reinforce content. The idea in the technique is to allow parts of the poem to drift sideways, like a boat in a current, in order to fill out either (1) the horizontal function of content (e.g., description, narration, exposition, argumentation, etc.), or (2) to purposefully digress in order to end up in some small but revealing detail that impinges upon and pressures the theme toward the surface (in which case the digression ends up indirectly affecting **vertical content**).

Lateral Moves

Here are several examples (in boldface) of lateral moves.

The following lines quickly characterize a woman's troubled relationship with a man she's in love with, and then by way of exaggeration characterize his irresistible allure, which is the reason he has become her problem.

> Mother is drinking to forget a man
> **who could fill the woods with invitations**
> (Lynn Emanuel, "On Waking after Dreaming of Raoul")

In order to acutely sketch in and anchor the unique quality of an experience, sometimes it is profitable to move laterally by extending a general state through a highly specific simile.

> Sometimes I remember my dreams **as if they were**
> **a movie I were in** when it was the movie that was in me.

Mining the Details

The poet James Wright half-kiddingly wrote: "There are some tiny obvious details in human life that survive the divine purpose of boring fools to death." But his point about really seeing "what is" is well taken. In the following example lines by Robert Long, the description of the speaker's surroundings succeed in creating through an elaboration of the details a sense of his being trapped under the crush and rush of urban life:

> The romance of police in their shiny cruisers washes
> Across television screens **as well as everyone's windows,**
> **Here in New York, through the first-floor triple-locked**
> **Kind as well as the big, barroom plate-glass type,**
> **Street level, blurred with transient figures: going to work,**
> **Going home, etc.**
> (Robert Long, "Have a Nice Day")

Correlatives

This term, similar in function to the psychological details in the poem above, is a lateral reference that, on one level, seems to be an objectively stated image, action, or event; but, when viewed in terms of the poem in which it resides, it has obvious implications that affect, nuance, and echo other parts of the poem.

THE ANECDOTAL CORRELATIVE In John Skoyles' poem "Once or Twice," the subject of having and not having, of hitting and missing, are **leitmotifs** subtly carried throughout the poem and brought sharply into focus in the little snowball fight incident near the end, which is a **correlative** in the form of an anecdote as to his hit-and-miss situation.

Once or Twice

1
You never let me have you
more than once or twice.
I guess these things
don't mean that much to you,
and I don't want to say
they have to be meaningful
in some silly psychological sense;
but for me at those times
watching your face,
for a moment each feature
took on a life of its own.
And I loved those little lives
in you, being someone
whose life is steady and controlled.
So it was a release for me
to see you lose yourself
passionately, once or twice.

2
Leaving your house one morning,
after a night with you,
I saw children dodging
each other's snowballs.
One said "Where did I get you?"
I mention this only because
I have nothing to say to you,
and there's a chance this detail
might soften up your heart a little.
(John Skoyles, "Once or Twice")

In other words, the correlative of the snowball fight is a substitution for what the speaker would like to ask his girlfriend.

THE ENTIRE POEM AS CORRELATIVE Sometimes, as in the genre of the **fable,** an entire poem can be a metaphorical correlative to an unstated concept or theme. In Russell Edson's poem below, the cracked logic of his fable allows us to see one explanation of the intersection between art and human sexuality from an entirely unexpected and odd point of view.

The Rat's Legs

I met a rat under a bridge. And we sat there in the mud
discussing the rat's loveliness.

I asked, what it is about you that has caused men to write odes?

My legs, said the rat, for it has always been that men
have liked to run their hands up my legs to my secret parts; it's
nature . . .

(Russell Edson, "The Rat's Legs")

Digressions

These lateral kinds of moves, seemingly away from the thematic centerline of a poem, appear to fly in the face of the rule imposed against allowing digressive material into good essay writing; yet, as with most poetic devices that rhetoricians categorize as fallacies of logic, structure, or form, these **digressions** and counter-intuitive moves have a very canny purpose quite the opposite to their seeming to be a defect that includes unnecessary material.

Yusef Kommunyakka keenly and succinctly captures the guilt, need, and loneliness that his speaker's father feels, by way of sparsely selected quotes from his love letters.

Words rolled from under
The pressure of my ballpoint:
Love, Baby, Honey, Please.

(Yusef Komunyakaa, "My Father's Loveletters")

Slyly and purposefully contradicting himself in order to draw attention to what to some may seem like a small matter (the death of a pet dog) but is, in fact, one of great import, the speaker below protests that his subject has nothing to do with the Norman Rockwell-like themes of American literature, which, in fact, it does seem to.

For this is about a dog and a boy
and has virtually nothing to do with Mark Twain
and the rest of American Literature

(Richrd Katrovas, "A Dog and a Boy")

In a kind of purposeful run-on description of what the speaker in the following lines senses, Mark Cox allows his speaker to end up describing his wife's fingernails as an oblique and savvy way of bringing to bear on the present situation her tense relationship with her mother.

I feel childish and gently pull
the blanket over my head, barely touching my lips
to the short, ragged fingernails she chews while talking
to her mother on the phone.
(Mark Cox, "The Word")

LATERAL AND DIGRESSIVE MOVES EXERCISE

Extend by filling out what could normally be considered a completed image or action with additional images or actions that (1) move the original images in a lateral direction into new territory on the same level of description, narration, or argument, or (2) move the images or actions by way of a digression, which ends up highlighting an insightful and significant point, trope, action, or image (see pp. 51–52).

LOGOPOETICS

This term, popularized by Ezra Pound in his seminal tract on Modernism, *The ABC of Reading,* refers to: (1) the imaginative and logical interaction of ideas and imagery in a poem, or, as Pound says, the "the dance of ideas" in a poem; and (2) the dynamics and effects that arise from the interaction of having employed different poetic techniques and word usage. The two main remaining Poundian terms that encompass aspects of poetry are **melopoetics** (sound and rhythmical effects) and **phanopoetics** (imagery). It should be noted that, as with other techniques, tactical moves of **logopoetics** can be amplified to the level of their being a structural strategy so that the poem evolves into a new form, such as the mosaic qualities of the **fractured narrative, montage, collage,** and **stream of consciousness.**

Pound, in the first sense of the logopoetics, in which different angles and levels of thought are placed contiguously, pointed to the multidimensional levels of tone and thought that the French poet Jules Laforgue was able to create in his work. The concept of logopoetics seems to be a precursor to Robert Bly's postmodernist idea of **leaping poetry,** in which the poet's imagination leaps from one level of consciousness to another, from dream image to realistic detail to spiritual realm to metaphorical musings, what Flannery O'Connor referred to as **anagogical writing** (originally a term referring to biblical writing that contained multiple levels). In other words, Bly seems to have capitalized on Pound's idea of admixing varying textures and used the same concept in terms of juxtaposing different kinds of consciousness. We'll look at both micro and macro levels of logopoetics, from switching domains of consciousness to the use of tactics within a poem that create the illusion of dimensionality by juxtaposing related but different forms of verbal expression, as employed in multimedia orchestrations. The basic tools needed for this kind of variegated composition are energy and a spontaneous and abiding sense of surprise.

Leaping Levels of Consciousness

Here we are focusing on the movement of the poet's mind, tracking the different dimensions and domain of consciousness it enters, flows through, and re-enters. In Jorie Graham's poem "Salmon," she begins by literally describing the upstream spawning habits of salmon, and then, in order to match levels of instinct, she jumps over to considering Platonic states of being and everyday life, then weaves her way through other levels of thought and sense.

	They leapt up falls, ladders,
(LITERAL)	and rock, tearing and leaping, a gold river
(SYMBOLIC/	and a blue river traveling
SPIRITUAL)	in opposite directions.
(CONCEPTUAL)	They would not stop, resolution of will
(RATIONAL	and helplessness, as the eye,
ANALOGY)	is helpless
(SCIENTIFIC)	when the image forms itself, upside-down,
	backward,
	driving up into
(PHILOSOPHICAL)	the mind, and the world
	unfastens itself
(LITERAL FACTS	from the deep ocean of the given. . . .
ACTING	Justice, aspen
SYMBOLICALLY)	leaves, mother attempting
	suicide, the white night-flying moth
	the ants dismantled bit by bit and carried in
	right through the crack
	in my wall. . . .
	(Jorie Graham, "Salmon")

Rhetorical Tactics

This term **rhetoric** is used to describe a series of different kinds of moves meant to persuade the reader and suspend his or her belief ("rhetoric" means "means of persuading"). It's an excellent way to add textural interest and flow to a work, and a way to drive and shape the poem thematically. In the poem below by Mark Halliday, which appears to be a **stream-of-consciousness** form, the poem is actually a choreographed, rich admixture of expressive modes—nearly cyclic in their appearance in the poem—whose forms are made up of narration, summary statements, characterizations, **meditative moments** (composed of **commentary**), rhetorical self-questions, self-corrections, and insights (as the *marginalia* indicates).

	Reality U.S.A.
Cycle # 1	I feel I should go to Norfolk Virginia and drink
(NARRATIVE)	gin with sailors on leave from the *Alabama,*
	talking baseball and Polaris missiles and Steve
	Martin movies, another gin with lime juice, then
	Balto, Balto, hitchhike in and out of Baltimore
	for days back and forth for days in a row dis-
	cussing the jobs of whoever gives me rides, sales-
	men, shippers, small-time dispatchers of the
	much that can be
(SUMMARY STATEMENT)	dispatched. For the ACTUALITY OF IT!
(CHARACTERIZATION)	Books dominate my head. I read in them, I read at them,
(SELF-QUESTIONING)	I'm well into my thirties. What about real life?
(MEDITATIVE MOMENT)	The woman in the light-blue skirt
	on the cigarette billboard has such big thighs!
	What is it about thighs? Smooth and weighty,
	weighty and smooth: you can tell there's really
(INSIGHT)	something *there.* And to think that
Cycle # 2	the woman must really exist, it's a photo after all
(NARRATIVE)	not a painting, she is somewhere in America—
	and to think that some guy gets to lie down
	on her and her thighs . . . She's a model,
(CHARACTERIZATION)	she probably lives in New York, New York
	baffles me. I know I could never find her there—but
(MEDITATIVE MOMENT)	listen, her sister lives in Baltimore,
(DESCRIPTION)	hanging out sheets to dry from the balcony
	of a light-blue house, lifting her arms—
(NARRATIVE)	reality. Along with
	her dimly dangerous ex-husband, her speed pills,
	his clumsy minor embezzlement of funds from
	Pabst Auto Supply, and what else? The boxing
	matches he goes to, and the stock-car races

(SELF-QUESTIONING)	and—maybe I should go to Indianapolis?
(SELF-CORRECTION)	But I feel sure I'd be bored in Indianapolis
	despite the smoky reality of Indianapolis.
(MEDITATIVE MOMENT)	But it's this idea of American experience how I don't have it, how I ought to know the way things are really and not just from Hemingway or Dreiser, John O'Hara or James T. Farrell or, say, Raymond Carver or Bruce Springsteen
(SUMMARY STATEMENT)	but directly: firsthand: hands-on learning.
(SELF-QUESTIONING)	What if I were to take a Greyhound to Memphis,
Cycle #3	quit shaving, learn to drink whiskey straight,
(NARRATIVE)	lift some weights (maybe I should do the weights before I go) and get a tattoo on one bicep saying KISS OFF and meet a guy named Eddie who chain-smokes and rob a record store with Eddie! Yes, we smash the glass at 3 a.m. on Davis Avenue in Memphis and grab 300 albums and 20 8-track tapes pile them into Eddie's red pickup and bingo, we're gone in five minutes. Next day we paint the pickup yellow
(CHARACTERIZATION)	and change the plates, no sweat. Eddie knows,
	he knows stuff, he knows how to fence the loot
	and he says next we hit a certain TV store, he
	slugs my shoulder laughing, I get my piece of cash
(MEDITATIVE MOMENT)	but really it's not the cash I care about
(SUMMARY STATEMENT)	it's the being *involved.*
Cycle #4	Eddie thinks that's weird,
(NARRATIVE)	he says "You're weird, man"
	and starts to act mistrustful so I leave town.
	Kansas City here I come.
(SELF-CORRECTION)	No, skip Kansas City, I want to save Kansas City.
	Just in case.
(SELF-QUESTIONING)	—In case what? What am I talking about?
	How many lives does a person get?
	one, right? and me,
(CHARACTERIZATION)	I love my life with books!—
(SELF-CORRECTION)	Of course it's *not* just books, I've got bills
(DESCRIPTION)	and friends and milkshakes, the supermarket,
	laundromat
(SELF-CORRECTION)	oh shit but still I keep feeling this thing about *reality*—
(MEDITATIVE MOMENT)	the world is so loaded: a green beer bottle is chucked half-full from a speeding Ford Mercury and that beer sloshes

(SELF-QUESTIONING) exactly like this loaded world—what?
(SELF-CORRECTION) Forget the world, just take America,
(MEDITATIVE MOMENT) sure there's the same hamburgers everywhere and
gasoline fumes but among the fumes and burgers
(SUMMARY STATEMENT) there's *detail,* tons of it, you can smell it.
There are variations . . . All the stuff Whitman
claimed he saw, there's the really *seeing* that stuff!

Cycle #5

There's—
(NARRATIVE) I don't know—there's a waitress in an Arby's
Roast Beef and her name is either Donna or Nadine,
you buy the Special on the right day and you get a
free Batman 10-ounce glass, she makes a joke about
it, you say "What time do you get off work" (only
this time it's really hapening) and that night Donna
or Nadine does for you what you thought they only
did in fiction . . . That's right. Next morning her bottom in the light from the window looks so pearly
(SUMMARY STATEMENT) it's like home, just glad to be home.
(NARRATIVE) It's April, all cool and sunny,
and across the street from Arby's there is a ten-
year-old black boy wearing red hightops and we
talk about the Braves (this is in Georgia, now, and
the asphalt glistens) and the kid says something
that I'll never forget. Good. So then, the kid's
uncle sells me some cocaine or teaches me how to
aim a pistol or takes me for a ride in his helicopter—
(SELF-QUESTIONING) there must be a few black men who own helicopters?
(NARRATIVE) Up we go roaring over Georgia
The roofs and poles and roofs
the components,
the components!
Ohhhh . . . Already they've worn me out.
(Mark Halliday, "Reality U.S.A.")

Tactical Maneuvers

Although the switching of states of consciousness in Jorie Graham's "Salmon" shows up, technically, in the form of different kinds of poetic devices, they are, so to speak, only the resulting symptoms of having traveled through different states of consciousness. The same is true of Mark Halliday's "Reality USA"; the changes in its surface rhetorical **tactics** appear because the writer's mind changed direction. The distinction between the writer's entering different states of consciousness and the writer's deciding to employ technically various tactics is admittedly an elusive and argumentative difference; but there is a difference, and it goes back to the etymology of the word *technique,* meaning "to make." It's just a matter of whether the techniques are being invented in the making or are being applied more consciously as devices a book such as this can teach.

LOGOPOETICS: POETRY PROJECTS EXERCISE

For the sake of economy, here's an exercise that's a lot of fun entitled "Twenty Little Poetry Projects," with which Jim Simmerman creates an interesting admixture of textures. He says it's his most popular exercise with students and one that has consistently produced good student poems. The prescribed list of rules has these directions by Simmerman: "Open the poem with the first project and close it with the last. Otherwise, use the projects in whatever order you like, giving each project at least one line. Try to use all twenty projects. Feel free to repeat those you like. Fool around. Enjoy."

1. Begin the poem with a metaphor.
2. Say something specific but utterly preposterous.
3. Use at least one image for each of the five senses, either in succession or scattered randomly throughout the poem.
4. Use one example of **synesthesia** (mixing the senses).
5. Use the proper name of a person and the proper name of a place.
6. Contradict something you said earlier in the poem.
7. Change direction or digress from the last thing you said.
8. Use a word (slang?) you've never seen in a poem.
9. Use an example of false cause-and-effect logic.
10. Use a piece of "talk" you've actually heard (preferably in dialect and/or which you don't understand).
11. Create a metaphor using the following construction: "The (adjective) (concrete noun) of (abstract noun) . . ."
12. Use an image in such a way as to reverse its usual associative qualities.
13. Make the **persona** or character in the poem do something he/she could not do in "real life."
14. Refer to yourself by nickname and in the third person.
15. Write in the future tense, such that part of the poem seems to be a prediction.

16. Modify a noun with an unlikely adjective.
17. Make a declarative assertion that sounds convincing but that finally makes no sense.
18. Use a phrase from a language other than English.
19. Make a nonhuman object say or do something human (**personification**).
20. Close the poem with a vivid image that makes no statement, but that "echoes" an image from earlier in the poem.

Here's Simmerman's own exercise poem he assigned himself from "Twenty Little Poetry Projects":

1. Morning comes on like a wink in the dark.
2. It's me it's winking at.
3. Mock light lolls in the boughs of the pines.
Dead air numbs my hands.
A bluejay jabbers like nobody's business.
Woodsmoke comes spelunking my nostrils
and tastes like burned toast where it rests on my tongue.
4. Morning tastes the way a rock felt
kissing me on the eye:
5. A kiss thrown by Randy Shellhouse
on the Jacksonville, Arkansas, Little League Field
because we were that bored in 1965.
6. We weren't *that* bored in 1965.
7. Dogs ran amuck in the yards of the poor,
and music spilled out of every window
though none of us could dance.
8. None of us could do the Frug, the Dirty Dog
9. because we were small and wore small hats.
10. *Moon go away, I don't love you no more*
was the only song we knew by heart.
11. The dull crayons of sex and meanness
scribbled all over our thoughts.
12. We were about as happy as headstones.
13. We fell through the sidewalk
and changed color at night.
14. Little Darry was there to scuff through it all,

15. so that today, tomorrow, the day after that
he will walk backward among the orphaned trees
16. and toy rocks that lead him
nowhere I could ever track,
till he's so far away, so lost
17. I'll have to forget him to know where he's gone.
18. *La poullet grave du soir toujours avec moi--*
19. even as the sky opens for business,
even as shadows kick off their shoes,
20. even as this torrent of clean morning
light comes flooding down and over it all.

SUBSTITUTION

Although the technique of **substitution** of content, which is parallel to the metrical substitutions of feet in traditional verse, arrives from the natural, unconscious, associative powers of the mind, it can be abstracted from the creative process and used consciously as a "bait and switch" element of revision for purposefully linking one level of meaning to another; for instance, literal to thematic or abstract, or the reverse. Usually, this tactical move opens up the vertical direction of a poem's content, whether it plumbs downward or transcends upward, but it can also be used on the horizontal plane of content.

Moving Through Levels of Meaning

SUBSTITUTING THE FIGURATIVE FOR THE LITERAL In the following passage from the poem "Traffic" by Holly Smith, as the speaker starts by referring to a literal situation of rush-hour traffic, she substitutes the literal "back up" of traffic for an emotional, metaphorical "back up," and then moves the content of the poem further along in the form of an opportunistic **segue** to a **flashback** (substitutions are boldfaced, the segue is italicized).

If you sit long enough
red flashes **of rage** [METAPHORICAL SUBSTITUTION]
break the exhaust haze.
Traffic backs up
further and further
into the back of my mind [METAPHORICAL SUBSTITUTION]

until I don't have to think
about the time last summer [SEGUE TO FLASHBACK]
when you said you would return
but never did.
(Holly Smith, "Traffic")

There's a great deal of work on two levels being done by the **substitutions,** and merely by the singular move of substituting the emotional for the literal, the poet has created an opportunity to fill in the reader deftly on the catalyzing, dramatic situation.

In the following passages from Robin Behn's poem "Station," she employs a very effective substitution in her closure in which the symbol of an imagined arriving train, set up and elaborated in earlier content, takes the place of a suicide scene. The substitution could be viewed as a kind of relief or euphemism, but it also adds an eerie emotional dimension to the action.

and the boy who brought the gun into the lunchroom
and raised it to the height of love which didn't yet

know forward or reverse,
and that we did sit together on the trestle
all one night of the history of earth and call it *hobo tracks,*
our lives swinging from the end of one stick.
But not. Or else not yet.

"Bundles" and "tracks" the doctors call it when
the aging brain snares itself on the dim past, blank future.
Are we there yet?

Where yet? Who?
With the small gray satchel.
Are there windows on the train?

And we would be on which side of the glass?
After the sun is bandaged?
And are the others ready yet?

The boy put the gun inside his mouth.
We thought we had forgotten that.
But what did it look like to the mouth?
Yes, the train, it's coming now—
(Robin Behn, "Station")

SUBSTITUTING THE LITERAL FOR THE FIGURATIVE Going in the reverse direction, from a symbolic dream image back to a literal one, John Engman very effectively shows in the closure of "Mushroom Clouds" a child switching from an apocalyptic fantasy he has during an atomic bomb air-raid drill to the actual, literal scene.

(FANTASY)	I imagined myself in crash helmet and bulletproof vest, Miss Nurvak's periscope rising from the blackened grass:
(LITERAL)	how happy [my teacher] would be to see **a successful graduate of Central Elementary** who had not been reduced to ash,
(FANTASY)	whose ideals had not been shaken by the atomic blast, who pushed the culprit forward with his bayonet,
(LITERAL)	**a boy with wet pants.**
	(John Engman, "Mushroom Clouds")

SUBSTITUTING THE LITERAL FOR THE ABSTRACT Here the poet follows two series of summary actions with an abstract, cause-and-effect conclusion, and then stays on the abstract level to characterize and evaluate the former abstractions.

	As first as a child I collected words, slurring them together into a single blur
(FIRST SUBSTITUTION)	**until I thought what I felt.**
	Then I collected others' words. words so wise and irreducible
(SECOND SUBSTITUTION)	**I thought they taught me how to grasp.**
(MEDITATION ON ABSTRACTIONS)	**They felt like a kind of immortality but they only insured I could never use them whenever I inquired after myself.**

Substitution as an Overall Strategy

Just about every device or technique used in a poem can be amplified to become a **strategy,** an overall plan for achieving a result; or, taken from a slightly different perspective, it can be considered an **organizing principle.** For instance, a metaphor can be enlarged to become a **controlling metaphor;** the voice of a character or thing can be magnified into a **persona poem;** a flashback can be leveraged into a full-blown **memory narrative,** etc. In the examples that follow, the poets have adopted, repeated, and complicated the technique of **substitution** so that it stands as their poems' strategy and type.

PARADOXICAL SUBSTITUTION A Rainer Maria Rilke poem, "Sometimes a Man Stands Up During Supper," puts forth the proposition that if one stays home and does not undertake a spiritual pilgrimage, then one's children will compensate by revolting and leading the life their father had forsaken. On the other hand, if one opts to wander the world on a spiritual quest, then one's children will necessarily choose to settle down and lead a more conventional and stable life. The same is true in Philip Larkin's "Poetry of Departures": no matter what the speaker does or doesn't do, he is fated to accumulate the same life he has led, as if there were a "prime directive" of no escape even though the urge for an opposite inner and outer journey remains.

Poetry of Departures

Sometimes you hear, fifth-hand,
As epitaph:
He chucked up everything
And just cleared off,
And always the voice will sound
Certain you approve
This audacious, purifying,
Elemental move.

And they are right, I think.
We all hate home
And having to be there:
I detest my room,
Its specially chosen junk,
The good books, the good bed,
And my life, in perfect order:
So to hear it said

He walked out on the whole crowd
Leaves me flushed and stirred,
Like *Then she undid her dress*
Or *Take that you bastard;*
Surely I can, if he did?
And that helps me stay
Sober and industrious.
But I'd go today,
Yes, swagger the nut-strewn roads,
Crouch in the fo'c'sle
Stubbly with goodness, if
It weren't so artificial,
Such a deliberate step backwards

To create an object:
Books; china; a life
Reprehensibly perfect.
(Philip Larkin, "Poetry of Departures")

SUBSTITUTION BY SUBTRACTION In Beckian Fritz Goldberg's poem "The Possibilities," she uses a unique, subtractive method of substitution whose series of replacements continuously unpeel, like an onion, the layers of external circumstance so that when all the objects of desire are removed, we see the basic condition of the human heart unmasked (subtractions in boldface).

The Possibilities

After a wife's death a man may talk
to his horse with a great tenderness
as if, just this morning, he had tried on
her pink slipper. **And if he has no horse**
he may crack his window a little
wider when it lightly rains to confirm
the roofs and trees are made
of paper. **If there is no rain**
he may make himself a meal at midnight,
sweet artichokes and Danish cheese,
a glass of red wine. **If there is**
no red, then white. He may suck
his knife clean with his tongue. Later

lying awake he may hear the wild lung
of a motorcycle far off on a far road.
If there is no motorcycle, a dog
trying for any syllable in any known
language. Something falling suddenly in
in the closet, according to some law.
Nearness in the dark is a kind of beauty
though it is only a lampshade, a shoulder
of the walnut chair. **If there is no chair,**
then a shelf. A shelf of books with the devil's
violet fedora tossed on top. Or something
exotic from the sea, manta ray

like the pulse in the ball of his foot.
A man may walk ten steps behind
his life. It may be sorrow or fear.
He may see her back like two doves rushing

up where a boy has flung a handful
of pebbles. **If no pebbles,** leaves
where a masked prowler hunches, his belt of
lockpicks, his bag of velvet like the one
from which memory snatches. These are

the possibilities, the immaculate
like miracles which are nothing
in themselves, but in this world a sign
of angels, ghosts, supernatural beings
who watch us. Who listen. Who sometimes
helplessly let us stumble on
their pyramids, their crude observatories
or let us, generation after
generation, speak to the broken horse
of the human heart.

(Beckian Fritz Goldberg, "The Possibilities")

SUBSTITUTION OF THE PHYSICAL FOR THE INEFFABLE In Mark Cox's poem "In This His Suit,"the implied assertion that drives the poem is that we are not the physical beings and artifacts that can be easily apprehended, but we are those haunting traits, beliefs, and experiences we take with us when we go, yet leave behind as human hieroglyphics.

In This His Suit

Not his clothes, but their chimerical creases,
not his body, but the gestures of the body
worn last and put unpressed
into its plastic. Not the hand,
but how he held it, palm buttressing head.
Not the meat, not words, but grace; not the mouth,
but the smoke, scratches on a plate, the
table's dulled edge.
Not absence, not presence. Not indentation,
but impression. Not not, but not is, not either
or neither. The hose's curve, the garden's
mounds, the slab walk's slope, the book's missing page
found in another book.
Not the death, but his dying.
Not male, not female, not young, old, compassionate,
bitter, peaceful or sorrowed.
Not the life, but the living.

(Mark Cox, "In This His Suit")

SUBSTITUTION OF TIME FRAMES In Kyle Vaughn's poem below, we witness a succession of "before and after" snapshots of the ways things were once beautiful and comfortable when love existed, all of which are purposefully juxtaposed against a later, more degraded quality of life when love is gone. The poem's unconscious strategy, which forms the basis of its conscious, structural strategy of substitution, is based on the psychological and poetic device of **selective perception,** in which what we naturally tend to see in the outside world is unconsciously selected to reinforce the intense emotional state we happen to be in at the time.

rewriting myself

there used to be something about love written here,
but now it is an old man feeling somewhat sick.

there were birds standing in for confession and revelation.
now there are new buildings, already being remodeled.

here was written the possibilities of falling down,
but now just the record of having fallen.

once the record of beauty and voices,
now burned lines and words turned to ash.

even when I was young and injured, I remembered certain
kinds of hope,
even just mother covering me with ice.

now I lie in the bathtub, pretending it is cool.
wool suits and almost reaching comfort in my shoes
now sweaters eaten away by something in my drawers
and buttons lost in the darkness behind them.

years ago I used my words to explain myself.
but they evolved into telescopic poems, which I use to stay far
away.

I do try, though like looking in the eyes of my friends,
trying to convince myself to be comfortable.

trying to earn degrees and hold conversations.
trying to listen joyfully to each morning cracking open.

trying to remember how to write music.
trying to pick up the phone and say what is perfect, what is right.

do what is right—be a good man, I tell myself
but nothing changes.

no, things change—

there used to be something about love written here.

(Kyle Vaughn, "rewriting myself")

SUBSTITUTION EXERCISE

Try salting in the following tactics into a poem you'll write or have already written.

a) After a literal detail, add a prepositional metaphor (e.g., "the red traffic light **of rage**").
b) Add in a fantasy stemming from the narrative.
c) Find a metaphor in your poem and then make a short list in which you subtract or substitute some of its characteristics or attributes.
d) Find some literal images in your poem and then add an abstract quality or specific detail to those images.
e) Right after a narrative event or a statement of condition, segue to the past or future, and/or another place or scene.

C H A P T E R

3

Connecting Content

THE IMAGE NARRATIVE

Cesare Pavese, the great twentieth-century Italian poet, spoke of a poem's "image story," or **image narrative,** by which he meant the story told, in coherent form, through a series of the poem's images and perceptions. The image narrative could be thought of as a story form of the **emblem** (see p. 123) in that its imagistic appearance is similar, but while the former is an elaborated, dynamic descriptive mode, the latter is a static, foreshortened, symbolic cluster of associated images. Pavese writes of his discovery of the image narrative.

> I had discovered the value of the image. And this new image of mine (*here* was my reward for my stubborn insistence on concrete narrative) was not imagery in the familiar rhetorical sense, i.e., a more or less arbitrary decoration imposed on realistic narrative. In some obscure sense, my image *was* the story itself.

This sort of shorthand, internal glimpse into a poem's visual aspects can be of great help during the revising process.

The poet Richard Jackson writes on the use and function of the image narrative.

> At the heart of every poem is a kind of tension, as Allen Tate calls it, a counter-pointing between the dynamic forces of language. We might call this the structural dynamic, an example of which might be how most "good" characters in *King Lear* speak a language of nature, while most "bad" characters speak a language of commerce, politics, and militarism: the collision of language types is a collision of vision. Emily Dickinson often creates tension by counter-pointing images that relate to the conservative religion of her time against images of erotic love. The images are arranged by way of their associative and connotative references into an image narrative, a shorthand plot summary, an "underplot" that props up the surface "plot" or structure and is really the essence of form. In the context of each poem's image

> narrative, words take on special, often different, or shaded meanings. The image narrative itself is what orchestrates and paces our responses and emotions as they and we move through the poem.

Jackson continues: "Being aware of the image narrative allows the poet to better see or intuit where the poem might take some other turn, or where it has taken a wrong or confusing turn."

In Pavese's poem "Summer," notice how he creates an image narrative between abstract and concrete imagery: abstract images of the memory and experience of light, smell, and sound on the one hand, and concrete images of sound and substance on the other (key words in boldface).

A garden between low walls, **bright,**
Made of dry grass and a **light** that slowly bakes
The **ground** below. The **light smells** of sea.
You breathe that grass. You touch your hair
And shake out the **memory of grass.**

I have seen ripe
Fruit dropping thickly on **remembered grass** with a **soft**
Thudding. So too the **pulsing of the blood**
Surprises even you. You move your head
As though **a miracle of air** had happened around you,
And **the miracle is you.** Your eyes have a **savor**
Like **the heat of memory.**

You **listen.**
You **listen to the words,** but they barely graze you.
Your face has a **radiance of thought that shines**
Around your shoulders, like **light from the sea. The silence**
In your face touches with a **soft**
Thud, exuding **drop by drop,**
Like **fruit that fell** here years ago,
And old pain still.
(Cesare Pavese, "Summer")

The interplay and extension of taste, touch, sight, smell, and sound begin to redefine each other so that the senses radiate out, embrace each other, and so that, on the surface level of meaning and plot, the poem can shift from its opening descriptive and external sense of nostalgia to its more internal sense of pain in its closure. The image narrative has transported us into ourselves by metamorphosing its own images, letting them develop, grow, and tell their own story. In this subliminal sense of "plot," we are looking at the unconscious, often archetypal, associations within a felt experience, and if we follow this narrative in its connective relation to the surface plot narrative, it allows us to see how we can give more depth and resonance to our ideas about revising.

A clearer example can be seen in Michael Ryan's following poem, in which description and action can be summarily categorized into three mutually shared general categories: (1) chaos, (2) normalcy, and (3) formlessness (key words in boldface).

TV Room at the Children's Hospice

Red-and-green leather-helmeted
maniacally grinning motorcyclists
crash at all angles
on Lev Smith's **pajama top**

and when his **chocolate ice cream**
dumps like a mud slide down its front
he smiles, not maniacally, still **nauseous**
from chemotherapy and **bald** already.

Lev is six but sat still four hours
all afternoon with IVs in his arms,
his grandma tells everyone. Marcie
is nine and was **born with no face.**

One profile has been built in increments
with **surgical plastic and skin grafts**
and the other looks like **fudge.**
Tomorrow she's having **an eye moved.**

She finds a **hand-mirror** in a **toy box**
and maybe for the minute I watch
she sees **nothing she doesn't expect.**
Ruth Borthnott's son, Richard,

cracked his second vertebra
at **diving practice** eight weeks ago,
and as Ruth describes getting the news
by telephone (**shampoo suds plopped**

all over the notepad she tried
to write on) **she smiles** like Lev Smith
at his **ice cream,** smiles also saying
Richard's on **a breathing machine,**

if he makes it he'll be **quadriplegic,**
she's there in intensive care every day
at dawn. The **gameshow**-shrill details
of a **Hawaiian vacation** for two

and **surf teasing the ankles**
of the couple on a **moonlit beachwalk**
keep drawing her attention
away from our **conversation.**

I say it's amazing how life can change
from one second to the next,
and with no apparent disdain
for this **dismal platitude,**

she nods yes, and yes again
at the gameshow's **svelte assistant**
petting a dinette set, and yes
to Lev Smith's grandma

who has appeared beside her
with **microwaved popcorn**
blooming like a huge
cauliflower from its tin.

(Michael Ryan, "TV Room at the Children's Hospice")

Segues

A **segue,** whose root word means "to follow," is simply a way to connect to and transit from one thing to another, whether it be among plot elements, different domains of imagery or thought, or from one level of a poem to another. One of the stickier narrative problems in the lyric-narrative genre of poetry, in which the organization of **time frames** (past, present, future) and physical or abstract space (place, interiority and exteriority, levels of consciousness) are constant considerations, is the inventing of ways to move smoothly, organically, and with a sense of unpredictable inevitability from one narrative element to another. Once again it should be noted that the techniques for achieving a seemingly seamless segue from thing to another is just a technical replication of the way in which our minds naturally process experience.

TO CHANGE SUBJECTS The segue below creates a subject change smoothly and easily because of the underlying characteristics held in common between the cat devouring the bird and the woman hunting for men: a sense of predation, a guiltless sort of guile, and a cold-hearted, instinctual, mercilessness.

Sometimes when I think about my cat
holding down a bird she's caught
and opened up as easily and neatly
as the cold light shining in her eyes,
I am reminded of a woman I loved

who let me be with her on selected nights
so she could more easily attract other men.

CHANGING FROM FIGURATIVE TO LITERAL BACK TO FIGURATIVE In Alberto Rios' poem "The Inquietude of a Particular Matter," he links the metaphorical portrait of a young woman to her literal, daily activities that, in turn, circle back again to a metaphorical, interior, mythic quality the young woman seems to possess for the speaker.

big clack teeth
Like in the cartoon, unconnected,
Almost, clacking, clacking so
She could not help
Sounding like the fat ducks
That every day she fed
After she stopped her work
In the peeling secretariat
Of a third but ambitious
Supervisor to the federal railroads,
Fed the ducks every day popcorn,
Palomitas, and the one day
She could not because of the snow,
Snow for the first time
She could remember this early,
This far to the south,
The ducks opened their mouths anyway
And ate the snow, the white bits
They thought had come from her.
(Aberto Rios, "The Inquietude of a Particular Matter")

White Space

Generally speaking, there are two fundamental ways by which poets make **white space** (the space between stanzas or sections in a poem) work in a poem: one is a simple, straightforward cinematic "wipe-out" that is meant to introduce a new topic, scene, character, plot point, or point of view, etc.; and the second is a more subtle "coloring-in" of meaning in the white space by the use of subtly implied content. The first kind requires a resetting or reloading of content with each new stanza, while the second type involves an implied interpolation of content in the white space. A third type, a combination of the two primary techniques, is one in which something new is introduced while there's also a concomitant further development of the poem's logic, argument, plot, or associative reasoning occurring in the white space.

THE WIPE-OUT In the following five stanzas from Donald Hall's poem "Ox Cart Man," he uses each stanza as a time and/or place unit that breaks away from what has just been described or thought. Stanza 1 deals with bagging potatoes; stanza 2 deals with other household goods and articles; stanza 3 deals with the marketplace; stanza 4 describes the ox cart man's selling off of his cart and ox used to haul the goods; and stanza 5 describes his starting from scratch again.

Ox Cart Man

In October of the year,
he counts potatoes dug from the brown field,
counting the seed, counting
the cellar's portion out,
and bags the rest on the cart's floor.

He packs wool sheared in April, honey
in combs, linen, leather
tanned from deerhide, and vinegar in a barrel
hooped by hand at the forge's fire.

He walks by his ox's head, ten days
to Portsmouth Market, and sells potatoes,
and the bag that carried potatoes,
flaxseed, birch brooms, maple sugar, goose
feathers, yarn.

When the cart is empty he sells the cart.
When the cart is sold he sells the ox,
harness and yoke, and walks
home, his pockets heavy
with the year's coin for salt and taxes,

and at home by fire's light in November cold
stitches new harness
for next year's ox in the barn,
and carves the yoke, and saws planks
building the cart again.

(Donald Hall, "Ox Cart Man")

COLORING-IN MEANING In the minimalist example below, characteristics of similarity and dissimilarity within the images of the poem travel across the white space in the same way that information and impressions travel across the synapses between brain nerve cells. Basically, the technique works the same way as **juxtaposition** of content in and between lines in a poem. Here's an example that'll help make the point:

Hands

Leaves

Wings

Ideas

The white space between the objects exhibits a back-and-forth progressive movement of thought, from human to vegetable to animal back to human, ultimately triangulating an equation between the functions of hands and ideas, that of grasping.

Track the different kinds of linked thinking traveling through the white spaces in the first six stanzas of Robin Behn's poem "Paper Bird" (editorial remarks are italicized in brackets between stanzas).

The way folding makes a weakness
in the paper, the way the weakness

[*now Behn considers the opposite*]

let the wings
move as if to fly,

[*Behn now correlates two subjects*]

the way, flying, he left me
and left behind this bird

[*now she takes meaning into consideration*]

as a token, I suppose, of how
we two

[*here she manipulates and fuses her bird image*]

were a bird with four wings
that seemed to lift

[*now she releases the image into a finality*]

our single body
a little off the ground;
(Robin Behn, "Paper Bird")

THE IMAGE NARRATIVE: WHITE SPACE EXERCISE

Write the first stanza of a poem. Then, in preparing to write your second stanza, make the white space contain some of your thinking about lines in the first stanza. For instance, if we were to write a first couplet as:

> The brown fox
> leapt over a fence

and then we thought about the symbolic character of foxes (wild and free nature) and fences (ownership of earth), we could connect the first couplet to the second couplet by having the white space contain that symbolic thinking, as in:

> The brown fox
> leapt over a fence
>
> then another and another until
> it had a sense of who built them

We could then continue thinking about the two levels we had just built up and add a new one-line stanza in a similar fashion in which the white space, again, contains our thinking; in this instance, a note on how pride and greed can separate us from our basic nature, as in:

> The brown fox
> leapt over a fence
>
> then another and another until
> it had a sense of who built them
>
> and why one gets lost.

CINEMATIC TECHNIQUES

We turn to the terminology and techniques of filmmaking when dealing with the manipulation of imagery and physical viewpoints in a poem, since cinematic techniques are primarily concerned with the cutting and splicing of film segments and setting up various kinds of visuals. Film editing has four basic purposes: (1) to expand or compress the actual time period of an event; (2) to show the **simultaneity,** emotional contrast, or equivalency of corresponding events (as in the use of **associational logic, metaphor,** and **symbol**); (3) to insert a repeated visual (and sometimes aural) comment that anchors a series of shots to a motif or *idée fixe* (as in a **refrain**); and (4) to fill in or project pieces of **plot** by inserting scenes from the past or future.

Techniques of camera movement and camera angles create distinct fields of vision that evoke specific emotional responses in the viewer, and that physical **point of view** determines the viewer's role in the action on a spectrum from participant to observer, which creates an attitude on the part of the viewer toward the action, and the felt-intensity of the drama.

Cuts

Cuts splice different shots together so that the first shot is immediately replaced by the second. In poetry we call this immediate proximity of images, actions, or ideas a **juxtaposition.** There are four basic kinds of cuts.

THE STRAIGHT CUT The **straight cut** is linear in direction, and acts to further the plot or theme in a straightforward way; for example, (cut 1) a girl sits by the phone; (cut 2) the phone rings and she picks it up. This cut offers a natural, easy sense of movement, and logical chronology.

THE CROSSCUT The **crosscut** shows actions taking place at the same time in two or more separate locations. In poetry, it's the construction known as the **cut-and-shuffle poem.** In filmmaking, D. W. Griffith invented the technique.

(CUT 1) a man is hit by a car
(CUT 2) an ambulance starts on its way for the rescue

The crosscut can also be used to show ironic contrast or philosophical resignation.

(CUT 1) our man who has just been hit by a car
(CUT 2) the ambulance on its way gets into a crash
and/or
(CUT 3) slow-motion close-up of snowflakes falling

THE CONTRAST CUT The **contrast cut** is also used to heighten the tension in a situation, but while the crosscut may use similar shots in juxtaposition, the contrast cut always uses opposing shots. After establishing the character of an American soldier fighting in Vietnam, contrast cuts might look like this.

(1) our man hit by a bullet
(2) his wife giggling and flirting with a shoe salesman

The possibilities are limited only by the imagination and experience of the writer.

THE JUMP CUT The **jump cut** is an editing device in which **actual time** (the time it actually takes to do something in "real life") is foreshortened into

felt time (the illusion of actual time). It is also known as **cutting-to-continuity,** a term that implies continuous but compressed action. Camera shots skip from action to action creating the illusion of continuous motion, but showing only a necessary small fraction of the action. An extreme example of this is illustrated in the following stanza from Alan Dugan's "On a Seven-Day Diary." He captures the boredom of his daily routine by listing in throw-away fashion the sequence of the general things he did.

Oh I got up and went to work
and worked and came back home
and ate and talked and went to sleep.
Then I got up and went to work
and worked and came back home
from work and ate and slept.
Then I got up and went to work
and worked and came back home
and ate and watched a show and slept.
Then I got up and went to work
and worked and came back home
and ate steak and went to sleep.
Then I got up and went to work
and worked and came back home
and ate and fucked and went to sleep.
Then it was Saturday, Saturday, Saturday!
Love must be the reason for the week!
We went shopping! I saw clouds!
The children explained everything!
I could talk about the main thing!
What did I drink on Saturday night
that lost the first, best half of Sunday?
The last half wasn't worth this "word."
Then I got up and went to work
and worked and came back home
from work and ate and went to sleep,
refreshed but tired by the weekend.
(Alan Dugan, "On a Seven-Day Diary")

Visual Transitions

Transitions are editing devices that bridge separate images or actions. Transitions can be smooth, abrupt, expected, or unexpected. The two types of transitions that are most sophisticated and adaptable to poetry are the **metaphorical dissolve** and the **form dissolve.** In addition, there are the distinct but related devices of the **thematic montage,** the **flashback,** the **flashforward,** and the **substitute image.**

THE METAPHORICAL DISSOLVE The **metaphorical dissolve** is a synthesis of two different actions or images united by their implied meanings. The first image is transformed into a second image that, in turn, then reinforces or changes the first image. For instance, a man who is about to have an automobile accident might be reading a "Dear John" letter behind the wheel of his moving car. The camera zooms in on the letter, which represents pain and loss, and then dissolves to the hospital sheet that covers the face of the now-deceased accident victim. The letter and the sheet then come to symbolize death. Similarly, in early gangster movies, it was common to see a man in a white hospital room that starts to spin; this image, in turn, dissolves into a spinning newspaper headlining the event. Here's a passage that exemplifies the device.

> Mornings I used to walk the dogs
> by Nacote Creek, months before their deaths,
> **I'd see the night's debris, the tide's vagaries,**
> **the furtive markings of creatures desperate to**
> **eradicate every smell not theirs.**
> (Stephen Dunn, "Loosestrife")

THE FORM DISSOLVE The **form dissolve** juxtaposes images with similar physical characteristics. For instance, a blaze that an arsonist has set might dissolve and flashback into a bonfire he lit 20 years earlier at summer camp; or a shot of a starry night might ironically dissolve into the view from inside the black hood of a prisoner being executed at high noon. **Sound dissolves** are also common in films. The sound (and image) of water spraying from a burst pipe might segue smoothly into an oil gusher. It's common for these images to be used as a **leitmotif** in film or poetry, and the ease with which they are employed is equaled by their effectiveness. While film accommodates the form dissolve with a simple blurring or superimposition of images, poetry uses the devices of **simile, metaphor, juxtaposition, slant imagery,** and **off-rhyme or perfect rhyme** to effect a form dissolve. Here's an example for the device from John Brehm's "When My Car Broke Down."

> My second thought was to **stare at the engine**
> for a while. I leaned over and looked
> down into it **as into the bowels of a ship**
> **or the cranium of some fantastic beast.**
> (John Brehm, "When My Car Broke Down")

THEMATIC MONTAGE The **thematic montage,** an extension and intensification of the dissolve technique, is based on the list (or catalogue) form. Through its repetitions and improvisations, it pumps up dramatic effect and widens the connotative range of a subject while staying focused on its theme. Philip Levine's "They Feed They Lion" and Section IV of Allen Ginsberg's *Kaddish* are examples of thematic montage in poetry. Here's another that centrifugally relates the color blue to sadness; that is, from the central image of blue it radiates outward in a series of associations.

> From where you sit it's hard
> to tell the color of her eyes, but you'd have to guess
> some shade of blue, the local color here:
> **Blue Plate Special, smoke on the rise from a dozen ashtrays,**
> **the cop sweet-talking another Danish he won't pay for,**
> **an entire row of songs in the jukebox, the blue-streak**
> **chatter of a woman on the pay phone fingering the dark**
> **blue bruise on the back of her neck . . .**
> (David Clewell, "We Never Close")

THE FLASHBACK AND FLASHFORWARD The **flashback** (see p. 38) is a shot or sequence that opens up in the middle of another **time frame** (e.g., present or future) in order to add emotional, psychological, logical, or narrative context and dramatic weight to a story. It mimics the way our mind works when in the middle of a present experience we suddenly flash back onto some related incident (through similarity or dissimilarity) we have experienced in the past. The **flash-forward** (see p. 38) is an opposite technique in which a past or present action leaps forward into a real or imagined future event or image in order to supply information, knowledge, warning, or moral lessons to which the characters who are bound by the present usually aren't privy.

THE SUBSTITUTE IMAGE The **substitute image** plays off of the predictable **stock response** a reader or film viewer is about to have by a closely related but unpredictable image. In many films before the advent of our current more explicit sexual images, full nudity was substituted with images that supplied an apt innuendo. Over the years these kinds of substitutions have become cliches. For instance, intense physical desire was often visually represented by a riptide or tropical storm, which parallels the present literal action. But substitutions can also be diametrically opposed or tangential images in relation to the image that's cut. In Tomas Tranströmer's poem "Loneliness," just as he is about to have a head-on car crash, he substitutes the predictable, violent imagery with surreal images of his fear being felt as mucoid egg whites and impossibly elongated hospital buildings. In the passage below, the sexual substitution acts as a visual euphemism.

> As he took off his shirt and undressed,
> she looked out the window at a bare-branched tree
> that looked like an iron sculpture.

View

The physical view in film language corresponds roughly to the **point of view** in literary criticism, but here we will be speaking of a physical view, the "eyes" through which we see the specific images and scenes that make up the work of art. There are two basic considerations that make up a physical point of view: **range** and **angle.** (The related concept of camera movement will be discussed separately.)

RANGE **Range** in filmmaking denotes how close or how far away we, the viewer, are from something, the distance from which a shot is taken. In order to quickly establish a comprehensive context for an upcoming scene and its details, directors use a long-range, wide-angled shot. Or a director might want to focus closely and tightly on an image (for instance, the glass ball of swirling snow in the opening of *Citizen Kane)* in order to reveal more meaning, give more emphasis to something, and move the viewer from the feeling of being merely an objective and passive participant to being more of a subjective, engaged observer.

The Establishing Shot The **establishing shot** frames a great deal of information and context because it is a long-range view of a scene. It can be used as an opening shot to establish terrain or action (as in *Lawrence of Arabia's* opening of a shot of the desert and rising sun) or used as a closing shot to make a comment (as in *Working Girl,* where the camera zooms out from a single office, within which most of the film took place, to imply the millions of other office workers vying with each other in the tens of thousands of other office windows glittering in the New York City skyscape). Each movie is made up of single shots put into a **sequence,** which, in turn, make up scenes. In the following lines, an establishing shot quickly sets up a scene within which more particular action is taking place.

> Inside a house squatting at night on the prairie
> a woman reads by a lamp, a cat curled on her lap.

The Deep Focus Shot The **deep focus shot** is the visual equivalent to the **omniscient point of view** in that it enables the viewer to see background, middle ground, and foreground (just as the omniscient point of view enables us to see the exterior and interior of characters) all in clear focus. The following lines set this up efficiently.

> She dipped her toe in the tide
> and looked up at her husband who seemed
> to be swimming out toward the cruise ship
> heading for the heat, the sambas, and blue skies of Havana
> where from an overturned boat a man was swimming
> toward him.

The Close-Up Shot The **close-up shot,** which is the opposite of the establishing shot, selects, focuses on, zooms in on, or tracks details so that their importance is heightened. Cinematic cliches of this type abound: the shot of sweat on someone's face in a difficult situation; a lizard scuttling under a bush just before an atomic blast; a drop of dew (about to drip off a leaf) that reflects a landscape in miniature. In poetry, a few highly specific **selected details** (what the French call *le mot juste image*) and the **objective correlative** (if it's specific enough) are equivalent devices to the close-up shot. They act as narrative or descriptive forms of implication and commentary (**narrator agents**). For instance, in a relationship that is souring, the poet or filmmaker might focus on a wilted flower in the room, a dead fly caught between screen and window, etc. The **close-up** makes the viewer scrutinize details that might have otherwise been overlooked. In Maura Stanton's poem "The Conjurer," the speaker has cast a spell on the other characters, shrinking them to insect-sized complainers who infest her dreams.

> . . . those lovers crawled
> inside my left ear with candles
> trying to find my brain in a fog.
> They moved deep among the stalactites
> searching for the magic spell they thought
> I'd lost in sleep . . .
> (Maura Stanton, "The Conjurer")

Angle

The **angle** of a shot is a term used to indicate two aspects of a field of vision: the vertical height and horizontal tilt of the camera's viewpoint. But they are not just physical perspectives, since subjective human experience attaches emotional and psychological meanings to these various positions. For example, if the point of view is lower than what is being viewed, feelings of intimidation and doubt can be implied; if the point of view is higher than what is being viewed, feelings of superiority or mastery might be summoned up, while a tilt to the camera's angle is often used by genre filmmakers to depict disorientation or psychosis. For the purposes of poetry, we'll look at the **bird's-eye view** and the **low-angle shot.**

THE BIRD'S-EYE VIEW The **bird's-eye view** is a shot taken above a subject. While it literally states a physical distance and an all-encompassing comprehensibility, it can emotionally imply arrogance, disinterest, omniscience, transcendence, accusation, or fear. If we were to write a poem or make a movie about Icarus' flight to freedom from the Minotaur's maze, we'd use this point of view to effect many of the emotions mentioned above.

THE LOW-ANGLE SHOT The opposite of the bird's-eye view, the **low-angle shot** establishes a perspective literally beneath what is being viewed. It can imbue a scene or perspective with a sense of guilt, smallness, intimidation, or helplessness, as in the countless scene in movies where shots of onrushing trains, stampeding herds, and car chases are taken at or beneath ground level. In poetry, if, for example, we were writing about being operated on, the natural and obvious point of view would be from a position where we are looking up from the operating table at the doctors and lights. In Donald Justice's poem "Anniversaries," the speaker remembers what it was like to be an infant.

Many drew round me then,
Admiring. Beside my bed
The tall aunts prophesied,
And cousins from afar,
Predicting a great career.
(Donald Justice, "Anniversaries")

Movement

THE PAN The **pan** is the view taken in by the flat, lateral sweeping movement of a stationary camera. It approximates the movement of our eyes when we are taking in images such as a wide, horizontal setting or various people in a room. Actually, the pan is merely a processing of the static establishing shot, and because it moves, it can build up a sense of mystery or create a lively sense of presence and immediacy, and offer the build-up of a sense of acquiring information and familiarizing ourselves with our surroundings. Richard Hugo's opening lines in "2433 Agnes, First Home, Last House in Missoula" use the pan shot to establish familiarity with the setting.

It promises quiet here. A green Plymouth
has been a long time sitting across the street.
The lady in 2428 limps with a cane
and west of me fields open all the way
to the mountains, all the way I imagine
to the open sea.
(Richard Hugo, "2433 Agnes, First Home, Last House in Missoula")

THE MOVING SHOT A **moving shot** creates a sense of action to, through, or away from a scene. And depending upon the speed of this movement, it also creates excitement (flying toward something), fear (being chased), relaxation (a pleasant walk), or torpor (induced by feeling stuck in stopped time). Watch how Bill Tremblay uses a series of shots to create the sense of movement in this stanza from his poem "Creation" (see full poem on pp. 225–226).

                    His mother
carried him and created the kitchen,

the bathroom, talcum, pleasure. She
made the air, the smell of hot toast.
His father walked him with both hands
and created doors, the world outside,
angel clouds, and telephone wires strung
above streets were how things're connected.
He created motion in a maroon Packard,
and colors for go, stop, and maybe.
(Bill Tremblay, "Creation")

Poets have used a number of compositional techniques for movement in a scene: quick juxtapositions of images, the piling and layering of "rhyming" or dissonant images as in the montage and collage, the cataloguing or listing of images passing by, or a fuller inventory and accounting by way of narration and description. Once again, as in the pan, movement creates a sense of immediacy and unveiling.

Poetry, one of the most eclectic forms of art since it contains many aspects of the other arts, probably contains more technical terms than any other art because it has freely borrowed some of its terminology from film, dance, painting, sculpture, photography, architecture, and music.

CINEMATIC TECHNIQUES EXERCISE

Cut shot

1. **Crosscut:** Next to an event in a poem of yours, juxtapose a simultaneous event that *parallels or enhances* the original event.
2. **Contrast cut:** Next to another event, juxtapose a simultaneous event that is *in contrast or opposition* to it.
3. **Jump cut:** Take an event from your poem and write out a series of action shots within that event so that the series is *one continuous sequence.*

Visual transition

1. **Metaphorical dissolve:** Choose an image from one of your poems and then add an image with a similarly implied meaning that creates a transition to another scene.
2. **Form dissolve:** Choose an image or sense detail from one of your poems and create another image or detail that has a similar physical mass, color, or shape that makes a transition to a new domain.

3. **Thematic montage:** Choose an image from one of your poems and write out a series of associated images that progressively lead to the next image in the poem.
4. **Flashback/flashforward:** Right after an image, detail, event, or statement in one of your poems, segue backwards or forwards to another time and place.
5. **Substitute image:** Choose a few predictable images in your poem and substitute other more unexpected but logical images in their place.

Camera

1. **Establishing shot:** Open a poem with a full shot of the room the speaker is in.
2. **Deep focus shot:** In the above establishing shot, make sure details of the foreground, middleground, and background are equally in focus.
3. **Close-up shot:** Select one or more images from the above shot and focus in closely on some detailed aspect of it.

SYNTACTICAL TRANSITIONS

Hypotaxis and Parataxis (Juxtaposition)

The apocryphal adage that one imagines hanging like a sign over the writer's workshop, "Writing is 99% perspiration and 1% inspiration," seems to contradict Keats' famous and stultifying caveat, "If poetry comes not as naturally as leaves to the tree then it had better not come at all." But most poems don't come naturally; they're worked on draft after draft and "worked up" so they seem to have been effortless to make. Ideas, images, and phrasings, which don't come with complementary male/female plug-in sides to facilitate connecting things, put the burden on the poet to draft ways of maneuvering, adjusting, and ordering content so that the connections, like plumbing, gas, and power lines hidden inside walls, serve their purpose rather than exhibiting the blueprints and hard work of the multiple levels of thinking involved. This section of the book takes up two general means of making connections.

HYPOTAXIS **Hypotaxis** is based on the operations of rational modes of thinking in which the ordering of content proceeds through conventional forms of logic and the conventions of syntax, grammar, and language as a medium. Here, connections are explicitly applied as routes are on a map. Hypotaxis ("arrangement or placement beneath") is based upon formal logic or ratiocination, the usual rational arrangements the higher brain perceives as structures to manage and order time and space (such as chronological order, cause and effect, sequence-as-cause, subordination, association, parallelism, induction, deduction, transformation, enhancements, etc.). These are conceptual substructures that move the poem along in an orderly, linear fashion and keep the meaning coherent. The common genres of strategies for telling or showing something in literature—narration, argumentation, **exposition,** description, analysis, definition, and allusion—use the hypotactical method, which offers explicit directions as to where content moves and as to the hierarchy of relationships among its parts, much as traffic signals direct and adjust the flow of traffic.

Explicit connector phrasings and words such as "even though," "nevertheless," "but," "furthermore," "on the other hand," and so on, function very pragmatically to signal the direction, relationship, and relative importance of parts of content among other parts of content.

Sequence Stephen Dunn's opening two stanzas to "The Routine Things around the House" use the hypotactical words "when," "now," "yet," and "since" to indicate the logic of sequence-as-cause and the dialectic of the speaker's thought.

> **When** mother died
> I thought: **now** I have a death poem.
> That was unforgivable
>
> **yet I've since** forgiven myself
>
> (Stephen Dunn, "The Routine Things around the House")

Subordination The same sort of explicit, imbedded hypotactical traffic signals (parts of syntax that indicate the direction of a thought) occur in the next few lines of Dunn's poem, when the speaker uses subordinate clauses to name his position in the family and a quality of character he contains.

> **as** sons are able to do
> **who've** been loved by their mothers.
>
> (Stephen Dunn, "The Routine Things around the House")

PARATAXIS (OR JUXTAPOSITION) **Parataxis** (or **juxtaposition**), the second mode of thinking, is based more on the unconscious, associative kinds of connections that form as **jump cuts** in film, moving, through implication, from one thing to another with no explicit transition or contexting commentary as to how these things are connected. It does without the verbal bridge building that hypotaxis uses, and relies on the reader's ability to triangulate an implied transition between things. **Parataxis,** or **juxtaposition** ("arrangement side by side") is based on the unconscious modes of the brain's operations (dreams, fantasies, imagination) in which things such as images, actions, and thoughts appear side by side without any intervening transition, context, explanation, or helpful commentary, without any of the explicit, supporting hypotactical words of the more rational first mode.

A more efficient, livelier, but, at times, more difficult style for the reader to interpret can be seen in the placing back-to-back of disparate images, actions, and thoughts (what film terms **jump cuts**) in order to effect an especially quick and sharp quality of perception. For instance, placing the words, cat/bobcat/lion in a row immediately creates two primary attributes of association by way of resemblances and logic: (1) that this family of animals is feline; and (2) that there's a progression or **flow** from small to large and possibly from domesticity to wildness. And this was implied without any intervening exposition, commentary, or context.

In the following made-up example, images of scale and emotion are associatively laid out in discrete and linear juxtapositions of scenes that have the feel of carefully arranged, separate sequences and jump cuts.

> Whenever he would feel anything, it would feel magnified
>
> like walking up to a drive-in movie screen and looking up
> at the gunfights, stampeding herds, and lovemaking.
>
> His microbiology teacher felt the same way about things
> on the cellular level.
>
> Entering the subway, he stopped to watch an old man
> orchestrating a flea circus for passersby.
>
> He felt like a falling snowflake who had acrophobia.

But in the following poem, the juxtaposed images and references flow unbroken from one to another, reminiscent of a flight of thought. Fusing both the hypotactical and paratactical methods of arranging syntax, as if rounding the corners of a square and squaring a circle, Roger Weingarten, in his poem "Jungle Gliders," arrives at a combination style that explicitly connects narrative elements on a complex time/space continuum, but also force-feeds the reader a veritable *tour de force* flow of juxtaposed associations in the poem's first sentence.

> I was kneeling with my daughter into a chaos
> of frog-shaped jigsaw cutouts guaranteed
> to coalesce into animal acrobats that range
> the upper levels of South Asian jungles, when,
> looking up at the Dragon Lizard's ribs spread
> into wings pictured on the box my son,
> making bomber sounds, held
> over my head, I remembered the roach that fell
> out of the fist-sized hole in the ceiling

of my first furnished room, almost
eighteen and kneeling
between your pale
knees in the air, mind dug into the heap
of coats and blankets that covered the concrete
carpet of my basement palace, where
we were struggling for warmth
and pleasure, when the gold-bellied
angel of retribution, like a miniature
landlord, dropped through the onion-scented
fumes from the heater jammed in the window
and landed on your freckle we'd christened
The Third Eye.

(Roger Weingarten, "Jungle Gliders")

Leaping

In a seminal little book on the creative process and the theory and aesthetics of poetry, Robert Bly, in *Leaping Poetry: An Idea with Poems and Translations,* raises the techniques we've just been discussing to the level of a consideration of the two main types of consciousness involved—the conscious and the unconscious—and the interplay or lack of interplay between them. He maintains that much of Western poetry is based mostly on the processes of the higher brain's ability to use rational logic, while in other cultures' poetry, such as South American, Asian, and European styles based on Surrealism and intuition, there's a high degree of interplay between the conscious and unconscious modes of mental operation. He categorizes the amount and mix of levels of consciousness in a poem into the following hierarchy: (1) Poets of Steady Light, who tend to use only rational, conscious operations of consciousness; (2) Hopping Poets, who mainly rely on the products of rational logic along with a modicum of unconscious material; and (3) Leaping Poets, who, through the process of association, freely roam back and forth from conscious to unconscious levels in poems that display a "leap from the conscious to the unconscious and back again, a leap from the known part of the mind to the unknown part and back again."

Bly's idea, based upon scientific research on the brain's three-stage evolution (triune brain theory) from primitive to mammalian to higher brain, is that a complete expression of an experience should carry with it materials from these three hierarchical modalities of human consciousness. His popularization of the psychological levels at work in the creative process behind poetry has offered poets great freedom and permission from many of the restrictions and conventions of traditional Western verse, and seems another cultural signal of the way our post-modern culture perceives the world through Einstein's theory of relativity.

In "Lace," Dean Young uses conscious and unconscious levels of thought operations, both rational, hypotactical, and associative, paratactical methods, all sewn together with basic poetic devices and tools of logic and grammar, to get at an evocation of the delicate and intricate "lace" of what it is to be human.

Lace

While crickets tighten their solitary bolts
and morning's still dark-tousled,
the steady fan, steady turbine of summer mist,
each engine, planet, floating spark,
each person roams a room in my heart,
mother snaps beans into a bowl, father
blows smoke out through the screen door
and my wife lifts her arm to look at her arm,
the amethyst-and-platinum bracelet, in slats
of amber light, caught like a bee in sap.

After the afternoon hammock, beer bottles
loosening their labels with sweat, after
fireflies ignite like far city lights
that tease, devouring and devoured like stars
that fall, hampered with lust and weight,
I wait for her to come to bed, the water
in the pipes a kind of signal like locking
doors, turning the sheets and sleep
like a shell smoothed in the waves' lathe
and the kiss cool with fatigue and mint.

Before the delicate downward yearning of snow,
the winter wools and wafts of cedar, naphtha
and dry winter heat, the opaque wrapping
done and undone, burning in the grate,
before the gray vaulted shape of each burned thing,
the bitter medicinal dust, old lace and its cobweb
dream breaking in my hand, each thread frays, knots
give and knot again like roots into stem,
the stem unraveling into flower, into flame,
into seed and wind, into dirt, into, into, into.

(Dean Young, "Lace")

SYNTACTICAL TRANSITIONS: JUXTAPOSITION EXERCISE

One of the methods of creating implication with efficiency and verve is the use of juxtaposition, the placing of an image, action, description, comment, flat statement, or trope directly next to another image, action, trope, etc. Basically, the proximity of the two terms forces the triangulation of a third, implied "comment" that the close reader will perceive. Here are some categories of juxtapositions. Try creating your own exercise examples from these:

Juxtaposing equal images:

It's a clear blue day. This must be what it's like
to see through Marilyn Monroe's eyes.

Juxtaposing opposite images:

The birds are building their delicate nests
among the girders of the overpass.

Juxtaposing an equal image and concept:

The branches of the trees are bare.
I feel the same way when I'm nervous.

Juxtaposing an image to an opposite concept:

The cat falls asleep
to awaken its dreams.

Juxtaposing equal concepts:

Man invented democracy
when he could feel what other men felt.

Juxtaposing opposite concepts:

What stays is
what doesn't last.

SEMANTIC SPRINGBOARDS (COMMITTING OR TRIGGERING WORDS)

Oftentimes, the connotative, resonant, linguistic, or sonic qualities of words we happen upon in writing give rise, consciously or unconsciously, to new content and new directions for the content. On the upside, poets look upon these words as opportunities for **triggering words** to open up new associations, a **semantic springboard** that uncoils enough upward lift to give the poem new momentum.

On the downside, the poet has to determine whether or not this word or phrase or image is worth committing the poem's progress to, or whether the poet, in being too cautious, might be "looking a gift horse in the mouth." It's very common to see a student-poet latch onto a good metaphor, and then, for better or worse, begin "milking the metaphor" so rigorously and systematically that it ends up preempting the arrival of other latent and potential content, and, ironically, by force of its aptness, over-controlling the poem. On the other hand, more often than not, poems in progress will contain committing words the poet saw only as regular content, not realizing the "gold in the ore."

The Triggering Plot Point

Watch how in "The Age of Reason," which describes an overloaded airplane driven by an overweight, drunken pilot who forgot to fill the plane with gas, Michael Van Walleghen is able to capitalize upon the occurrence of a scatological remark (**triggering words**) his father makes, use it as a **plot point,** and then lift it to the epiphanic level of a religious blessing.

> Then suddenly
> there were we, lumbering
>
> down a bumpy, too short runway
> and headed for a fence
>
> *Holy Shit!* my father shouts
> and that's it, all we need
>
> by way of the miraculous
> to lift us in a twinkling
>
> over everything—fence, trees,
> and powerlines. What a birthday!
> (Michael Van Walleghen, "The Age of Reason")

The Triggering Riff

A good deal of jazz improvisation is composed of **riffs,** which are impromptu variations on a phrase formerly laid down in the composition. From David Clewell's poem "We Never Close," here is a one of a series of scooter push-offs, equivalent to a jazz riff, in which the triggering word "blue" kicks off a chain of associations swirling within and around the diner scene.

> From where you sit it's hard
> to tell the color of her eyes, but you'd have to guess
> **some shade of blue, the local color here:**

Blue Plate Special, smoke on the rise from a dozen ashtrays,
the cop sweet-talking another Danish he won't pay for,
an entire row of songs on the jukebox, the blue-streak
chatter of the woman on the phone fingering the dark
blue bruise on the back of her neck, and suddenly
any blue you brought here with you pales in comparison.
(David Clewell, "We Never Close")

Triggering Controlling Emblem

At other times, the effect of a triggering word can be deeper and more widespread, as in the following lines from sections of a poem by Sharon Olds, "The Quest," in which the word "strand" acts as a springboard to lift up into an imaginative riff on things that are woven or used to tie one thing to another, and then drive deeply back through memory.

un-
do her, **fine strand** by fine
strand. These are buildings full of **rope,**
ironing boards, **sash, wire,**
iron cords woven into black-and-blue spirals like
umbilici

* * *

remembering the time my parents **tied me to a chair**

* * *

my wrists like birds the
shrike **has hung** by the throat from **barbed wire.**
(Sharon Olds, "The Quest")

The Matrix for Metaphor

The aptness and power of a metaphor often depends very much upon its context, in the same way that a punch line to a joke or the closure of a poem depends upon the material that sets it up. A metaphor that is organically derived from its context shines new meaning and energy back onto its context. When taken out of the context of the poem, what seems to be a highly original and effective metaphor may diminish in its former intensity and striking power. In other words, the matrix or context of a poem, whether local or systemic, can act as a trigger or springboard for the creation of powerful metaphors.

Following are some metaphors and similes, excised from full poems, that both soar away from and then connect back to their matrices.

Here's a metaphor from Mark Cox's poem "The Word."

> **When my heart**
> **is not wrapped in layer after layer of daylight, not prepared**
> **like some fighter's taped fist.**
> (Mark Cox, "The Word")

Even standing alone this is a strong and suggestive metaphor. But in order for us to see how this is an **organic metaphor** whose resonant and multiple levels of meaning throw light back throughout the poem, we would have to know the poem's **dramatic situation** (a tense, personal relationship) and its ***idée fixe*** or **hyper-figure** (i.e., of not speaking), along with the context of the speaker's silent embattlement within himself. But merely by adding the metaphor's preceding paradoxical sentence, we can see the effect that context has on metaphor in the newly revealed figurative correlation between the speaker's unconscious speaking in his dreams, and his not consciously speaking while awake. Also, notice how the poet uses the **laddering** technique that first imagines a fist wrapped in the metaphorical full consciousness of daylight that then smoothly telescopes (by way of the **scooter** technique) into a boxing metaphor.

> I speak best and most fully in my sleep. **When my heart**
> **is not wrapped in layer after layer of daylight, not prepared**
> **like some fighter's taped fist.**
> (Mark Cox, "The Word")

The next example poem by Rita Dove contains a central **organic metaphor** of negative containment, which, again, is interesting and strong by itself; but watch the economic, political, and social levels of meaning that accrue when it's placed back into the context of its poem. Here's the metaphor on its own.

> he was a bubble of bad air
> in a closed system.

Here's Rita Dove's entire poem (with the resonating context in boldface).

Elevator Man, 1949

> **Not a cage but an organ:**
> if he thought about it, he'd go insane.
> Yes, if he thought about it
> **philosophically,**
> he was a bubble of bad air
> in a closed system.
>
> He sleeps on his feet
> until the bosses enter from the paths

of Research and Administration—
the same white classmates
he had helped through Organic Chemistry.
A year ago they got him a transfer
from assembly to Corporate Headquarters,
a "kindness" he repaid

by letting out all the stops,
jostling them up and down
the scale of his bitterness
until they emerge queasy, rubbing
the backs of their necks,
feeling absolved and somehow
in need of a drink. **The secret**

he thinks to himself, **is not**
in the pipe but
the slender breath of the piper.

(Rita Dove, "Elevator Man, 1949")

SEMANTIC SPRINGBOARDS: TRIGGERING WORD EXERCISE

1. **Triggering word:** In one of your poems, find a seam among images or actions and insert a word or phrase that acts as a springboard to trigger a new direction or impulse that eventually leads back to the next image or action in the model poem.
2. **Triggering riff:** Choose a detail, image, or action in your poem, and then improvise a series of associated images, details, or actions.
3. **Controlling emblem:** Choose an image in one of your poems, and then salt into the poem a number of other images, tropes, and/or actions that resonate with characteristics similar to the one you have chosen.

THEMATIC SHAPES OF POEMS

Poems, like types of expository writing, contain inner geometrical shapes formed by the way their themes are developed: for instance, a common, simple "V" shape is formed by proceeding from the general to the specific, and the inversion of that type, the "Λ," is created by going from the specific to the general. Moving from a linear configuration, poems can move curvilinearly, centrifugally outward, or centripetally inward from a central point. Or they be circular in nature. Generally speaking, the most suitable inner thematic shape of a poem should reflect a logic of an aesthetic ordering of the experience being offered, so that a kind of "Platonic" inner, abstract shape, or "inscape," is formed.

The typographical arrangement of the poem on the page may or may not necessarily literally mirror the **thematic shape** of the poem; in other words, it is possible for an **open field** thematic shape to be represented in couplet stanzas (or any kind of **strophic** poem), or as a block poem (termed **sticchic**). And, conversely, it is entirely possible for a straightforward inductively shaped theme to appear in any typographical arrangement the poet feels is effective. But either intuitively or consciously, the poet will correlate the inner thematic shape and the outer formal structure so they are in some kind of harmonic, progressive, opposing, or productive tension with each other.

Basically, the poet's aesthetic sense and the perceptions stemming from the topic create the organizing principle that composes the poem's thematic shape. And that shape can be represented visually in the following simple line drawings.

The Deductive Thematic Shape

Alan Dugan's "Love Song: I and Thou" is an example of the **deductive thematic shape;** that is, it's funnel-shaped. It begins with a general, abstract statement that is subsequently supported by various concrete (metaphorical) examples of evidence. The shape of the poem's argument or thesis narrows down to the very last word, "wife," which seals up the poem.

Love Song: I and Thou

Nothing is plumb, level, or square:
   the studs are bowed, the joists
are shaky by nature, no piece fits
   any other piece without a gap
or pinch, and bent nails
   dance all over the surfacing
like maggots. By Christ
   I am no carpenter. I built
the roof for myself, the walls
   for myself, the floors
for myself, and got
   hung up in it myself. I
danced with a purple thumb
   at this house-warming, drunk
with my prime whiskey: rage.
   Oh I spat rage's nails

into the frame-up of my work:
  it held. It settled plumb,
level, solid, square and true
  for that great moment. Then
it screamed and went on through,
  skewing as wrong the other way.
God damned it. This is hell,
  but I planned it, and I
  will live in it until it kills me.
I can nail my left palm
  to the left-hand crosspiece but
I can't do everything myself.
  I need a hand to nail the right,
a help, a love, a you, a wife.

(Alan Dugan, "Love Song: I and Thou")

The Inductive Thematic Shape

The **inductive thematic shape** is the converse of the deductive thematic shape. It begins with something specific and ends with the general, and is represented as an inverted funnel. In Yusef Komunyakaa's poem below, he uses a series of particular descriptions and features of the boiler room, and as the poem progresses, its vision widens until the speaker is able to evoke what his father's life has come to mean emotionally to him.

Temples of Smoke

Fire shimmied & reached up
From the iron furnace & grabbed
Sawdust from the pitchfork
Before I could make it across
The floor or take a half step
Back, as the boiler room sung
About what trees were before
Men & money. Those nights
Smelled of greenness & sweat
As steam moved through miles
Of winding pipes to turn wheels
That pushed blades & rotated
Man-high saws. It leaped
Like tigers out of a pit,

Singeing the hair on my head,
While Daddy made his rounds
Turning large brass keys
In his night-watchman's clock,
Out among columns of lumber & paths
Where a man & woman might meet.
I daydreamed some freighter
Across a midnight ocean,
Leaving Taipei & headed
For Tripoli. I saw myself fall
Through a tumbling inferno
As if hell was where a boy
Shoveled clouds of sawdust
Into the wide mouth of doubt.
(Yusef Komunyakaa, "Temples of Smoke")

The Deductive-Inductive Thematic Shape 

The **deductive-inductive thematic shape** is a combination of the two previous basic shapes, the deductive stacked on top of the inductive so that they reflect one another. In John Skoyles' poem, "No Thank You," the speaker begins with a **rhetorical question** of a general nature, proceeds to specific references to action within the overall situation, and finally opens out into a general flashback. The focus of the poem is not the woman on the bench he is observing, but his reaction to her.

No Thank You

(GENERAL) Who'll be the lover of that woman on the bench?
If she wants to hurt someone, she can use me.

↓ Did she mean it, or was she trying to be
unforgettable?
If she wants to use someone, she can hurt me.

(SPECIFIC) I'll use my manners to stay in one piece,
but I end up believing every excuse that I make.

(SPECIFIC) I always sigh when I see a woman like this;
I don't know where it comes from and I don't
↓ know where it goes.

(GENERAL)

I thought I'd enjoy a beautiful day like today;
I took a walk in the park and then something
like this happens.
(John Skoyles, "No Thank You")

Inductive-Deductive Thematic Shape 

The **inductive-deductive thematic shape,** in the form of diamond, is the converse of the previous shape; it begins with the particular, which then enlarges into a statement or image, begins again with the general and, as it develops toward its conclusion, that ends with the specific again. In Tess Gallagher's poem "Now That I Am Never Alone," she begins with particulars in the form of a description of a moth, and lapses into a flashback that drives toward the statement-in-imagery in the middle of the poem about her cold state. Then the poem concludes with the specific, metaphorical images of her departed husband in the presence of the fluttering moth, and herself as the light to which he is attracted.

Now That I Am Never Alone

In the bath I look up and see the brown moth
pressed like a pair of unpredictable lips
against the white wall. I heat up
the water, running as much hot in as I can stand.
These handfuls of water over my shoulder—how once
he pulled my head against his thigh and dipped
a rivulet down my neck of coldest water from the spring
we were drinking from. Beautiful mischief
that stills a moment so I can never look
back. Only now, brightest now, and the water
never hot enough to drive that shiver out.

But I do remember solitude—no other
presence and each thing what it was. Not this raw
fluttering I make of you as you have made of me
your watch-fire, your killing light.
(Tess Gallagher, "Now That I Am Never Alone")

Circular Thematic Shape 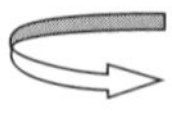

In "Poetry of Departures," Philip Larkin ponders the possibility of overthrowing his old, stultifying way of life for one that promises adventure and freedom. Toward the poem's ending it curves back upon itself (via its **circular thematic shape**) with the realization that ultimately the speaker would only end up re-creating the same sort of staid, settled existence by which he presently feels trapped. Although the specific content of the beginning and ending are different, the implied scene behind the opening lines and the explicit scene in the ending are the same.

Poetry of Departures

Sometimes you hear, fifth-hand,
as epitaph:
He chucked up everything
And just cleared off,
And always the voice will sound
Certain you approve
This audacious, purifying,
Elemental move.

And they are right, I think.
We all hate home
An having to be there:
I detest my room,
Its specially chosen junk,
The good books, the good bed,
And my life, in perfect order:
So to hear it said

He walked out on the whole crowd
Leaves me flushed and stirred,
Like *Then she undid her dress*
Or *Take that you bastard;*
Surely I can, if he did?
And that helps me stay
sober and industrious.
But I'd go today,
Yes, swagger the nut-strewn roads,
Crouch in the fo'c'sle
Stubbly with goodness, if
It weren't so artificial,
Such a deliberate step backwards
To create an object:
Books; china; a life
Reprehensibly a life
Reprehensibly perfect.

(Philip Larkin, "Poetry of Departures")

Centripetal Thematic Shape

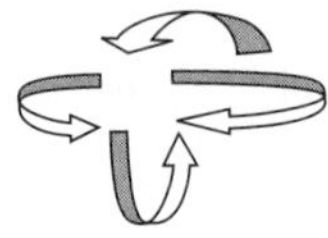

In some **open field composition** poems, the stated or unstated thesis acts as a magnet that associatively draws content from various outside levels and angles of thought, which cluster around the nuclear thematic center. For example, in Louis Simpson's "The Silent Piano," the theme, around which disparate content is arranged, is the question: "Where is it ['the inner life']?".

The Silent Piano

We have lived like civilized people.
O ruins, traditions!

And we have seen the barbarians
breakers of sculpture and glass.

And now we talk of 'the inner life',
and I ask myself, where is it?

Not here, in these streets and houses,
so I think it must be found

in indolence, pure indolence,
an ocean of darkness,

in silence, an arm of the moon,
a hand that enters slowly.

*

I am reminded of a story
Camus tells, of a man in prison camp.

He had carved a piano keyboard
with a nail on a piece of wood.

And sat there playing the piano.
This music was made entirely of silence.

(Louis Simpson, "The Silent Piano")

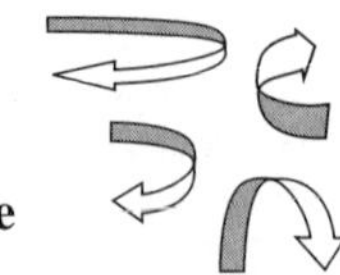

Centrifugal Thematic Shape

The opposite of the centripetal thematic shape is the **centrifugal thematic shape** in which content leaps outward from a stated or unstated center to associate itself with disparate but associated images, actions, and concepts. In some **open field composition** poems, the stated or unstated thesis acts as a magnet that draws a cluster of associated content from various outside levels and angles of thought toward its nuclear thematic center. For example, in Leslie Ullman's meditative identity poem, "Desire," her philosophical musings, psycho-emotional content, self-reflexive apprehensions, and superimposed imagery of land and sea worlds all emanate from her central feeling that something's wrong, that somehow she's in a kind of trouble that only living in two worlds can erase.

Desire

While the pulse in my neck
taps "trouble, trouble," I think about
deep sea fish—their calm gills,
eyes like iced flowers, cold hearts
pumping. I think, *tons of water*
could be holding me down, the vast
blue pressure shot with light that doesn't
break the darkness, but turns
whole fields of minnows into stars.
How slowly they move in the immense
privacy, while grasses wave in slow motion
as they have forever, fanning time,
not this fever, not tongues of flame
springing from this face . . .

I imagine I breathe water,
suddenly skilled at drawing
what little air I need and sending
the rest back to its heavy world—
that's the miracle of fish, what I
envy—then I remember the striped bass
I once lifted from fresh water to my
natural element, this giddy vanishing
of all substance, that drowning.

(Leslie Ullman, "Desire")

Centripetal/Centrifugal Thematic Shape

The **centripetal/centrifugal thematic shape** combines outward and inward-moving thematic developments that, through association, refer inwardly to the poem itself and outwardly to associatively related images and concepts. Michael Burkard's "Strange Meadowlark" records the vacillating movement of the narrator's mind, which sets up a tension between the two argumentative movements of the poem and between concrete and abstract considerations.

Strange Meadowlark

My mother died recently in a home.
I've wondered about that line,
it requires a trench in a field.
I wonder about that line too,
the trench traveling like this,
from here to there, a black reflection.

The lupin trembles. It trembles.
Like the snow:
isn't my mother black winged?

On page 73: the black reflection
of the moon's book: a boat collapses
in the little vigil light.
The boat eclipses this coincidence.

When the pages choose 74:
how would you live?
Okay. I acknowledge the sleeves
in the flowers, how facile
the light breathes.
The trench ignites the pointlessness
of the field, of the line in the field,
of the trench in the field.

A black vase situates the hill.
The hill listens, the hill
is page 73. It is 1975
and the hill is all that is on my mind.
The hill leaves a little reflection.
(Michael Burkard, "Strange Meadowlark")

Thematic Shapes from Nature

When Mary Anne Redmond was a graduate student in creative writing, for her paper's topic she researched and catalogued designs that occur in nature and that fall under four main categories: the unit, dual symmetry, multiple expanding, and repetitive or continuous. She then matched these naturally occurring shapes to poems that she felt fit these shapes. Following is the chart of designs.

	The Unit	Dual Symmetry	Multiple Expanding	Repeat
R O	point	closure	gradient	mosaic
U N D	circle	rays	spiral	wobble
S T R A	line (vector)	parallel	plane (intersection)	node or chain
I G H T	counterforces	axial symmetry	dendritic branch	jagged continuity

Here are some poems that illustrate several of the natural designs above.

● **THE POINT** W. S. Merwin's "The Room" basically stays focused on that one image, one point. It is the reader who, after the poem is read, enlarges the frame of the symbolic image.

The Room

I think all this is somewhere in myself
The cold room unlit before dawn
Containing a stillness such as attends death
And from a corner the sounds of small of a small bird trying
From time to time to fly a few beats in the dark
You would say it was dying it is immortal
(W. S. Merwin, "The Room")

◯ **THE CIRCLE** A good example of **circular thematic shape** is Mark Strand's "Keeping Things Whole," in which the speaker ends up where he began (with an enriched restatement) in his existential, logical proof.

Keeping Things Whole

In a field
I am the absence
of field.
This is
always the case.
Wherever I am
I am what is missing.

When I walk
I part the air
and always
the air moves in
to fill the spaces
where my body's been.

We all have reasons
for moving.
I move
to keep things whole.
(Mark Strand, "Keeping Things Whole")

THE SPIRAL Maya Flamm's poem "Display" exemplifies a spiral thematic shape, both in the way that its syntactical structure builds incrementally through repetition and variation on previously stated content and in the meaning and movement of the content itself. Key phrases that create the shape are highlighted in boldface.

Display

like everything fanned out to sheerness filigree of spines ugly
and raw as spines

like everything fingers or claws or hairs grip open-ended
molecules to pull along the distance is nothing at all

like everything sparrows choke or drown or bludgeoned

like everything it all washes back to sea or desert or tropical
wind specked with husks

like everything the bodies of energy toss back and forth
between the distance

like everything tossed the energy tugs as the hairs skin
sponge vein scattered out in what looks a certain way

like everything a certain look transfers from the eyes to
the heaps to the valleys

like everything that certain way the eye moves from thing to
thing makes days

like everything days reach out into the wilderness brush past and
over the hips of arenas

like everything smoke is loved as breath fire is fought from the
center and **the center insists on itself.**

(Maya Flamm, "Display")

_______ **PARALLEL PLANES** In Philip Dacy's poem "Skating," both the literal image of himself skating and the symbolic image of his reflection on the ice form parallel planes of his exterior/interior existence in which his character's chronic dissociation from himself is brilliantly drawn.

Skating

Skating on the surface of my life,
I saw myself below the ice,
another me, I was moving fast
above him, he was moving slow,
though he kept up. There must have been
some warp of being twisting
us together so, two different speeds
head to head, or feet to feet, or,
better, shoulder to shoulder, brothers,
that's the way it felt, but separated
by a death, an ice, a long wall
laid down upon the world to lock us
into rooms. Knock, knock. Are you
there? He was, and waving, though
it was a distant wave, an outer-space
wave, as if he were umbilicaled
and drifting off between the stars. The stars
skated on that ice, too, and went so fast
they seemed not to move at all. Perhaps
he was the one sped swerveless home,
an arrow, while I dream-skated,
my two blades, for all their dazzle,

leaving the ice unchanged, and top was
bottom and bottom top, but who could say?
I only knew I wanted to break through.
I wanted the ice to melt to let
us sink together, two lovers in a bed,
or crack, a warning sign missed, while
the stars swam around us like fish
lit up from within by something
we could never name, nor wished to,
lest the light fade. But the ice held,
because it was wiser than I was,
because two is more than twice one,
because the air and water made a pact
to disagree while I skated on
the surface of a life I thought was mine.
(Philip Dacey, "Skating")

╳ **INTERSECTING PLANES** Intersecting planes, which can be composed of crisscrossing themes, plot elements, or the differing motivations of characters, etc., is exemplified in the poem below by Robert Cochran, where the speaker's haunting dream of a painting and a child's chalk drawing intersect, an event that resolves the question of to whom can one give one's heart.

An Offering

(for Azesha Buchanan)

I reach into my body
and take out my heart
as drops of red blood
run down my white arm.
I stumble across the street
and offer my heart to a waitress
working the graveyard shift
at an all-night diner next to a hospital.
When she refuses
I see a woman sitting in a booth
sipping black coffee and smoking a cigarette,
her three young children asleep beside her.
I offer her my heart but she says
she doesn't talk to strangers
so I tumble outside to the blare of

streetlights, headlights, and horns
and stagger back across the street to my car.
I put my heart in the passenger seat
fasten both seatbelts and speed home.
Then I grab my heart and open the door and coast through the
unlit house
with the familiarity of a blind man.
I sleep hard. When I wake it is 2:30 in the afternoon
and I remember dreaming about this beautiful painting by Otis
Dozier
of a softly surreal blue-green cactus with purple blossoms and a
big black crow
and in my dream I was surrounded by the image
falling through purple blooming cacti and big black crows and the
blue moon.
I check my mail and then read the sports page
I shave and grab my heart and get into my car and head to West
Dallas
and just as I drive across the Trinity River I see a little black girl
drawing with colored chalk on the sidewalk.
I stop the car and get out
and the girl is drawing a beautiful blue-green cactus
with purple flowers and a big black crow
and I tell her she is missing a purple flower right there
and she says that I can draw it in if I want
and after we finish drawing on the sidewalk
I reach into my coat pocket
and pull out my heart wrapped in newspaper
and carefully place it in her hands
like a thousand-year-old prayer wrapped in silk.
(Robert Cochran, "An Offering")

DENDRITIC BRANCH In the following five-stanza excerpt from Robert Long's poem "Time and Its Double," the poem purposefully keeps branching off in different directions of thought, which gives it a very contemporary urban feel.

St. Lucy is the patron saint of eyes. A friend told me
She was haunted, in childhood, by a statue, in Corona, Queens,
Of Lucy holding a dish full of eyeballs. This is part of the dream
I had last night, brought on by a tv commercial:

Me, in a chaise, basking on the sands
Of St. Bart's, or one of those other chichi isles
Named for men who were shot full of arrows, or stoned by the populace,
Or each other, or wandered around mumbling to themselves.

As we drive off into the slate early evening, we think of Lucy.
Send her a prayer. You know, every month around this time
I get a package from the Dessert-of-the-Month Club, to which I've belonged
For going on three years. One time,

L' isle flottante came to my door, and Carol Ann had to take a valium.
Carol Ann wore tanktops and cutoffs and slept a lot. Awake,
She worked on her dissertation of Keats, read Bachelard
Over and over, went to writing seminars, while I fed the cats,

Worked in the garden. One day, it was over.
"No man hath seen God at any time," Scripture insists,
And that includes all our acid trips and eerie feelings
Atop Irish hills at the feet of which our ancestors were buried.
(Robert Long, "Time and Its Double")

⟶ ⟵ **COUNTERFORCES** Alexander Pope, famous for the opposing forces marshaled in his **heroic couplets,** is a good example in form and sense of this type. Here are some lines from his "An Essay on Man."

1. Say first, of God above, or man below,
What can we reason, but from what we know?
Of man, what see we but his station here,
From which to reason, or to which refer?
Through worlds unnumbered though the God be known,
'Tis ours to trace him only in our own.
(Alexander Pope, "An Essay on Man")

THEMATIC SHAPES: ARGUMENTATIVE AND NATURAL SHAPES EXERCISE

Using one of your poems, see if you can rework it into the following inner thematic shapes.

Argumentative shapes

1. **Deductive shape:** Begin the poem with a general statement that takes into consideration the whole experience the poem addresses, and then follow that with a progressive series of more particular material.
2. **Inductive shape:** Reverse the order of the exercise above and begin the poem with specifics and move toward more general material that ends with your opening general line above.
3. **Deductive-inductive shape:** Combine the shapes of the previous two versions above so that the model poem opens with a general statement, moves to the particular in the middle of the poem, followed by a new general statement that again moves to closure with specifics.
4. **Circular shape:** Begin and end the model poem with the same image or scene or statement, but make sure the repeating material in the closure has an enriched meaning because of its previous, preparatory context.
5. **Centripetal shape:** Holding the thesis of your poem in mind, associate images, scenes, and tropes located outside the immediate situation but whose connotations move the material inward toward the unstated central thesis.
6. **Centrifugal shape:** Holding the thesis of your poem in mind, begin it with images, actions, scenes, and tropes from the immediate dramatic situation, and then move the material outward toward the unstated thesis.

Natural shapes

7. **The point:** Focus on a specific image in your poem, and develop material that stays within that image/symbol.
8. **Circular shape:** In your closure, return to that same idea that your opening lines suggest, but do so as an "enriched restatement."

9. **Intersecting planes:** See if you can make different but parallel actions cross paths. (This can be easily done using a flashback that opposes the action in the present or future.)
10. **Counterforces:** At some point in your poem, present two different but equal opposing actions, thoughts, or images that create forces in which both terms are true.

C H A P T E R

4

Imagery

ASPECTS OF IMAGERY

By consensus, **imagery,** whether it's specific or general, literal or figurative, is the most translatable aspect of poetry, probably because the image—from the archetypal and culturally universal to the highly specific and localized—is a universal language based upon the unconsciousness's language mode—the visual image. Imagery *shows* first and then, with its literary statement implied inside it, it *tells.* In fact, it was Ezra Pound who maintained the distinction between a picture and an image in saying that a picture is a flat, visual representation, whereas an image is a picture with a statement or idea implied inside it. With the twentieth century's new internationalism in cultural and geopolitical domains, it is not surprising that there has been since the early part of the twentieth century an increased emphasis and focus on the image, whether it has been through the lens of the **Symbolists, Surrealists,** the Imagists, or the **Deep Imagists.**

In this section, we'll look at the many intersecting aspects in which images are employed (on a scale ranging from the factual to the detailed to the general to the abstract), and what effects and kinds of leverage can or cannot be achieved in using the types along this scale. All along this scale of magnitudes are two assumed kinds of positions or distances: (1) the speaker of the poem in relation to his or her subject, and (2) the reader of the poem in relation to the experience of the poem, what in critical terminology is termed **aesthetic distance.** This is noted because the distance between one thing and another is obviously crucial to the topics of size and presence that the images create.

Kinds of Seeing

Images are indirect, concrete, abstract, or concrete-abstract translations from (1) sensory data, (2) cognitive operations of feeling, thought, and **felt-thought,** (3) proprioceptive sensations (sensing the state of the body and self), and

(4) **selective perception** (perception filtered through "where we're at"). While the basic skill in making an image accessible is dependent upon the finesse with which we are able to balance our subjective immersion in an experience with our being able to view it from a more objective distance, there are various levels and kinds of "seeing" that we can classify within the image. Here are some types that are presented as categories, though they need not be mutually exclusive.

THE WITNESSED IMAGE This is a very highly specific testimonial image whose power lies in its exactness, texturizing effects, and particularity, as in "the chair strung with cobwebs and cottony cocoons."

THE LITERAL This is the fundamentally flat, three-dimensional visual representation of what is seen. It offers simplicity, clarity, and a strong sense of presence or "hereness," as in "the cement floor."

THE FIGURATIVE This is a fusion of the literal image with an image from another domain. It adds energy and rings of connotative meaning to the literal, as in "the frogs of meaning are ugly."

THE SELECTIVELY PERCEIVED IMAGE This is an image that is both selected and colored by our projected emotion, state of being, or personality (see **location**). Its power comes from the force of our emotional, physical, or intellectual connection to what is outside us (as a device it is termed **pathetic fallacy**), as in "The rain cried as freely I did."

THE PENETRATIVE IMAGE This is an image that links the literal image to some aspect of its function or meaning, which is brought up from a deeper, more universal level, as in "The chair held its notion of rest as my open hand offered a welcome." The power of the penetrative image lies in its capacity to connect levels of thought and feeling, and its breadth of comprehension.

Specificity vs. Generality

Specificity is one level up from the use of factual naming. It, too, adds **texture** and a sense of "being there," but it also contains one of the basic, paradoxical secrets of poetry: that the power of poetry lies in the specific. As the poet Richard Hugo admonished: "Think small. If you have a big mind, that will show itself. If you can't think small, try philosophy or social criticism." One of the most common mistakes young poets make is to reach for the large instead of the specific when feeling highly emotional, the "O gray day" kind of sweep when a highly selected, specific image would anchor the feeling much more accurately and securely.

In the following exercise poems, "Hell (A)" and "Hell (B)," by Jonathan Holden, he offers two versions of the same experience that differ widely in effect and in the amount of reader interaction, because, according to whether one employs specificity or skates along the surface of general description and narration, very different experiences inside the poem and between poem and reader are created. Here is the general version.

Hell (A)

You will wake up
in the class you hated
most in high school.
Everything will be
the same
as it was,
the same disgusting
students doing
the same
disgusting
things
they used to do.
Even your desk,
a typical high school
desk in a typical high school
room, will be the same.
It will be spring,
and as you sit
there listening
to another dull
and meaningless lecture,
you will be so
bored
and horny
that you will kill
time
through idle sex fantasy
and daydreams
about sports,
wishing you were out
of school.

(Jonathan Holden, "Hell A")

Some readers will enjoy this highly generalized portrait of the "bad old days" because like a meditation object, it allows them to focus in on and supply their own personal experiences back in high school. In other words, we are being asked to go more than half way toward creating the "experience" the poem is purporting to capture. (Note: There are poems and kinds of poems, culturally, that require the reader to do a great deal of work to "get" the poem, but the issue of reader participation in the creation of the poem in this instance is different from using generality because of a lack of skill or laziness.) In "Hell (A)" there is nothing concrete that the mind's inner senses can latch onto because everything is so generic: the high school, the students, the desk, the time of year, the lecture, the sex fantasy, etc. If you like what this version is doing, it is because you, the reader, are the one putting detail and emotion into it from your own memory.

Here's the much more specific version.

Hell (B)

You will wake up
in your old seat
behind Peter Bowerbank
in 8th-period Driver
Ed. Tommy Conger will
be there too, in back of
you, squelching his
Wrigley's, breathing
spearmint down your neck.
And Lyle Smith,
who had the loudest
artificial burp—
bulked against the side
board, honking
snores. Your desk
will be the same scarred
tablet, prehistoric,
with the purple fossils
in it—the blue rune
that said *Eat the*
Root, the one that read
Bird Bites. Chuck
Spine will have his comb
out to lubricate his hair.
It will be May,
and as you wait
in the lighted cave
of Room 101—wait to
evolve while Mr. McIntyre
repeats leave forty

miles an hour—
you will think and
think of the little wet
click Mary Devore's
lips make as she smiles,
imagine the voltage
in her sweater, try
to think how
outdoors on the tight
green diamond
the throw from third
to first is easy—a lilt,
a flicker, bullseye,
and McIntyre will go on,
and the lukewarm New Jersey
haze, like a light
perfume, will stretch
south almost to the bridge,
to Bayonne.
(Jonathan Holden, "Hell B")

The first thing we experience in "Hell (B)," of course, is the experience, which is imparted by way of the images, actions, names, tropes, and qualities (there's lots of **texture** in the poem), whereas in the previous "Hell (A)" generalized version, we had to supply our own memories to make the poem work. The poet has reversed the percentage of interaction so that now we, the reader, only have to go much less than halfway to complete making the poem with the poet. Aside from the use of "real" names of people, Holden selects highly specific sensual details, such as Tommy Conger's spearmint breathing down the speaker's neck, Lyle Smith's burp and snoring, the little click Mary Devore's lips makes when she smiles. The poet literally adds blue and green colors to "color in" the scene; he creates the **leitmotif** and **controlling metaphor** of prehistoric references (scarred tablet, purple fossils, lighted cave) to give a "stopped time" quality to the experience; and he lyricizes the last third of the poem so that its **melopoetics** express and embody its songlike feeling.

The Fixed vs. Free (or Floating) Image

While we are discussing the merits of specificity versus the problem of generality, it is an appropriate time to introduce an umbrella classification of images: whether they are "fixed" or "floating." The **fixed image** is a specific, detailed picture or series of pictures created and presented by the poet in an effort to control the reader's imagination and act as a guide as the complication and complexity of the poem develop, as in an image such as "The cold, black stove with lion's paws for legs." The **free** (or floating) **image** is a more generalized, impressionistic picture that depends upon the reader's subjective experience, memory, or imagination for its specificity, as in "the baleful, leonine, dark stove." Since this type of floating image supposedly relies more on our willing participation, the poem with free imagery is thought to have a more personal effect and to offer the sort of looseness of control and structure appropriate to the aesthetics and philosophy of the twenty-first century. On the other hand, the fixed image is said to produce a stronger sense of unity, completeness, and coherence in a poem. However, in keeping with Aristotle's principles of moderation and balance, most poems employ a combination of the two types.

ASPECTS OF IMAGERY: SPECIFIC IMAGE EXERCISE

Write a poem about your high school days using general images. Then in a second draft, go back through the poem and substitute more detailed images for the general ones. In a third draft, see if you can create an overall, general metaphor that could ne accrued from the detailed imagery, and salt the metaphor into the poem in various places.

FROM FACTOIDS TO ABSTRACT CONCEPTS

Facts

Around the middle of the twentieth century in the United States, Beat poets, the New York School of poetry, and unaffiliated poets such as James Wright began using the names of real persons, places, things, and events. This began to break the very same kind of taboo against the personal that forbade using the first-person pronouns "I" and "we" in the formal essay. But, possibly taking their cue from the influences of fiction and journalism, poets found that using specific names of people, names of places, exact dates, and terms for things gave a poem a ready-made quality and power of displaying an almost tactile surface **texture.** One could effect grittiness, or smoothness, or slickness—any kind of characteristic that specific names might evoke. Think of the connotative power of peoples' names: Ethel, Germaine, Jake, Li Po, Rachel; the nuances and flavors embedded through time and association in the names of places: Kalamazoo, Big Sur, Morocco, Kashmir, Kokomo. Specific dates and events were also used, not just for their inherent ability to add specificity or connotation, but for the added impact of texture and of creating the "real," the kind of doubling of the dramatic effect one experiences in thinking that a movie or story is based upon a real event. In current practice, the range of naming included in poetry seems wide open: from the highly scientific terminology someone such as Albert Goldbarth uses in his essay-poems to the slangy cultural terms slam poets freely employ in their work. Facticity is now a convention. Look at how specific the title of David Wojahn's poem is: "The Assassination of John Lennon as Depicted by the Madame Tussaud Wax Museum, Niagra Falls, Ontario, 1987." It covers four of the five "W's" of journalism: who, what, when, and where.

The Power of the Specific

This type of detail or specific image is referred to as a **fixed image.** It offers strong gripping power in terms of the reader's ability to grasp something visually. A good test of whether an image is specific or not is to ask, "If this image were in a movie, would it be clearly seen and experienced?" Many of the images in the poems of Elizabeth Bishop are known for their realism in terms of their metaphorical and literal exactitude, the particularity of their coloration and texture, as if she had the technical eye of a painter. In her famous poem "The Fish," she describes a fish she caught—its eye, skin, and general appearance with great specificity and fidelity to the real image.

On the other hand, sometimes an image seems to the writer to be specific but fails when put to the litmus test of imagining it in a visual medium. For example, if we think about the phrase "the old door," which seems specific, actually there's only the generic concept of an object there. We have no idea what material the door is made of, its color and texture, where it's located, whether it's hanging straight or not, nor of the door's location. The poet must go back and add qualifying words or phrases, or tropes, or associative images in order to make the door a visual virtual reality. Look at the dazzling way Jimmy Santiago Baca portrays his visual impression of what it's like to be let out of a dark jail into daylight.

> From a dark cell
> as if from the hull of a slave ship,
> I emerge into blinding noon deck-streets,
> where sun hacksaws tin sheets of glistening air.
> (Jimmy Santiago Baca "I Am Here")

Notice that because Baca uses the tropes of simile and metaphor as tools for his description, we automatically create the visual image he is evoking. In processing the connotative level of the tropes, we first have to establish the screen of a literal image (hot sun) upon which to process the substituted figurative image (screeching hacksaw).

The Power of the General

This kind of image is often referred to as a **free** or **floating image.** It is general in nature and relies upon more of our active co-creating with the poet than do images and tropes of a more specific character. Although the opening of this section on imagery warned, as a basic rule, against the use of general names, images, and descriptions, in the hands of skilled poets, generality can show a collective, sweeping, multidimensional power at a time when texture, solidity, and the illusions of what is "real" and "true" might be impediments to larger aims. Look at the very generic level of nouns and adjectives and the cliches (in boldface) that Charles Simic uses in his poem that follows. And yet Simic is able to fuse layers of dark feeling, a psychological state of alienation, and a dreamlike consciousness to his general, literal images so that the larger than life quality of the fable or mythopoetic is evoked. This is the method and effect of the **deep image** poets, though Simic does not claim to be of that school of poetry writing.

Tragic Architecture

School, prison, trees in the wind,
I climbed your **gloomy stairs,**
Stood in your **farthest corners**
With my **face** to the **wall.**

The murderer sat in **the front row.**
A mad little Ophelia
Wrote **today's date** on **the blackboard.**
The **executioner** was **my best friend.**
He already wore **black.**
The janitor brought us **mice** to **play with.**

In **that room** with its **red sunsets—**
It was **eternity's** time **to speak,**
So we **listened**
As if our **hearts** were **made of stone.**

All of **that** in **ruins** now.
Cracked, peeling walls
With **every window broken.**
Not even a **naked light bulb** left

For **the prisoner** forgotten **in solitary,**
And **the school boy** left behind
Watching the **bare winter trees**
Lashed by **the driving wind.**

(Charles Simic, "Tragic Architecture")

Fusing the General to the Specific

Oftentimes, a poet will want to introduce an image or state of being with an all-encompassing, general statement, and then immediately follow that up with a specific image or trope that anchors, countersinks, and seals over the poem's opening generality. W. S. Merwin performs this move often and brilliantly. Here are two examples from his poems.

My words are the garments of what I shall never be
Like the tucked sleeve of a one-armed boy.
(W. S. Merwin, "When You Go Away")

* * *

My mind is divided
like a stockyard seen from above.
(W. S. Merwin, "Plane")

The Processed Image

Poets will often establish a static or fixed image, and then manipulate that image so that it "bends" and "moves" like a blues note, into something else. This is referred to as a **processed** (or **moving) image.** The **processed image** begins as a static image and then undergoes a change by telescoping into a new type of image. The transformation is meant to take the reader into a new domain of understanding, to manipulate the narrative elements of time and space by way of the imagery. Here is an example of this technique.

I do not believe for a moment that the last
poet in the last standing building
while the world splits up and caves inward
like the crust of a rich cake
will be trying to make a line come out right
(Marvin Bell, "Against Stuff")

The Reach of the Diffuse

Typically, as another basic rule, young writers are warned not to use the abstract in poetry, as with generality, because it has less focus and less striking and sticking power. But, just as most poetic devices were once classified as defects of grammar or fallacies of reasons by Renaissance rhetoricians, poets will often break with established rules in order to invent new ways of expressing something. In the following poem, William Bronk adamantly creates an indefinite, generic level of imagery that he then blurs, and then, further, erases in order to evoke the feel of a larger, almost impalpable process embedded in the existential experience of being.

Against Biography

We came to where the trees, if there were trees,
say, a little group of them, or a house
maybe, something there, whatever it was,
a man standing, someone, it would be clear
enough, sharp at the edges, but everything else
was blurred, all running together or else
moving—sideways, back and forth—or the scale
was wrong, some of the things close by
were smaller than those set farther back, so that though
we saw something, and saw it plain enough,
we saw it nowhere, there wasn't any place
for it to be, or any place for us.
We wandered. Not quite aimless. Man here, though,
would live without biography; it needs
a time and place: there isn't any: who
could say, not smiling, me and my world
or so and so and his time, and stage a play
clothed properly in front of sets,
and believe that this made time and place of the world?

No we had come too far for that belief
and saw ourselves as ghosts against the real,
and time and place as ghosts; there is the real.
It is there. Where we are: nowhere. It is there.

(William Bronk, "Against Biography")

The Power of the Abstract

Although novices are warned against using easy, abstract terms in poetry writing in the hands of a master who has a firm grip on its referential level, the abstract can deftly cover the huge geography of metaphysical, intellectual, and spiritual terrains. Here's an example from Samuel Hazo, who uses the rhetorical devices of paradox, contraries, and chiasmus (a crisscrossing of semantic meaning and syntax between parallel yet opposite terms) to map out the uncharted, subjective world of the human spirit.

Silence Spoken Here

What absence only can create
needs absence to create it.
Split be deaths or distances,
we survive like exiles
from the time at hand, living
where love leads us for love's
reasons.
We tell ourselves
that life, if anywhere, is there.
Why isn't it?
What keeps us
hostages to elsewhere?
The dead
possess us when they choose.
The far stay nearer than we know
they are.
We taste the way
they talk, remember everything
they've yet to tell us, dream
them home and young again
from countries they will never leave.
With friends it's worse and better.
Together, we regret the times
we were apart.
Apart, we're
more together than we are
together.
We say that losing
those we love to living
is the price of loving.
We say
such honest lies because
we must—because we have
no choices.
Face to face
we say them, but our eyes
have different voices.

(Samuel Hazo, "Silence Spoken Here")

The Verbal Gesture

The **verbal gesture** is a loose workshop term for creating generic imagery. It is a generalized, imagistic shorthand meant for us to fill in or not fill in. But its power lies in the economy and evocation of the gesture. As a basic rule in poetry writing, verbal gestures are thought of as a defect, in the same sense that the use of cliches is. But, of course, any defect can be capitalized upon and, in the hands of a skillful poet, made into an effective device. Michael Burkard's poem, "A Feeling from the Sea," is, basically, a chain of verbal gestures meant to evoke a kind of existential dislocation. The purposeful semantic vagueness, the looseness in attitude that amounts to futility, the obliqueness of feelings, and the casually sketched-in thoughts and actions all contribute quite effectively in accurately focusing in on and portraying a state of mind, not unlike ennui, that lies between the border of consciousness and unconsciousness.

A Feeling from the Sea

I was feeling all this magic
and so I wrote this thing
and I made it up as I went along.
And two days later, actually a day,
I thought it must have seemed silly, and untrue,
that I attributed it to magic and to voices
in the air, in the room, and a feeling
from the sea. But it was not bravado
and I believed it.

I believed her too. And the face
of Pasternak, and the book I borrowed,
and half read, and the streets I half walked
and half looked while walking.

And then today I read some lyrical poems,
just a few, and a portion, a small piece,
from another one which was not so lyrical.
And I thought these lyrics were a truth,
equal to many, and I thought of disappointment
at these feelings. They are made this way, these lyrics,
like a hill you are meant to take into yourself,
and so better understand the world and fools.
And the power of people when they truly believe.

And I wrote some letters, and made some calls,
and tried to write, and it seemed falsely

lyrical. And I put it away. And I felt in that closeness
there is still something, many things, I don't understand,
or am afraid of, or find, later, unexpected.
And I thought myself foolish.

I could not find a tone for things.
I could not find a moment.
(Michael Burkard, "A Feeling from the Sea")

The Deep Image

The **deep image,** which fuses inner and outer states of being, tying them into a recognition of an archetypal experience, enacts an intuitively understood spiritual, emotional, and psychological realm of experience that evokes a universal feeling. In Charles Simic's portrayal of public education, all the nouns and adjectives have a generic quality that take on the added consciousness of victimization and mysteriously transcend their obviously hackneyed character.

Tragic Architecture

School, prison, trees in the wind,
I climbed your gloomy stairs,
Stood in your farthest corners
With my face to the wall.

The murderer sat in the front row.
A mad little Ophelia
Wrote today's date on the blackboard.
The executioner was my best friend.
He already wore black.
The janitor brought us mice to play with.

In that room with its red sunsets—
It was eternity's time to speak,
So we listened
As if our hearts were made of stone.

All of that in ruins now.
Cracked, peeling walls
With every window broken.
Not even a naked light bulb left
For the prisoner forgotten in solitary,
And the school boy left behind
Watching the bare winter trees
Lashed by the driving wind.
(Charles Simic, "Tragic Architecture")

The Surreal Image

This **genre** of imagery uses spontaneous and odd juxtapositions of disparate images, improbable size, color, shape, and magnitude, and the appearance of images in odd, unreal, or unexpected contexts. Its agenda is to subjectively portray a quality of mind and aesthetics based upon the unconscious associative mode of image-thinking that dreams feature. Its founding aspiration was to leap over the boundary of duality, contradiction, and opposites in which the rational mind tends to think. Following are the opening two stanzas from Charles Wright's "Nightdream."

> Each day is an iceberg,
> Dragging its chill paunch underfoot;
> Each night is a tree to hang from.
> The wooden knife, the mud rope
> You scratch your initials on—
> Panoply, panoply.
> Up and up from his green grave, your father
> Wheels in the wind, split scrap of smoke;
> Under him stretch, in one file, Bob's Valley, Bald Knob,
> The infinite rectitude
> Of all that is past: Ouachita,
> Ococee, the slow slide of the Arkansas.
> (Charles Wright, "Nightdream")

The Magical Realism Image

Magical Realism features wild and transformational imagery and tropes, the kind Americans are familiar with in cartoons, as when Bugs Bunny literally paints himself into a corner, then paints a door in the wall, opens it, and walks out. The images and tropes are not just static one-on-one equivalencies, substitutions, or comparisons, as in similes and metaphors, nor do they depend upon unexpected juxtapositions and uncommon contexts, as in Surrealism. They telescope, leap, and morph from one thing into another in a visual streaming. One of the foremost practitioners of this genre in America is the poet Victor Hernandez Cruz, whose rich and colorful imagination and sense of playfulness suffuse his work. Here are lines from his poem (with the symbol of "dot" as its title).

> ●
> You can get involved with a dot
> when you're high on some drug
> A dot becomes everything in the world
> A dot can appear bigger than a dot

Take heroin and look at a dot
till the dot massages your eyelids
Between the eye opened and the eye closed
your mental gear works with that dot
You think it's got a mouth, maybe some feet
What's dot doing up there?
You get convinced that the dot is a speaker
and you hear some music
Suddenly you realize your head is between your knees
People who take acid can go inside a dot
Under the influence of cocaine one dot
would become seven dots
I saw a real coked-up guy take a broom inside
a dot, dust, paranoia written all over his face
Don't ever give a junkie a broom
In pursuit of debris he would redefine the
outline of the dot and go on further to make
a hole at the center
Coffee can make a dot appear where a dot
cannot be
The caffeine eyeball pretends to see a roach
on the distant wall every 2 minutes
How many times have you slammed your hand
on the wall trying to hit a moving dot?
(Victor Hernandez Cruz, "**.**")

The Emblem

The **emblem** is a shorthand cluster of resonating, thematically integral images, acting for a poem much in the same representative way symbols on a medieval heraldic shield signify qualities of character (and history). The emblem may be taken from the surface rhetorical imagery of a poem, or its cluster of images may be gleaned from a deeper, more unconscious and intuitive location in the poem. In the poem "Tuba," by Morton Marcus, the emblematic content of the poem is made up of the slant-rhymed images that form the character's transcendence: a flaming tuba, a brass kite, an implied fat uncle, the mouth of the sun.

Tuba

a flaming tuba
blazes on the boulevard

the flames are wings
and the tuba rises

above the city and up
through the sunlight

a brass kite
sailing to the clouds

harrumping like an uncle
tying his shoelace

who has sprouted wings
that sear through his back

and who finds
he is no longer sitting

by the side of the bed
but flying, flying

over bridges and shops
still doubled over

still tightening the laces
while he wheezes and grunts

all along he had known
this would happen

had been waiting
for the day

when he would be flying
waving to the crowds

smiling and nodding
to his astonished friends

but not this way
not bent over

pulling at his shoelace
harrumping harrumping

as he disappears
into the **mouth of the sun**
(Morton Marcus, "Tuba")

The emblem is akin to the **image narrative** (see p. 67), but the latter is a more dynamic aspect of visual representations in a poem.

FROM FACTOIDS TO ABSTRACT CONCEPTS: RANGE OF IMAGERY EXERCISE

1. **The general image:** Write a stanza or two containing general images tha resonate strongly with one another so that their overall effect creates a powerful atmosphere.
2. **Fusing the general to the specific:** Make a general statement and then follow it with a highly specific image that "shows" the meaning of the statement.
3. **The processed image:** Create an image and then process that image by stages so it becomes transformed into something else.
4. **The diffuse image:** In an effort to establish a sense of indefiniteness (as in something that is indefinable, lost in memory, or cannot be concretely experienced), create a dramatic situation in which images are vague and blurred, and your word choice is purposely indefinite and overly general.
5. **Abstract images:** In an effort to cover a great deal of conceptual territory, write out an image that contains an abstract notion and then fuse an opposite abstract notion to it in order to create a paradox in which both terms are true at once.
6. **The deep image:** In order to capture archetypal and instinctual levels of consciousness, write out an important experience in which you use elemental kinds of iamges.
7. **The surreal image:** To create irrational states of mind and experiences, try:
   a. enlarging or diminishing the size of objects in a poem,
   b. changing their usual contexs for unusual contexts,
   c. juxtaposing odd and disparate images.
8. **The Magical Realism image:** Imitate Magical Realism by writing out a series of images that associatively transform themselves into other images which have new and unexpected shapes, colors, and contexts.
9. **The emblem:** Create an emblem in a poem by employing images that have similar symbolic qualities and harmonic meanings.

CHAPTER

5

Free Verse

The term **free verse** merely indicates poetry that doesn't feature the traditional rhyme and meter of **fixed forms** such as the sonnet, sestina, villanelle, etc. Or, as poet Stanley Plumly describes it: "The chief distinction between the verse line and the free-verse sentence is the distinction between a poetry that continually returns and one that continues, that turns, that goes on." But there are specific technical measurements, reliable guiding principles and rules, and sets of conventions and expectations that poets rely on in the practice of writing in the free verse mode. There is a general **prosody** that has stabilized, defined, and somewhat standardized the current Postmodern poetry built upon the principles of the Modernist movement of the twentieth century.

TENSION

In free verse the most important element of control is **tension,** creating through the element of a poem a combination of proportional dynamic relationships that act as cohesive forces to unify the work. The effect is felt as a result of establishing complementary, contrasting, or contrary elements, such as meter against propositional sense, rhythms against counter-rhythm (**syncopation**), diction against action, abstract statement against concrete image, the general against the specific, what is said against what is meant (**irony**), and appearance against reality. The **New Criticism** school focuses on the term "tension," embodied in the ideas of the poet Allen Tate, who explains tension as the pulling and pushing of the literal level of language ("extension") against the connotative and metaphorical levels of language ("intension"). More specifically, according to Robert Penn Warren, "conflict structures" expressed in the technique of the poem (meter against **sentence sounds, formal limits** versus **variations,** the **image narrative,** etc.) create both the paths toward the poem's expression and the means by which to judge and evaluate the poem's art.

The elements of tension in free verse can be as systematically conceived as the structural and formal architecture of Metaphysical and New Critics' poems, whose paradigm might be the **controlling metaphor** or conceit, or as loose and organically derived as the work of Postmodernists such as John Ashbery, John Cage, and Robert Hass. The basic building block is some form of order that pits predictability against surprise to create a new order of understanding held together, framed by, and set off by the cohesive forces of tension. Aesthetic order is brought into being by the quality of perception of the artist, no matter how or where he may have come upon his materials. Artistically, there's no difference between a **found poem** and a seventeenth-century **sonnet** except for style.

Kinds of Tension

The following is a list of elements in a poem that can create kinds of tension.

1. **Tone** Some poems set tone against form, as in Anne Sexton's "And One for My Dame," in which the speaker's hostile attitude toward her father and husband sets itself in contradistinction to the ghosted presence of its "Baa Baa Black Sheep" nursery rhyme form. Here are a few stanzas from the poem.

   My husband,
   as blue-eyed as a picture book, sells wool:
   boxes of card waste, laps and rovings he can pull

   to the thread and say *Leicester, Rambouillet, Merino,*
   a half-blood, it's greasy and thick, yellow as old snow.

   And when you drive off, my darling,
   Yes sir! Yes, sir! It's one for my dame,
   your sample cases branded with my father's name,

   your itinerary open,
   its tolls ticking and greedy,
   its highway built up like new loves, raw and speedy.
   (Anne Sexton, "And One for My Dame")

2. **Voice** Some poets, such as Charles Bukowski and Alan Dugan, have used the aspect of **voice** as a foil or *contretemps* to content. In the poem that follows, watch how the hard-bitten, sardonic speaker's character works in tension against the traditionally time-honored and wise themes of beauty, love, mortality, and loss.

I don't know about love.
No one ever took the time
to tell me it's an acetylene torch
smelling like a wine-soaked rose
that can burn through years of nights
and leave you loving it.

3. **Form** Another commonly employed strategy is to pit a poem's thematic, argumentative, narrative, or typographical shape against the way the poem paces itself and moves down the page. Elements such as line length against sentencing, line endings that fragment syntactical phrases, and the supply or lack of transitions can be effective tools to create resistance and tension. For instance, the stylized form of many of Robert Creeley's poems—fragmented, rhetorically stressed, multi-faceted **autologues**—work well to create uncertainty, hesitation, and doubt, and are set inside tender musings and philosophical meditations on the nature of experience.

Song

What do you
want, love. To be
loved. What,

what wanted,
love, wanted
so much as love

like nothing
considered, no
feeling but

a simple
recognition
forgotten sits

in its feeling,
two things,
one and one.

(Robert Creeley, "Song")

4. **Imagery** Imagery often has the task of carrying a visual expression of thought, emotion, physical sensations, mood, atmosphere, consciousness, and attendant implied "statements" in its language. A strong example can be found in Charles Simic's ***dinggedicht*** imagery, which often sets the surreal and the mythic against the quotidian. He excels in evoking visuals that have an

unsettlingly eerie effect, as in this Edward Hopper-esque, slice-of-life snapshot of life on Main Street, USA.

True History

Which cannot be put into words—
Like a fly on the map of the world
In the travel agent's window.

That empty street in the afternoon heat
Except for my old father
Pressing his head against the glass
To observe her better
As she drags her threadbare shadow
From New York to Shanghai.

He not sure whether to alert his friend,
The barber, napping next door
With a sheet draped over his head.
(Charles Simic, "True History")

5. **Thematic correspondences** The connotative interrelationships resonating among the elaborated parts of a poem, when interpolated by the reader, create theme. A breathtaking example of a simile that surgically portrays a mood of spiritual despair can be seen in the way the simile of the first and last stanzas of Emily Dickinson's description of the soul's threshold experience in her poem "# 258."

There's a certain slant of light,
Winter Afternoons—
That oppresses, like the Heft
Of Cathedral Tunes—

* * *

When it comes, the Landscape listens—
Shadows—hold their breath—
When it goes, 'tis like the Distance
On the look of Death—
(Emily Dickinson, "#258")

6. **Narration** Unless a story, in and of itself, is exceptionally unique, instructive, or highly entertaining in some way, a poem's narrative should serve to contribute to a higher, deeper thematic purpose in a poem. In Lynn Emanuel's comic excoriation of the conventional baggage and boredom of prose, she takes over from her character's complaint about the burdensome

rituals of romance and matches these with the very same problems she, as a poet, has with the narration of prose. In this long, self-reflexive, postmodern comic diatribe against the block-and-tackle machinery it takes to lift a piece of fiction to the level of feeling, Emanuel's own **prose poem** violates her principles concerning the evils of narrative. But this seemingly unintended strategy of her having created a surfeit of **horizontal content** overrides the violation of her aesthetic since it's so very entertaining.

The Politics of Narrative—Why I Am a Poet

Jill's a good kid who's had some tough luck. But that's another story. It's Friday, and the smell of fish from Tib's hash house is so strong you could build a garage on it. We are sitting in the Blue Lite where Carl has just built us a couple of solid highballs. He's okay, Carl is, if you don't count his Roamin' hands and Rushin' fingers. Then again, that should be the only trouble we have in this life. Anyway, Jill says, "Why don't you tell about it? Nobody ever gets the broad's point of view." I don't know, maybe she's right. Jill's just a kid, but she's been around; she knows what's what.

So, I tell Jill, we're at the Blue Lite just like now when he comes in. And the first thing I notice is his hair, which has been Vitalis-ed into submission. But honey, it won't work, and it gives him a kind of rumpled, your-boudoir-or-mine look. I don't know why I noticed that before I noticed his face. Maybe it was the highballs doing the looking. Anyway, then I see his face, and I'm telling you—I'm telling Jill—this is a masterpiece of a face.

But—and this is the god's own truth—I'm tired of beauty. Really, I know, given all that happened, this must sound kind of funny, but it made me tired just to look at him. That's how beautiful he was, and how much he spelled T-R-O-U-B-L-E. So I threw him back. I mean, I didn't *say* it, I say to Jill, with my mouth. But I said it with my eyes and my shoulders. I said it with my heart. I said, Honey, I'm throwing you back. And looking back, that was the worst, I mean the worst thing—bar none—that I could have done, because it drew him like horseshit draws flies. I mean, he didn't walk over and say "Hello, girls. Hey, you with the dark hair, your indifference draws me like horseshit draws flies."

But he said it with his eyes. And then he smiled. And that smile was a gas station on a dark night. And as wearying as all the rest of it. I'm many things, but dumb isn't one of them. And here is where I say to Jill, "I just can't go on." I mean, how we get from the smile into the bedroom, how it all happens, and what all happens, just bores me. I'm kind of a conceptual storyteller. In fact, I'm kind of a conceptual liver. I prefer the cookbook to the actual meal. Feeding bores me. That's why I write poetry. In poetry you just give the instructions to the reader and say, "Reader, you go on from here." And what I like about poetry is its readers, because those are giving people. I mean, those are people you can trust to get the job done. They pull their own weight. If I had to have someone at my back in a dark alley, I'd want it to be a poetry reader. They're not like some people who maybe do it right if you tell them, "Put this foot down, and now put that one in front of the other, button your coat, wipe your nose."

So, really, I do it for the readers who work hard and, I feel, deserve something better than they're used to getting. I do it for the working stiffs. And I write for people like me who are just tired of trickle-down theory where some guy spends pages and pages on some fat book where everything, including the draperies, which happen to be *burnt orange,* is described, and further, is some *metaphor* for something. And this whole boggy waste trickles down to the reader in the form of a little burp of feeling. God, I hate prose. I think the average reader likes ideas.

"A sentence, unlike a line, is not a station of the cross," I said this to the poet Mark Strand. I said, "I could not stand to write prose. I could not stand to have to write things like 'the draperies were burnt orange and the carpet was brown.'" And he said, "You could do it if that's all you did, if that was the beginning and the end of your novel." So, please, don't ask me for a little trail of bread crumbs to get from the smile to the bedroom and from the bedroom to the death at the end, although you can ask me a lot about death. That's all I like, the very beginning and the very end. I haven't got the stomach for the rest of it.

I don't think many people do. But, like me, they're either too afraid or too polite to say so. That's why the movies are such a disaster. Now *there's* a form of popular culture that doesn't have a clue. Movies should be five minutes long. You should go in, see a couple of shots, maybe a room with orange draperies and a rug. A voice-over would say, "I'm having a hard time getting Raoul, the protagonist, from the hotel room into the elevator." And bang, that's the end. The lights come on; everybody walks out full of sympathy because this is a shared experience. Everybody in that theatre knows how hard it is to get Raoul from the hotel room into the elevator. Everyone has had to do boring, dogged work. Everyone has lived a life that seems to inflict upon every vivid moment the smears, fingerings, and pawings of plot and feeling. Everyone has lived under this oppression. In other words, everyone has had to eat shit—day after day, the endless meals they didn't want, those dark, half-gelatinous lakes of gravy that lay on the plate like an ugly rug, and that wrinkled clump of reddish-orange roast beef that looks like it was dropped onto your plate from a great height. God what a horror: getting Raoul into the elevator.

And that's why I write poetry. Honey, in poetry, you don't do that kind of work.

(Lynn Emanuel, "The Politics of Narrative—Why I Am a Poet")

7. **Implication** What is said, juxtaposed against what is not said, creates an unstated, inner dimension of meaning evoked by controlled, predetermined assumptions on the part of the poet. In Jack Gilbert's poem that follows, a **rite of initiation poem,** he implies that imperfection has another, higher order in the magnitudes of beauty other than that which can be seen in the merely physical.

In Umbria

Once upon a time I was sitting outside the café
watching twilight in Umbria when a girl came
out of the bakery with bread her mother wanted.
She did not know what to do. Already bewildered
by being thirteen and just that summer a woman,
she now had to walk past the American.
But she did fine. Went by and around the corner
with style, not noticing me. Almost perfect.
At the last instant could not resist darting a look
down at her new breasts. Often I go back
to that dip of her head when people talk
about this one or that one of the great beauties.

(Jack Gilbert, "In Umbria")

8. **Syntax** The grammatical order and the logical sequencing of phrases, clauses, and sentence types, when artfully arranged, can contribute, like sound and rhythm and diction, their own intelligence and feeling to a poem. Watch how Lynn Emanuel, in the opening sentence/stanza of "On Waking after Dreaming of Raoul," gathers speed while elaborating her metaphor into a **conceit** to demonstrate the feeling and force of lust.

   If Freud was right and dreams of falling are
   dreams of having fallen then you must have been
   the beautiful declivity of that hill, Raoul,
   the speed so seductive and the brakes so
   unreliable, and so intricate and so abstract
   that when I touched them they squealed like a jar lid
   coming loose and I was embarrassed, but not sad,
   at being the one flat wheel that bumped down the hill
   in an unsteady gulp of denial—oh no oh no oh no—
   until I woke up chilly, damp, my breath unsteady.
   (Lynn Emanuel, "On Waking after Dreaming of Raoul")

9. **Rhetorical and grammatical devices of balance** The **concision** of the epigram, the balletic movements of grammatically balanced phrasing, and the play of parallel syntax against opposing or telescoping content can create very dramatic effects. John Kennedy well knew the memorable power of rhetoric when, in copying the rhetoric of a Latin orator, he said: "Ask not what your country can do for you, but what you can do for your country." The forms of how what is said can create containers that, in and of themselves, are indelible. Here, as a small token against the enormous amount of examples extant, is a poem by Jon Anderson that features very strong grammatical and rhetorical features.

   The Secret of Poetry

   When I was lonely, I thought of death.
   When I thought of death I was lonely.

   I suppose this error will continue.
   I shall enter each gray morning

   Delighted by frost, which is death,
   & the trees that stand alone in mist.

   When I met my wife I was lonely.
   Our child in her body is lonely.

   I suppose this error will go on & on.
   Mornings I kiss my wife's cold lips,

Nights her body, dripping with mist.
This is the error that fascinates.

I suppose you are secretly lonely,
Thinking of death, thinking of love.

I'd like, please, to leave on your sill
Just one cold flower, whose beauty

Would leave you inconsolable all day.
The secret of poetry is cruelty.

(Jon Anderson, "The Secret of Poetry")

TENSION EXERCISE

Here are a number of different exercises to help you create **tension** in a poem. Use one of your own poems to perform the following tasks.

1. **Tone:** Change its **tone** from serious to playful by setting its rhythm in a nursery rhyme pattern.
2. **Voice:** Change the **voice** into one that is more intellectual by using a more formal level of **diction** and **syntax.**
3. **Lineation:** Change the form of **lineation** by employing short, rhetorically stressed line endings.
4. **Imagery:** Change the images in the poem from their present level to levels that are more specific or more general.
5. **Thematic correspondence:** Substitute **tropes,** images, and references that do not **nuance** the poem's theme to tropes, images, and references that **connote** it.
6. **Narrative:** Add new **plot** elements that make your poem's **narrative** more interesting in terms of unexpected twists and occurrences.
7. **Implication:** Locate explicit actions in your poem and then add another, higher level of understanding and meaning to those actions.
8. **Syntax:** Create more elaborate and complex syntactical structures by adding nonrestrictive, appositional, and subordinate phrases and clauses.
9. **Balance:** Add phrasing in your poem that is repetitive but parallel and opposite to that in the poem.

THE CONVERSATIONAL MODE

A culture's literature develops and will continue to develop as long as its roots are planted in and remain connected to its spoken language and that form's evolution. This is how American poetry separated and distinguished itself from its progenitor, English poetry, and continues to evolve today, in "trickle-up" fashion, from the bottom up, as it gathers new energy, flavor, subjects, and themes from African American, Hispanic, Native American, and gay dictions, rhythms, and issues.

The **conversational mode** of writing stands on the shoulders of American innovative forebears such as Robert Frost, who composed blankverse "spoken poetry" and gave us his theory of **sentence sounds**—the musical phrasing found in the fluid sentences of conversation; Denise Levertov's model of **organic composition** (probably developed from Coleridge's ideas on composition in his *Biographia Literaria*); Robert Bly's theory of **leaping poetry** that pays attention to the origination of content in different levels of consciousness; William Carlos Williams' "variable foot"; Frank O'Hara (and the New York School of poets) who focused on the immediacy and dailyness of American life and language; and the Beat poets and Confessional poets who helped loosen taboos concerning poetic language and subject matter. These, and many others, helped relax the revolutionary and necessary Modernist dictums about compression, concreteness, detail, image, and architecture. While these early rules and practical standards for poetry writing are, in some measure, virtually unassailable as basic principles and a kind of grammar for modern poetry, they are by their strict nature difficult to apply to the more relaxed medium of the conversational poem. One does not casually speak in tightly organized resonant, epigrammatic, iambic utterances. On the other hand, while the conversational mode loosens these sorts of strictures, it should not do so at the expense of becoming slack. Casual, offhand expressions in the conversational idiom, such as "on the other hand," could be used effectively if the poet can make them connect to deeper, thematic aspects and carry more than one level of meaning. The aesthetic ideal is to create art while seeming somewhat artless as the speaker of the poem shapes form, development, and content more from and toward character and sensibility and voice, than to some pre-ordained formal concept of measurement. It is in the distinctions of character and personality that new and original strategies, forms, perceptions, and concepts will emerge.

What follows is a scattering of the conversational mode that selects various kinds of effective approaches and techniques used in the conversational mode by a number of poets.

CONVERSATIONAL POEM BASED ON PERCEPTION

In Romania
        the exotic is
                a McDonald's hamburger.

* * *

THINGS TO DO AROUND NEWARK

go over somebody's grandmothers place
and eat a lot of stale candy
(Michael Lally, "THINGS TO DO AROUND NEWARK")

POEMS BASED ON DROPPING OR RAISING LEVELS OF REFERENCE

I told him his handkerchief
could stop the war,
could bring us home and erase
the horror, or just be something
he could blow his nose in.

USING METAPHOR IN THE INFORMAL IDIOM

I remember Galileo describing the mind
as a piece of paper blown around by the wind,
and I loved the sight of it sticking to a tree
(Gerald Stern, "I Remember Galileo")

TROPE EVOLVING INTO PLOT AND CHARACTER

As far as birds, I am more like a pigeon than a hawk.
I think I am one of those snow-white pigeons with gold
eyes and a candy-corn beak, with a ruffled
neck—a huge white hood—and ruffled
legs, like flowers or long white pantaloons,
shamelessly exposed under my white dress
and hopelessly drooping when I run in
fear and slip and fall on the dirty newspapers.
(Gerald Stern, "The Angel Poem")

IDIOMATIC USE OF REPETITION (ANAPHORA)

like everything fanned out to sheerness filigree of spines ugly and raw as spines

like everything fingers or claws or hairs grip open-ended molecules to pull along the distance is nothing at all

like everything sparrows choke or drown or bludgeoned

like everything it all washes back to sea or desert or tropical wind specked with husks

like everything the bodies of energy toss back and forth between the distance

like everything tossed the energy tugs as the hairs skin sponge vein scattered out in what looks a certain way

like everything a certain look transfers from the eyes to the heaps to the valleys

like everything that certain way the eye moves from thing to thing makes days

like everything days reach out into the wilderness brush past and over the hips of arenas

like everything smoke is loved as breath fire is fought from the center and **the center insists on itself.**

(Maya Flamm, "display")

CONVERSATIONAL MODE EXERCISE

1. Choose a traditional, formal poem, and rewrite it in the **conversational mode.**
2. Write a series of lines on a formal level of diction, and, in closing, write a line or two in which the level of diction and syntax drops down to the conversational style.
3. Using one of your poems, locate a trope in it and extend it by adding a long, informally styled narrative that includes description, **characterization,** and plot.
4. Using the poem above, add your own idiomatic phrase to introduce a sentence, and then repeat that phrase (**anaphora**) several times, where appropriate, throughout the poem.

VOICE

Voice, the character and stylistic features of a poet's work, is the signatory aspect indelibly embedded in a poet's poems. It is comparable to the unique feel, texture, phrasing, and weight of any skilled musician's or painter's style, and it ultimately derives from the character and vision of the artist. As Denise Levertov succinctly says, "To be human is to be a conversation," and that very sense of humanness is the "news" that Ezra Pound claimed people died for lack of every day. It is that presence of a sentient, seeking, living human voice in a poem, that aspect of a poem that poet Stanley Plumly termed "the rhetoric of voice" that is the main vehicle and interlocutor in mainstream American contemporary poetry.

Voice, not to be confused with the ad hoc device of **tone** in a poem, might at times be carried by tone, and it may be imbedded in a poem's **persona;** but more often than not tone and persona can be very different and distinguishable from the larger qualities of voice, just as the voice of someone you know well has larger and deeper characteristics than the particular tone that person in a particular mood may be using in talking about whatever's at hand. The rhetorician I. A. Richards points out that the way someone speaks to an audience will have imbedded in his or her voice the person's concept of social level, intelligence, and sensitivity of the audience, as well as the quality of relationship he or she has with them. The literary critic Wayne Booth referred to voice as an invention of "whole character," "an ideal, literary, created version of the real man." It is important to distinguish the voice of a writer or poet from the speaker of a poem; while voice emanates from the writer's vision of the world and his relation to it, the ethos and pathos of a speaker in a specific work may only be an adopted mask for the purposes of the poem, just as an actor may well have a certain recognizable style but may adjust that to a particular role he or she is playing.

The element of voice has an integral relationship to other technical aspects of a poem, such as its aesthetic sense, prosody (rhythm, sonics, rhetorical devices), and structure, because all of these aspects of a poem are organically derived from the unique way in which the personality of the poet sees and experiences the world. In contemporary free verse, where almost every poem is filtered through a speaker who stands in for the poet, the element of voice is inextricably woven into, and may be a revelation of, style. It arrives through an accomplished poet's work with the same force of recognition that we experience when we lift the phone and instantly recognize, in all its resonance and context, whose voice is at the other end.

Following are a few stanzas from Robert Long's poem "Chelsea." In it we can hear a poetic voice Long typically displays, which has an urbane, down-at-the-heels colloquial feel to it.

Chelsea

I'm comfortable here, on 50 mg. of Librium,
Two hundred bucks in my pocket
And a new job just a week away.
I can walk the streets in a calm haze,
My blood pressure down to where I'm almost human,
Make countless pay-phone calls from street corners:
Buzzing, they go by in near-neon trails,
People, people like me, headed for black bean soup,
For screams in alleyways, for the homey click
Of the front door's closing, heading home
Past all those faces you know you've seen before:
Like a rear-screen projection in an old movie,
The actors pacing a treadmill or pretending to steer,
And the same '56 Dodge weaving in the background.
(Robert Long, "Chelsea")

Switching over to the rage of engaged, activist politics that are out at all costs for change in the socioeconomic-cultural arena in the United States, there is this first sentence of Amiri Baraka's "A Poem for Black Hearts."

For Malcolm's eyes when they broke
the face of some dumb white man, For
Malcolm's hands raised to bless us
all black and strong in his image
of ourselves, For Malcolm's words
fire darts, the victor's tireless
thrusts, words hung above the world
change as it may, he said it, and
for this he was killed, for saying,
and feeling, and being/change, all
collected hot in his heart
(Amiri Bakara, "A Poem for Black Hearts")

Franz Wright's voice, in a **tone color** similar to that of the artist Edward Hopper, portrays a sensitive, introverted paranoid living on the edge of society in his poem "Certain Tall Buildings." Here is the first half of the poem.

I know a little
about it: I know
if you contemplate suicide
long enough, it
begins to contemplate you.
It calls to your attention

the windows of certain tall
buildings, wooded snow fields
in your memory where you might cunningly vanish
to remotely, undiscoverably
sleep. Remember your mother
hanging the cat
in front of you when you were four?
Why not that?
(Franz Wright, "Certain Tall Buildings")

Then there's the fresh and indelible voice of the great Sufi poet Jelaluddin Rumi, whose musical, universal call for a return to our nature as lovers and to the love of the nature of the self sounds like this:

The minute I heard my first love story
I started looking for you, not knowing
        how blind that was.
Lovers don't finally meet somewhere.
They in each other all along.
(Jelaluddin Rumi, "The Minute I Heard . . ." trans., Coleman Barks)

The point here is that every poet worth his or her salt has an unmistakable voice, a trademark, that courses underneath and through his or her poetry. It is, ultimately, the spirit of the poet behind the poem.

VOICE: IMITATION EXERCISE

Across the arts, one of the most common, rudimentary, and quickest ways to learn craft is to closely imitate others' work. **Imitation,** the studying and copying of various elements of style such as voice, syntax, diction, use and formation of tropes, point of view, rhythm, the **logopoetics** of how things connect, types of imagery, levels of reference, and the use of various other surface textures, moves, and poetic tactics not only gives us a deeper understanding of how the poet went about creating the work, but also adds those tools to our workshop. Any good poet with a strong style will do as a subject for imitation, and this exercise invites you to follow your own enthusiasms for whatever poets you'd like to try imitating. In the meanwhile here's a representative Richard Hugo poem (he has been much imitated over the years), and its stylistic elements cited from the first stanza of "Goodbye Iowa." See if you can imitate the technical aspects of his work after you've read the poem and the list of characteristics.

Once more you've degraded yourself on the road.
The freeway turned you back in on yourself
and found nothing, not even a good false name.
The waitress mocked you and you paid your bill
sweating in her glare. You tried to tell her
how many lovers you've had. Only a croak came out.
Your hand shook when she put hot coins in it.
Your face was hot and you ran face down to the car.
(Richard Hugo, "Goodbye Iowa")

Hugo's Stylistic Features

1. Second-person, masked "I" point of view
2. Impacted and syncopated rhythms
3. Monosyllabic, heavily stressed words
4. Midline juxtapositions that create implied commentary
5. Similar sentence constructions, but of varying lengths
6. Subject matter: identity and low self-esteem issues
7. Slant rhyming and heavy **sonics**

TONE

Tone, in its popular, colloquial sense, usually refers to what degree a person sounds positive or negative; but in literature it typically defines: (1) an author's attitude toward his or her subject and/or audience; (2) the mood set in a speakerless (or transparent) poem; and (3) how emotionally close or distant (subjective or objective) a speaker seems in terms of what his or her relationship is to the subject and theme. The emotion that the poet projects seems to be the primary mechanism in establishing tone, but, technically, beneath the emotion and **selective perception** of the poet, the desired effects stem from the choice of the level of **diction,** word choice, phrasing, **point of view,** and mode of **horizontal content** (e.g., exposition, argumentation, narration, etc.), as well as the choice of rhetorical structures such as argumentation, **irony,** various forms of **poetic fallacies,** and devices such as metaphor and image. The emotional effects of tone and its position on a spectrum ranging from subjective to objective is termed **aesthetic distance,** and is a subject that is instructive to take up.

Aesthetic Distance

This is also known as *physical* or *psychic distance,* figuring out what tone to use—for instance, whether a poem about the death of a loved one is most comfortably and effectively written from a personal, lyric stance taken by the poet, or from one that is willfully objective and holds back its emotional power as a leveraging device. The level of aesthetic distance is best decided by the poet by measuring his or her feelings about an experience in relation to how best to tell it to others. Here is a partial sampling of various uses of aesthetic distance or tones.

FORMAL TONE In the following lines from W. H. Auden's poem, "Musée des Beaux Arts," the delayed and heightened syntax, the generic, allusive character of the nouns, and the statement-oriented rhetoric prepare a formality well-suited to the poem's lofty philosophical subject matter about the juxtaposition of tragedy and innocence.

About suffering they were never wrong,
The Old Masters: how well they understood
Its human position; how it takes place
While someone else is eating or opening a window or just
walking dully along;
How, when the aged are reverently, passionately waiting
For the miraculous birth, there must always be
Children who did not specially want it to happen, skating
On a pond at the edge of a wood. . . .
(W. H. Auden, "Musée des Beaux Arts")

HUMOROUS TONE Here is Robert Francis' funny, ditty-like celebration, which is as much about the weight and feel of words as it is about its subject: the clowns, boors, and incompetents that populate the earth. Francis is a poet well-known for his investment in lots of word play.

Yes, What?

What would earth do without her blessed boobs
her blooming bumpkins garden variety
her oafs her louts her yodeling yokels
and all her Breughel characters
under the fat-faced moon?

Her nitwits numbskulls universal
nincompoops jawohl jawohl with all
their yawps burps beers guffaws
her goofs her goons her big galoots
under the red-faced moon?
(Robert Francis, "Yes, What?")

ANGRY TONE Again, word choice, phrasing, level of diction, and syntax have everything to do with how Heather McHugh is able to create a driving, heatedly angry voice in the following stanzas from "Earthmoving Malediction."

Bulldoze the bed where we made love,
bulldoze the goddamn room.
Let rubble be our evidence
and wreck our home.

I can't give touching up
by inches, can't give beating
up by heart. So set the comforter
on fire, and turn the dirt

to some advantage—palaces of pigweed,
treasuries of turd. The fist
will vindicate the hand,
and tooth and nail

refuse to burn . . .

(Heather McHugh, "Earthmoving Malediction")

DISCONSOLATE TONE Notice the words and striking images emanating from and surrounding the concept of death, and the **personification** of objects that form an **emblem** in the following lines from Lorna Dee Cervantes' poem "Colorado Blvd."

I wanted to die so I walked
the streets. Dead night,
black as iris, cold as the toes
on a barefoot drunk. Not a sound
but my shoes asking themselves over,
What season is this? Why is the wind
stuttering in its stall of nightmares?
Why courage or the bravery
of dripping steel?

(Lorna Dee Cervantes, "Colorado Blvd.")

EXULTANT TONE Lynda Hull is able to create a breathless, high-flying mood, through acute imagery, striking word choice, a syncopated, jazzy rhythm, and **sonics,** in these lines from "Shore Leave," in which a romantic and slick sailor on shore leave takes his star-struck young daughter for a flashily dizzying day outing.

He's all charm with the car dealer and fast-talks
them a test-drive in a convertible like the one

on display, a two-tone Coupe de Ville. But once
around the corner he lowers the top and soon
they're fishtailing down dump-truck paths,
the Jersey Meadows smoldering with trash fires.
He shouting *Maybelline why can't you be true,*
and seagulls lift in a tattered curtain across
Manhattan's hazy skyline. Dust-yellow clouds
behind him, he's handsome as a matinee idol,
wavy hair blown straight by sheer velocity.
(Lynda Hull, "Shore Leave")

IRONIC TONE It is in his seemingly straightforward supposition that there should be a special jail for women who have lost their looks that Thomas Merton exposes our society's prejudice in estimating a woman's value and character according to her age and beauty, or, rather, lack thereof, in these lines from "There Has to Be a Jail for Ladies."

There has to be a jail where ladies go
When they are poor, without nice things, and with their hair
down.
When their beauty is taken from them, when their hearts are
broken
There is a jail where they must go.
There has to be a jail for ladies, says the Government,
When they are ugly because they are wrong.
It is good for them to stay there a long time
Until the wrong is forgotten.
(Thomas Merton, "There Has to Be a Jail for Ladies")

Point of View

Point of view refers to whether the speaker in a poem is talking from a first-, second-, or third-person perspective. It usually has more to do with the topic of narration and storytelling in terms of the speaker's physical or emotional distance from a subject, or from what level of consciousness and with what degree of intimacy or objectivity the subject is being addressed. But it is relevant here to the general topic of **tone** because it is one of the main devices that helps establish and leverage various shades of tone and distance in the voice of a speaker.

FIRST-PERSON POINT OF VIEW Up through the middle part of the twentieth century, it was untoward to use the first-person point of view (the personal pronouns "I" and "we") in a formal essay and literary works unless it was in the voice of a devised character. One was not allowed to use "I" to indicate the self, the writer as real or invented speaker. But in contemporary poetry, particularly after the breakthrough in Victorian literary mores and proprieties, with the work of the Beat poets, the New York "walkin'-talkin" School of poetics, and the Confessional poets, among others, many psychological and sexual barriers fell by the wayside, and language usage in poetry aligned itself more closely with the spoken, rather than the written, word.

The convention of the first-person point of view provides several kinds of ready-made characteristics to a poem: (1) an intimacy developed out of the subjectivity of the first-person reportage; (2) the verisimilitude of first-hand experience and knowledge since the speaker is a participant or witness; (3) an implicit sense of built-in trust because the speaker is "sharing" something and thus bonding with the reader; (4) a sense that the reader, affected by the sincerity of the point of view, is being told the "truth"; and (5) a feeling of immediacy.

Here, in the first stanza of Larry Levis' "The Poet at Seventeen," written in the first-person singular point of view, the speaker establishes a sense of intimacy, confession, lyricism, and heart-felt regret.

> My youth? I hear it mostly in the long, volleying
> Echoes of billiards in the pool halls where
> I spent it all, extravagantly, believing
> My delicate touch on a cue would last for years.
> (Larry Levis, "The Poet at Seventeen")

If the point of view is changed to the second person, an entirely different effect is created. The poem sounds accusatory, judgmental, and presumptuous. There's no room in this version for the hope of salvation triggered by the surrender of regret. If the point of view is further removed to the third person, a coldness in the form of objectivity and preordained resignation invades the speaker's voice.

SECOND-PERSON POINT OF VIEW This point of view, which in its strict form and intention addresses another person directly with the pronoun "you" (see the **masked pronoun,** p. 147, for other, looser usage), gives up a degree of subjectivity and intimacy, but gains another, more direct kind of emotional leverage, a comparatively enlarged perspective beyond the limitations of the "I" point of view. Feel the one-on-one kind of monologue established in the opening of Stephen Berg's "The Coat," a **letter poem** to his poet-friend Gerald Stern.

> Here's one of those warm simple letters in that big six-year-old
> scrawl of yours, filling the whole page with your statement,
> clear, sweet, kind, associating values with detail with Nietzsche
> with the glory of poetry with some local flower or creature you
> bumped into yesterday and fell in love with
> (Stephen Berg, "The Coat")

THE INSTRUCTIVE, COMMAND FORM OF SECOND-PERSON A more traditional use in earlier times of the second-person point of view was often employed as an implicit, general address, and was didactic, meant as an overt device of instruction. As you would expect, it has the leveraging power of formality and authority, but in contemporary times may seem off-putting for its presumptuous tone. Here's the opening stanza from William Blake's "Never Seek to Tell Thy Love."

> Never seek to tell thy love
> Love that never told can be;
> For the gentle wind does move
> Silently, invisibly.
> (William Blake, "Never Seek to Tell Thy Love")

THE "MASKED" OR FALSE SECOND-PERSON PRONOUN Almost as popular as the first-person point of view in contemporary American poetry from the 1960s to the 1980s was the "masked," second-person point of view, which has an all-inclusive, collective, reader-directed gesture of address implied in it. It is termed "masked" because its unrevealed but tacit identity is the first-person "I" or third-person "he," "she," or "they." Critics in recent times have thought to devalue its use, partly because of its ubiquity and partly because it is a rather easy device to get the reader included; but, nevertheless, it still has its own special power. Here's a well-known example from Richard Hugo's "Degrees of Gray in Phillipsburg."

> You might come here Sunday on a whim.
> Say your life broke down. The last good kiss
> you had was years ago. You walk these streets
> laid out by the insane, past hotels
> that didn't last, bars that did, the tortured try
> of local drivers to accelerate their lives.
> (Richard Hugo, "Degrees of Gray in Phillipsburg")

THIRD-PERSON POINT OF VIEW This is the most commonly used point of view in literature. It offers the most freedom in terms of leveraging an objective and all-inclusive overview and inner view of a situation, character, or experience since the speaker has unlimited license to work in, among, within, and beyond the limitations of the characters and action.

The first, general type, the third-person **omniscient point of view,** is characterized by its unlimited perspective: it offers the largest amount of freedom from which to view the experience about which the poem is written. It can interpret the psyches, actions, and thoughts of its characters, give an overview of a situation that is larger than what any character might have access to, and can include subjective commentary, judgments, and references on a situation, and/or remain impersonal.

1. **Third-person omniscient point of view.** Notice the leverage that the third-person **omniscient point of view** gives Bill Tremblay's speaker in moving from the an objective report of what nuns taught into Duhamel's inner feelings and perceptions.

Creation

In school the nuns taught God
made the heavens and earth in six
days. Duhamel never believed it.
He saw his mother and father make it
in one day.
At first it *was* dark.
His mother lifted the curtain and made
light shine through the glass windows
and the wooden crossbars, making their
children, the shadows.
(Bill Tremblay, "Creation")

2. **Third-person limited point of view.** From the **third-person limited point of view** or perspective, the speaker of the poem limits his or her vantage point to only what the character knows of his own actions and thoughts. Watch how effective the limitations of this point of view can be when, as in an instance such as David Lehman's poem below, the subject is about limitations and the unknown.

Fear

The boy hid under the house
With his dog, his red lunch box, and his fear
Thinking God is near
Thinking it's time to leave the things that mean
Just one thing, though you can't tell what that is,
Like God or death. The boy held his breath,
Closed his eyes, and disappeared,
Thinking No one will find me here—
But only when his parents were watching.
When they weren't, he slipped away
And hid under the house
And stayed there all night, and through the next day,
Until Father (who had died that December)
Agreed to come home, and Mother was twenty
Years younger again, and pregnant with her

Darling son. Hiding under the house,
He could see it all, past and future,
The deep blue past, the black-and-white future,
Until he closed his eyes and made it disappear,

And everyone was glad when he returned
To the dinner table, a grown man
With wire-rim glasses and neatly combed hair.
Fear was the name of his dog, a German shepherd.
(David Lehman, "Fear")

TONE: POINT OF VIEW EXERCISE

In order to see the substantial difference in aesthetic distance, immediacy, intimacy, maneuverability, and leverage that a change in point of view can make, switch the point of view in one of your poems so that there are at least four versions experienced from different perspectives.

FORM

Lineation

The line is one of the basic units of measurement and pacing in free verse. In fact, the word *verse* itself means "to turn," as opposed to *prose,* which means "direct," or without turns (although the **prose poem** format, which allows whatever kinds of devices and "moves" free verse offers except line breaks, is a common form). Writing in lines offers a number of opportunities: first and foremost, it is a way to control and manipulate levels of meaning, the interrelationships in content, and the speed and pacing for both the writer and reader. It is a way to rhythmically shape and sculpt the mood, feel, and general movement of a poem as it develops, whether it's based on syllabic count, rhythm, imagery, syntax, content, previous forms, or theories of form such as Allen Ginsberg's "mind breaths." But beyond the merely technical considerations of how lines are shaped are the aspects of voice and character. John Haines' dramatic dictum that "to change your line you must change your life" has validity to it if, as many poets feel is true, every aspect of a poem—its sonic values, rhythms, word choice, selectivity or ranginess—reveals one's vision, attitudes, values, and character. From Robert Creeley's highly restricted short-lined poems to C. K. Williams' margin-to-margin long lyric-narrative lines, poets will always have a definitive reason for choosing the kinds of lines they employ, whether their rationale is based on technique employed for effect or on an unconscious, intuitive sense of what feels right.

Aside from each poet's reason for choosing how long a line to make and what technical effect line breaks will have (whether lines feature **enjambment** or end-stops), there are some general principles that can be observed. For instance, paradoxically, the fact that short-lined poems read more slowly than long-lined poems is a technical aspect that translates easily into creating emotional effects. For example, if a poet feels the need to create a sense of suspense, hesitation, weightiness, doubt, or careful exploration, then a very short line works well for this, as in this example from the first four stanzas of Robert Creeley's "For My Mother: Genevieve Jules Creeley."

> Tender, semi-
> articulate flickers
> of your
>
> presence, all
> those years
> past
>
> now, eighty-
> five, impossible to
> count them
>
> one by one, like
> addition, sub-
> traction, missing
>
> not one.
>
> (Robert Creeley, "For My Mother: Genevieve Jules Creeley")

Now look at the entirely different effects created by the lengthening and shortening of lines from Dave Smith's first stanza of "In the House of the Judge."

> All of them asleep, the suspiring everywhere is audible weight
>   in the winter-shadowed house where I have dreamed
>   night after night and stand now trying
>   to believe it is only dust, no more than vent-spew
>   risen from the idiotically huffing
> grandfather of a furnace in the coal room's heart of darkness.
>
> (Dave Smith, "In the House of the Judge")

CHARACTERIZING THE LINE IN FREE VERSE Looking generally at the way lines are constructed, the way they move in free verse, David Wojahn has come up with four main categories: poems that use (1) **anaphora,** a rhetorical device that employs repetition of phrasing and/or syntax; (2) **parsing,** which breaks up the line into conversational and/or whole syntactical units; (3) **fevered**

enjambments, which constructs and breaks lines according to fragmented syntactical or phrasal units; and (4) **fixed form ghosting,** which echoes or is strongly based upon traditional fixed forms. Here are examples from each category.

1. **Anaphora** (stanzas from James L. White's "Naming"). Note the repetitions of address and parallel phrasings.

    Old woman, my mother,
    let's do the world again you and me,
    this time in the desert outside Gallup, New Mexico
    where the sky's as bright as cut ribbons.

    * * *

    Old woman, don't die.
    Take me to your first words again,
    to say there are plants that live as people,
    that certain animals carry dreams,
    that the hawk is itself where the canyon drops to air.

    * * *

    Old woman, my mother,
    so full of sickness it becomes acquaintance,
    don't die. The world is nearly empty for me.
    Take me near your river of first words again.
    (James L. White, "Naming")

2. **Parsing** (opening stanza of Robert Mezey's "White Blossoms"). Notice how the lines are built out of the regular separations of syntactical phrases.

    Take me as I drive alone
    through the dark countryside.
    As the strong beams clear a path,
    picking out fences, weeds, late
    flowering trees, everything
    that streams back into the past
    without sound, I smell the grass
    and the rich chemical sleep
    of the fields. An open moon
    sails above, and a stalk
    of red lights blinks, miles away.
    (Robert Mezey, "White Blossoms")

3. **Fevered enjambment.** Notice the fracturing of syntactical phrases featured in the **fevered enjambment** (technically termed **rhetorical stress**) in about half of the following lines.

I came to
believe his notion of
flying around the
moon was not
as crazy as
it sounded if you
were high on
something.

4. **Fixed form ghosting.** Notice how the combination of the **villanelle** (here, repeating phrases instead of whole lines) and **sestina** (repeating words) create the lyrical form of this poem.

The Secret of Poetry

When I was lonely, I thought of death.
When I thought of death I was lonely.

I suppose this error will continue.
I shall enter each gray morning

Delighted by frost, which is death,
& the trees that stand alone in mist.

When I met my wife I was lonely.
Our child in her body is lonely.

I suppose this error will go on & on.
Mornings I kiss my wife's cold lips,

Night her body, dripping with mist.
This is the error that fascinates.

I suppose you are secretly lonely,
Thinking of death, thinking of love.

I'd like, please, to leave on your sill
Just one cold flower, whose beauty

Would leave you inconsolable all day.
The secret of poetry is cruelty.
(Jon Anderson, "The Secret of Poetry")

LANGUAGE MODELS Another large-scale way to look at **lineation** is to think of the level of diction upon which poems are based: the written prose model, semiformal speech model, or the everyday spoken word. The following poem by Belle Waring is based upon recognizable rhythms.

1. **The prose model**

Baby Random
tries a nosedive, kamikaze,
when the intern flings open the isolette.

The kid almost hits the floor. I can see the headline:
DOC DUMPS AIDS TOT. Nice save, nurse,

Why thanks. Young physician: "We have to change
his tube." His voice trembles, six weeks

out of school. I tell him: "Keep it to a handshake,
you'll be OK." Our team resuscitated

this Baby Random, birth weight
one pound, eyelids still fused. Mother's

a junkie with HIV. Never named him.
Where I work we bring back terminal preemies,

No Fetus Can Beat Us. That's our motto. I have
a friend who was thrown into prison. Where do birds

go when they die? Neruda wanted to know. Crows
eat them. Bird heaven? Imagine the racket.

When Random cries, petit fish on shore, nothing
squeaks past the tube down his pipe. His ventilator's

a high-tech bellows that kicks in & out. Not
up to the nurses. Quiet: a pigeon's outside,

color of graham crackers, throat oil on a wet street,
wings splattered white, perched out of the rain.

I have friends who were thrown into prison, Latin
American. Tortured. Exiled. Some people have

courage. Some people have heart. *Corazon.*
After a shift like tonight, I have the usual

bad dreams. Some days I avoid my reflection in store
windows. I just don't want anyone to look at me.

(Belle Waring, "Baby Random")

2. **Semiformal speech**

Sometimes you hear, fifth-hand,
As epitaph:
He chucked up everything
And just cleared off,

And always the voice will sound
Certain you approve
This audacious purifying
Elemental move.
(Philip Larkin, "The Poetry of Departures")

3. **Idiomatic speech**

this babe in the back of the bus
gives me the hi-sign
like she's on to where I'm at
and when I get there
turns out she only wants a match.

Miscellaneous Bases

BREATH UNITS Allen Ginsberg uses a very long form of **breath units,** which are lines based upon what he calls "mind breaths," the amount of time it takes his mind to express a thought. Lines from his poem "Howl" exemplify this unit of measurement.

I saw the best minds of my generation destroyed by madness,
starving, hysterical, naked,
dragging themselves through the negro streets at dawn, looking
for an angry fix

CONVERSATIONAL UNITS The lines that follow are sculpted and phrased according to the rhythms and music of conversational speech.

I don't know,
she told me to go about my business,
sent me on my way
with a kind of half-wave and a wink,
a sort of hello and goodbye.

THOUGHT AND SENSORY UNITS In this category, some poets form up line units according to **thought** or **sensory line units,** in which lines are based on the dealing out of image units.

When the smell of cilantro
sprayed the air,
I realized stars
might be the pheromones
from God's celestial garden.

RHETORICAL EMPHASIS In the lines below, the last word in each line, juxtaposed against the line's previous content, persuasively emphasizes the character of the speaker's depressing and stressful home life.

I was tired of home. Mother was
always upset, my father was
far away, and there was no
sister or brother to help share the load.

INCREMENTALLY DEVELOPED UNITS William Carlos Williams' "snapshot technique" of crafting the following lines from "A Negro Woman" creates frozen moments in time that, through the accumulation of **incremental line units,** build a striking image.

A Negro woman
carrying a bunch of marigolds
wrapped
in an old newspaper:
she carries them upright,
bareheaded
the bulk
of her thighs
causing her to waddle
as she walks
looking into
the store window which she passes
on her way

(William Carlos Williams, "A Negro Woman")

FORM: LINE UNIT EXERCISE

1. **Anaphora:** Using one of your own poems, form the poem's lines and line lengths according to the repetition of a phrase (**anaphora**) you've created at the beginning or end of your lines.
2. **Parsing:** Rewrite whatever rhetorically stressed lines are in your poem so that you **parse** all its lines; that is, so they end with complete syntactical units (but not necessarily the ends of sentences).
3. **Fevered enjambments:** Now reverse the line endings so that each line ends with a **rhetorically stressed** (fevered enjambment) unit (incomplete syntactical phrase or clause).
4. **Fixed form ghosting:** Rewrite your poem using the echo of a **fixed form** behind it (**sonnet, sestina, villanelle,** etc.).

THE MOVEMENT OF LINE ENDINGS IN FREE VERSE

How the eye and mind coordinate and move when reading a line and what kinds of semantic expressions and implications are evoked by way of rhythm, syntax, and word choice within and at the end of lines are major craft issues in free verse.

When fixed forms lost their preeminence to free verse, the places for pausing (the initial, medial, or terminal **caesura** within a line and the **line break** that once depended upon devices of rhythm and rhyme) became transformed into opportunities for word play and interesting juxtapositions that focused more on the element of meaning than on **melopoetics** (rhythmic and sonic effects). While there is no prescribed system for categorizing free verse lines, the following classifications will be very helpful in becoming more conscious of the kinds of opportunities available in line making.

The Internal and External Movement of Lines

1. **The end-stopped line** The **end-stopped line** is one of the two basic ways the movement of a line is completed. It simply stops by using normal sentence-ending punctuation (period, question mark, exclamation point, semicolon, colon) or by way of implied punctuation evoked in the phrasing.

    He that was foe now is our friend.

    The symbol for the end-stopped line is a long sideways "T": ——|

2. **The enjambed line** **Enjambment** indicates that the line does not stop when it ends, but is carried over rhythmically to the next line by simply not ending a sentence or breaking a syntactical unit before it is completed. Any unfinished sentence automatically creates an enjambed line.

    I bought a
    loaf of bread at
    the circus but I didn't
    ever want to eat it.

    The symbol for the enjambed line is: ——>

3. **The end-stopped/reflexive line** Here the syntactical movement of the line stops at its end, but there is an inner, reverse movement (that aspect known as the **reflexive line ending**) created by what the end-word refers to, as in these lines in which the last word, "misty," makes the reader link up the previous reference to the "fog" with subsequent adjective "misty."

The fog was like his mind. Misty.

The symbol for the end-stopped/reflexive line is:

4. **The end-stopped/enjambed line** This is a two-directional line that combines the two primary movements of end-stopped and enjambed. The syntax indicates an enjambment, while the phrasing calls for what could be called an end-stopped pause. Here is an example from several lines from W. H. Auden's "Musée des Beaux Arts":

   They never forgot
   That even the dreadful martyrdom must run its course
   Anyhow in a corner, some untidy spot
   Where the dogs go on with their doggy life,
   (W. H. Auden, "Musée des Beaux Arts")

   The symbol for the end-stopped/enjambed line is this:

5. **The enjambed/reflexive line** This is another two-level line in which the syntax of the line indicates that it carries over to the next line, yet the end-word refers to something previous in the line, making the mind bounce backward. Here is an example (lines 2-5) from Richard Hugo's "Degrees of Gray in Phillipsburg":

   You might come here Sunday on a whim.
   Say your life broke down. The last good kiss
   you had was years ago. You walk these streets
   laid out by the insane, past hotels
   that didn't last, bars that did, the tortured try
   of local drivers to accelerate their lives.
   (Richard Hugo, "Degrees of Gray in Phillipsburg")

   Notice, also, that there are some interesting semantic triangulations in the juxtaposition of first half-line against second half-line in lines 2–5.

   The symbol for the enjambed/reflexive line is:

6. **The enjambed/reflexive/end-stopped line** This is the triple toe-loop of line endings. It syntactically refers forward to the subsequent line, semantically refers backwards to content in its line, and, with its heavy pause at the end of the line that makes an autonomous unit of the line-as-sentence, could be considered end-stopped. Here's another example (lines 1–3) from Hugo's "Degrees of Gray in Phillipsburg."

Isn't this your life? That ancient kiss
still burning out your eyes? Isn't this defeat
so accurate, the church bell simply seems
a pure announcement: ring and no one comes?
(Richard Hugo, "Degrees of Gray in Phillipsburg")

The symbol for the enjambed/reflexive/end-stopped line is:

The Semantics of Line Endings

TRANSFORMATIONAL LINE ENDINGS Aside from anticipatory enjambed line endings that create suspense, or emphatic line endings that highlight and emphasize previous content in a line or stanza, there is a category of line endings whose **semantics** change in meaning when the right word choice is made. Here are the major types of transformational line endings.

1. **Grammatical change.** Watch how the end-word, which at first seems to be not only a noun but also one that implies surprise, changes into a simple, descriptive adjective when the second line is revealed.

    She walked in out of the **blue**
    morning.

2. **Synesthetic change.** Here the end-words in the first two lines, which seems to indicate sounds, change their character and meaning—from aural sense to visual sense—in the context of their succeeding lines.

    The dragster had a **loud**
    color that made **ring**
    as it zoomed around the track

3. **Ambiguous change.** The first line's end-word seems to say "no" in no uncertain terms, but in the context of the second line the meaning reverses itself, an effect that can humorously show the complex character of relationships.

    They necked until she yelled **"Don't**
    let my parents see us!"

4. **Literal to metaphorical change.** This is the most basic and easiest kind of metaphor to construct, the prepositional metaphor, in which what at first appears to be literal becomes metaphorical in the context of the subsequent line.

She was lost in the **backwaters**
of her desire.

5. **Fused syntax line ending.** This type of line ending can be used to create action-reaction types of plot elements. In the example that follows, different emotional attitudes are shown.

    She called up **Frank and her boyfriend**
    got mad.

6. **Emotional/physical change.** Here the intention is to transform what at first seems to be an emotional attitude into a physical change in the context of the second line.

    When my ex waved hello I **sank**
    beneath the waves.

7. **Play on words (the pun).** In this type of line ending, the end-word plays off a double meaning, which creates a purposeful misdirection and effects drama, surprise, and etymological associations for the reader.

    She dressed so loud she might've been **call**
    girl.

LINE ENDING EXERCISE

In addition to shaping a poem rhythmically, well-crafted line endings can create surprise; control the direction of thought, argument, or plot; create new semantic and thematic levels of meaning; and offer, through implication, multiple associations that help contribute to a poem's **resonance.** In the category of **transformational line endings,** see if you can create your version for each one of the eight types that follow.

1. **Grammatical change (noun/adjective change):**

   The images in the mind of the artist were dark blue.

2. **General to specific change:**

   Every time he got he got angry he smoked cigarettes.

3. **Synesthetic change:**

   The sports announcer had a loud shirt on.

4. **Ambiguous line ending:**

   The mother crab told her babies, "Now just hold on, I'll be right there."

5. **Literal to metaphorical change:**

    He hid in the thicket of his feelings.
6. **Fused syntax:**

    We cheered for the hero and the villain slunk back into the shadows.
7. **Emotional to physical change:**

    When the fly landed on her nose, she looked cross-eyed at it.
8. **Pun line ending:**

    Marlene Dietrich's seductive voice came on the radio.

STANZAS

The word **stanza** is derived from the Italian word for "stopping place" or "room." It is a traditional **strophic** format made up of a coherent unit of lines, set off by space above and below, based upon one or a combination of logic, music, or imagery, within which elements such as rhythm, subject, plot, character, theme, rhetoric, and syntax operate. In traditional fixed-form, stanzaic verse, there is a large array of forms such as the ballad stanza, Chaucer stanza, elegaic distich, epigram, in memoriam stanza, quatrain, heroic couplet, Spencerian stanza, terza rima, triolet, and tercet, to name only a few. Poems composed merely of lines without stanza breaks are termed **sticchic** or "block poems."

In free verse, the number of lines in a stanza can range from one up to any amount the poet deems appropriate to his subject and methods. In the commonly employed stanza lengths of one to four lines, there are certain principles of organization and effects at work. Here are the characteristics featured by these stanzas.

The Monostich

This is a one-line stanza whose form creates a sense of focus, thrust, penetration, and succinctness. Oftentimes, the **monostich** is used to turn the direction of the narrative or argument of a poem. In W. S. Merwin's poem "Fly," after he has admitted to inadvertantly killing his pet pigeon by repeatedly trying to get him to fly, he skillfully focuses all of the narrative weight of his story on his failure to see that merely yelling the command "fly!" will not make his bird do so. In the middle of the poem he uses the focusing monostich: "So that is what I am" (see pp. 186–187 for the full poem).

The Couplet

Because the **couplet,** one of the most common stanzaic forms in Western poetry, has the strengths of brevity (in terms of length) and succinctness (in terms of compression of expression) and is usually bound by the parameters of a complete logical structure and grammar, it offers the important quality of being memorable, whether in an open (unrhymed) or closed (rhymed, as in the distich) form. The open couplet form, which is unrhymed, sometimes uses a stanza composed of two lines for its cinching, closed quality, and at other times for its elastic, anticipatory qualities.

Although Andrew Marvell's "To His Coy Mistress" seems to be written in non-stanzaic, block style, it is really composed of 23 consecutive couplets (see entire poem on pp. 207–208). The main character of the closed couplet is the way in which it can present opposing views, arguments, or events.

(CLOSED)

Had we but world enough, and time,
This coyness, lady, were no crime.
We would sit down, and think which way
To walk, and pass our long love's day.
(Andrew Marvell, "To His Coy Mistress")

The Triplets

The **triplet** is an unrhymed, three-line stanza, as opposed to the rhymed three-line **tercet** (as in Robert Herrick's "Upon Julia's Clothes" and the contemporary poet Molly Peacock's "Say You Love Me"). It offers one of the best formal opportunities for resolving, opening up, or mediating between two opposing or parallel arguments or events. Watch the way Sydney Lea uses the triplet to present and balance two states of consciousness and then, in his third-line comment, address the qualities of both in "Museum."

(OPEN)

Small thunder cuts my autumn doze on the porch.
Trotting by, two thoroughbreds—skittish,
slender.
Dream is at once a heavy and delicate thing.
(Sydney Lea, "Museum")

The Quatrain

The **quatrain,** because of its even number of lines, has the same features of balance and containment that the couplet offers. In the two quatrains of William Stafford's "Traveling through the Dark," each quatrain functions as and contains separate plot and comments that imbue the incident with philosophical and ethical resonance. Each quatrain also builds upon a previous quatrain, so that the "rooms" of this house are both discrete and complementary, a house whose area feels larger than the sum of its parts.

(OPEN) **Traveling through the Dark**

Traveling through the dark I found a deer
dead on the edge of the Wilson River Road.
It is usually best to roll them into the canyon:
that road is narrow; to swerve might make more dead.

By glow of the tail-light I stumbled back of the car
and stood by the heap, a doe, a recent killing;
she had stiffened already, almost cold.
I dragged her off; she was large in the belly.
(William Stafford, "Traveling through the Dark")

In the tradition of metered and rhymed verse, the closed quatrain has the same **mnenomic** quality that the closed couplet has. Walter Savage Landor, emulating the ancient Latin and Greek forms of terse, artfully wrought, philosophical lyrics, offers this single bittersweet quatrain.

(CLOSED) **Dying Speech of an Old Philosopher**

I strove with none, for none was worth my strife:
 Nature I loved, and, next to Nature, Art:
I warmed both hands before the fire of Life;
 It sinks; and I am ready to depart.
(Walter Savage Landor, "Dying Speech of an Old Philosopher")

STANZA EXERCISE

Taking one of your poems written in **sticchic** form (one block stanza), try recasting the lines in the following manner:

1. Rewrite the poem in open **couplets.**
2. Now rewrite the above version in **closed couplets.**
3. Next rewrite the poem in **quatrains,** using the above closed couplet form.
4. Finally, rewrite the poem using **triplets.**

SECTIONING

Sectioning is a structural device, using roman or arabic numerals, asterisks, or a decorative symbol to create stops and separations that are a bit longer than stanzaic breaks but shorter than the separation of acts in a play. Usually, the device is found in poems longer than fifty lines. In student writing, sectioning is typically a sign that the poet is at a loss as to how to narratively, argumentatively, or lyrically connect what should be stanzas, and so resorts to the characteristic breaking off of sectioning (from one topic, scene, character, or event to another). The sections in a contemporary poem typically hang together in associative and meditative ways in a thematic clustering rather than, say, sectioning in older, more traditional verse, by chronology or narrative. Sometimes, sectioning forms as a reflection of the way the parts of a poem are received or imagined by the poet. Organizationally, the units are more akin to the floating parts of a hanging mobile sculpture than a fixed, linear structure.

Here is an example of an effectively sectioned poem by Jack Driscoll whose discrete parts are scenes from memory, as the title indicates, centripetally arranged around the subject and experience of the mother's deafness.

Memories of My Deaf Mother

My mother takes down her hair
long and heavy
like so many nights of snow.
In bed she dreams
me knocking sound from these boards, each nail
a whisper driven deep into her ear. I am building
a coffin, my dead voice trying hard to call her back
through all this silence.

* * *

The deaf have poor balance. Undressing
by the stairs she always imagined falling, fear
alive in her spine. I was nine
the first time I saw her naked, her pale arms
hugging the railing like a neck.

* * *

I learned to talk with my hands, to close them
sometimes in anger, a door
slamming in my throat. I remember
how often water on the stove whistled itself dry
how the pickup's horn stuck one night

while my mother, smiling, parked it full of hay
in the barn. I woke, ran barefoot through the cold,
found four stalls battered, the horses
crazier than fire.

* * *

My father died dragging bales
through the deep snow. My mother, finding him,
exhaled a single word;
I choked it down,
listened to it thaw for years.

* * *

I am always coming home, wind
stuttering on the lip of a hill.
There is a cow;
she pulls her tongue across a saltlick,
where my mother opened her fur coat,
pulled my mouth around her nipple
like a scream.
            All winter
I curled next to her, dreamed
absence was a sound, the moon
tapping in her blind ear.

* * *

For the last time
I step into childhood,
unfold these memories, notes
pushed like a groan across the snow
     where she is hauling water
on a sled. I follow
ringing a bell for the horses
who step now from under the pines.
(Jack Driscoll, "Memories of My Deaf Mother")

SECTIONING EXERCISE

Create several stanzas that center upon an image. Then break off from those stanzas and begin a new section of stanzas that treat the same image or idea from an entirely different perspective. Continue creating new sections until you feel they encompass the image with a sense of wholeness, completeness, and unity.

FLOW

Syntax

Technically speaking, **syntax** is the ordering of words, or the grammatical structure of words, in a sentence. But syntax itself is considered one of the "intelligences" in a poem, a tool or order and **flow** by which the poet can evoke or nuance meaning by subordinating, sequencing, installing degrees of complexity of levels of thought, extending and elaborating content, counterpointing, or purposefully violating normal sentence conventions. It is, basically, the line of ordered words that connects things, people, places, and their actions, reactions, and ideas. Furthermore, syntax can create character because its arrangements can express straightforwardness, brutality, elegance, simplicity, floridness, madness, intelligence, vivacity, pomposity, etc. How the elements in a sentence are arranged harmonically with or against lines so that selected phrases and syntactical units are broken up, fused, continued through, or juxtaposed can make for some very interesting and skillfully wrought tensions, surprises, and releases as a feature in the flow of the poem.

THE SIMPLE SENTENCE AS LINE The simple sentence—organized as the sequence of subject, verb, object—has directness, impact, simplicity, and thrust. Notice the two simple sentences Franz Wright uses to effect the quickness and torque of a joke. Here Wright syncopates the rhythm of his first sentence with a shorter, reversed rhythm in his second sentence.

> They think that they can scare me.
> I'm always scared.
> (Franz Wright, "Certain Tall Buildings")

David Wojahn does the same sort of counterpointing of rhythms, using the music of colloquial phrasing, as he creates first a run-on double sentence, and then a two-sentence line.

> *David, fill the glass for me, I've got such a thirst.*
>
> * * *
>
> *Johnny, fill the syringe for me. All the pain's come back*
> (David Wojahn, "White Lanterns")

THE SENTENCE-LENGTH POEM One kind of syntactical *tour de force* is the poem composed of one sentence. Pattiann Rogers often uses a rhetorical and syntactical setup to string together multiple modifying and subordinated phrases and clauses rich in musicality. In the poem below, after 29 lines of delaying, introductory phrases and clauses that build expectation and pressure, she releases the main clause in her closure.

The Hummingbird: A Seduction

If I were a female hummingbird perched still
And quiet on an upper myrtle branch
In the spring afternoon and if you were a male
Alone in the whole heavens before me, having parted
Yourself, for me, from cedar top and honeysuckle stem
And earth-down, your body hovering in mid-air
Far away from jewelweed, thistle and beebalm;

And if I watched how you fell, plummeting before me,
And how you rose again and fell, with such mastery
That I believed for a moment *you* were the sky
And the red-marked bird diving inside your circumference
Was just the physical revelation of the light's
Most perfect desire;

And if I saw your sweeping and sucking
Performance of swirling egg and semen in the air,
The weaving, twisting vision of red petal
And nectar and soaring rump, the rush of your wing
In its grand confusion of arcing and splitting
Created completely out of nothing just for me,

Then when you came down to me, I would call you
My own spinning bloom of ruby sage, my funneling
Storm of sunlit sperm and pollen, my only breathless
Piece of scarlet sky, and I would bless the base
Of each of your feathers and touch the tine
Of string muscles binding your wings and taste
The odor of your glistening oils and hunt
The honey in your crimson flare
And I would take you and take you and take you
Deep into any kind of nest you ever wanted.

(Pattiann Rogers, "The Hummingbird: A Seduction")

HYPOTACTICAL CONNECTORS One of the main problems in creating long, complex sentencing lies in how to connect the various phrases and clauses together. An instructive example for seeing how this is done is shown in the opening stanza of Bruce Weigl's "The Black Hose," in which Weigl creates a sense of the trance state his young hero is in through his stanza-length single sentence. The barely noticeable, small hypotactical words (indicated in boldface) are what bolt together larger units of syntax.

A boy **who** knew enough to save for something
like the whim **that** took me downtown on the bus

one lost Saturday, morning of my mother's birthday,
I sat in the back **where** the gasoline smell
made me dizzy **and** I closed my eyes **but** didn't
think of her, **only** of myself basking in the light
and love **that** would fall down on me **when** I
handed her the box **and** she untied the bow to save
and lifted something shining out **and** held it up before us
like a promise taking shape for once in her hands
though I didn't know what to buy, the bus door
hissing behind me **because** I'm in some kind of
state now, **a trance that** comes **when** you pull at
the cords of light **that** connect the mother to the boy,
the 1959 department store opening up before me
like a jeweled city.
Bruce Weigl, "The Black Hose")

LINE AGAINST SENTENCE Given the potentially interesting and widely varied strategic features of sentencing, skilled poets tactically work the line against their sentence for various sorts of effects. They are working with two units of measurement: the line itself, like a road with dips and bends, rises, hairpin turns, and dead ends, that can focus on and emphasize aspects of thought, rhythm, images, details, plot elements, character, etc., and can even change grammatical units from, say, verbs to abstract nouns, while the larger unit of the sentence pulls the reader through the manipulations of the lineation.

Notice the way Stephen Dunn, with lines composed of full syntactical units, parses out plot, thought, rhythm, and drama in the reasoned argument of his opening two sentences of "The Routine Things around the House."

When mother died
I thought: now I'll have a death poem.
That was unforgivable

yet I've since forgiven myself
as sons are able to do
who've been loved by their mothers.
(Stephen Dunn, "The Routine Things around the House")

VARYING THE SENTENCE TYPES Beyond, but stemming out of, what is being said and the feeling fused to that, the combinations of sentence types and lengths have their own rhythmic and musical intelligence that they contribute to a poem. Pulling back and listening to the way sentences move in a poem is akin to the way painters **squint** at a painting in progress, blurring the painting's textures and details, so that they can see the larger design qualities and juxtapositions of shape and color. This aspect of the poet listening to the poem's sentences, sharpening his or her "ear," is the same process the sculptor goes through when he or she pulls back and focuses simultaneously on the positive and negative spaces in the piece being worked on. It is like listening for the patterns of dots and dashes in Morse code (See Robert Frost in **Sentence Sounds,** pp. 177–178). The act of artfully constructing the flow of syntax is called **sentencing.** Following are several examples of the kinds of effects that can be achieved.

The opening stanza of Barry Goldensohn's "Post Mortem as Angels" uses a long and flowing complex, introductory sentence to process the contrasting conditions between life and the afterlife. After that sentence, Goldensohn employs a series of short, punchy, rhythmically counterpointing declarative statements, all bound by a lyrical sheathing.

> When we meet then after death we will merge
> easily, without the forced reserve
> of our betraying bodies, the great routine
> or the restraint with which we kept ourselves, alive.
> There will be no husband then, or wife.
> We will be all truth. Nothing to defend,
> not one boundary. We will be one great friend.
> No drama of discovery, nothing left to find.
> (Barry Goldensohn, "Post Mortem as Angels")

In David Rivard's stanza below from "Earth to Tell of Beasts," notice all the dancelike counterpointing going on. Rivard opens the poem with a series of snappy, abrupt, colloquial parallel sentencing, follows that by opening up the rhythm of the next sentence into a more flowing, lyrical **epiphany,** and ends the stanza with short bursts of phrasing that echo the opening.

> It's a good bet.
> It's easy. It's a sure thing. That the warmth & abiding
> plentitude of this morning would permit me
> to call your pain a fugue, an intricately feathered
> spiral, because it sounds lovely. And lovely implies consolation
> and accuracy. But all the while, buried inside, hurt
> is still hurt, shame still shame.
> (David Rivard, "Earth to Tell of Beasts")

Instead of employing a series of different sentences, a poet will sometimes perform rhythmic variations within one long sentence that acts as a series. The last stanza of Dean Young's "Lace" uses a **litany** form of parallel clauses that break down into smaller clauses, and then into a tightening spiral of prepositional phrases that paradoxically imply an open-ended process of devolution, in which meaning gets larger and more diffuse as the syntactical units get smaller and smaller.

Before the delicate downward yearning of snow,
the winter wools and wafts of cedar, naptha
and dry winter heat, the opaque wrapping
done and undone, burning in the grate,
before the gray vaulted shape of each burned thing,
the bitter medicinal dust, old lace and its cobweb
dream breaking in my hand, each thread frays, knots
give and knot again, like roots into stem,
the stem unraveling into flower, into flame,
into seed and wind, into dirt, into into into.
(Dean Young, "Lace")

RECOMBINANT SYNTAX Just as geneticists recombine biochemical components of DNA to form different genes that result in new characteristics, poets will often play around with the elements of syntax (order of words) and morphology (form of words and phrases) to arrive at new and transcendent kinds of phrasing. **Recombinant syntax,** often just simple, linear re-formations, will lead to surprising alchemical changes in the quality and substance of the words' meaning. Here are some basic kinds of recombinations.

1. **Relocating modifiers.** In the following examples, the modifying clause "certain as the year just passed" changes its modification, in the first instance, from the plural, first-person "we," to, in the second instance, the geese, a change that calls into question the strength of the revelers' resolutions.

1

We stood with our New Year's resolutions
as certain as the year just passed
and watched the geese fly back home north.

#2

We stood with our New Year's resolutions
and watched the geese fly back home north
as certain as the year just passed.

2. **Switching agents.** In the models below, the more explicit first example becomes subsumed by and implicit in the second example merely by exchanging subjects.

#1

All night **in the barren wind, I**
carved out symbols: the owl
for what was lost; the moon
for what was forgotten.

#2

All night **the barren wind**
carved out symbols: the owl
for what was lost, the moon
for what was forgotten.

3. **Changing literal to metaphorical.** In the first instance in the models below, the cliff is literal, but in the second example the cliff takes on both literal and metaphorical resonance.

(LITERAL) They climbed the cliff with fear.

(METAPHORICAL) They climbed the cliff of their fear.

4. **Combining separations.** Sometimes separate, sequential elements can become more effective when they are smoothly linked together so that they generate new and complex ideas.

(SEPARATE) The year was filled with the losses.
The dandelions gone to seed.

(COMBINED) The year was filled with the losses
we didn't know were **the gains**
of a dandelion gone to seed.

FLOW: SENTENCE EXERCISE

1. **Simple sentence:** See if you can break down a poem with several very long sentences into as many short, simple sentences as seems feasible.
2. **Sentence-length poem:** Try fashioning a poem you've written into one, long sentence.
3. **Line against sentence:** Re-line one of your poems so that it contains short but authoritative lines that hold the reader's interest while the larger units of the sentences accrue.
4. **Varying sentence types:** Taking one of your poems, mix the variety of sentence types and lengths so that the poem then exhibits a new and interesting rhythm.
5. **Progression:** Progressively decrease the size of your sentencing in one of your poems until you end up with mere fragments.
6. **Recombinant syntax:** See if you can take parts of one of your poems and recombine its elements so that new and richer meanings are achieved.

PUNCTUATION BY MEANS OTHER THAN PUNCTUATION

Punctuation adjusts the speed, pacing, overall flow, emphasis, and direction of a poem's content, just as traffic signals regulate, with varying degrees of intensity (flashing yellow, steady yellow, flashing red, steady red), the flow of traffic. Punctuation marks are abbreviated, necessary symbols that indicate the duration and finality of a pause, the setting up of a sequence, subordination or parallelism, and the quality of energy that a syntactical unit will possess.

There's no need to go over what, basically, a rhetoric/grammar text can explain about punctuation, so here is a consideration of some kinds of poems that, for effect, have implied punctuation, or have preempted the need for explicit punctuation through their phrasing, lineation, and stanzaic structure.

Punctuation by Means of Syntax

The following poem by Hugh Seidman can be read easily without punctuation because he has parsed lines and stanzas into discrete, whole syntactical units.

Tale of Genji

In Murasaki's time
they wept at the sunsets

It was easy

                    If you were the Prince
                    & in love

Calligraphy could do it

                    The total life
                    in the nuance of a line

& later

            The sun that had changed

The cold light defining shadow
Poetry leading nowhere

Occurrence made meaningless
The injustice of history

Not that it mattered

                              Or the light
                              they wept at

(Hugh Seidman, "Tale of Genji")

Punctuating by Means of the Line

Lucille Clifton's poem, which is made up of eleven sentences, doesn't need punctuation or multiple readings in order to understand the syntax and logic because she has used the line as a unit of measure and used the conjunction "and" to replace punctuation and indicate phrasing. Notice that the refrain "good times" is presented as a couplet and needs no comma.

Good Times

my Daddy has paid the rent
and the insurance man is gone
and the lights is back on
and my uncle Bud has hit
for one dollar straight
and they is good times
good times
good times

my Mama has made bread
and Grampaw has come
and everybody is drunk
and dancing in the kitchen
and singing in the kitchen
oh these is good times
good times

oh children think about the
good times
(Lucille Clifton, "good times")

Punctuation by Means of Conversational Phrasing

The ear that is accustomed to hearing **conversational phrasing** will have no trouble following how the example poem below is parsed into lines whose measure is based upon conventional colloquial phrases as units that help control the pace and meaning of the poem, even though it's only one sentence.

Here I am again,
worrying about the usual,
which is to say
whatever's small and insignificant
while the really big things
I dream and care about
slide by unnoticed
if you know what I mean.

Pacing by Means of the Syllable

Usually, the flow and **pacing** in a poem occur in large units by way of the line, sentence, or stanza. In the following poem by Robert Lax, he breaks his lines into monosyllabic units of words and syllables to indicate the confusion and indecision that the protagonist is undergoing. Notice how Lax reverses the usually minor role of punctuation and gives his question mark at the end of section 2 as much space as a word. In fact, the question mark could be termed the thesis of his poem.

Novel/

1.

oh
well

(she
con-
soled

her-
self)
some-
thing

good

is

bound
to
hap-
pen
(I'll
die)
&
go
to
heav-
en

which
has
al-
ways

sound-
ed

so
love-
ly

or
to

hell
which
sounds

even
worse

2.

why
does-
n't
any
one

ever
die
&
go
to

(new
port)

?

3.
sud-
den-
ly

she
real-
ized
that
there
was-
n't

a
resort

in
the
world

she
want-
ed

to
go
to

any-
way

so

that
was
that

(Robert Lax, "Novel/")

Fusion through Lack of Punctuation

W. S. Merwin, particularly in his middle books, *The Moving Target* and *The Lice,* achieves a sense of timelessness and "con-fusion" by running his sentences together; in fact, they seem almost to move through each other. Here is an example of the type of syntax and sentencing Merwin employs.

> I get up I think there is almost no time
> left I guess I change that by changing
> the things I might do there it is just
> in front of me I don't think I will.

PUNCTUATION BY OTHER MEANS EXERCISE

1. Compose a stanza that exhibits implied punctuation by first writing out a long sentence, and then cutting it into lines that end with completed syntactical units. (See *Punctuation by Means of Syntax.*)
2. Compose a stanza of lines containing full independent clauses that can be read as independent units. (See *Punctuating by Means of the Line.*)
3. Compose a stanza of lines, each of which is made up of normal, conversational phrasing. (See *Punctuation by Means of Conversational Phrasing.*)
4. Compose a stanza mde up of monosyllabic lines. (See *Punctuation by Means of the Syllable.*)
5. Compose a stanza made up of lines in which the juxtaposed beginnings and ends of phrases and clauses are ambiguous. (See *Fusion through Lack of Punctuation.*)

SONICS

The term **sonics,** one of the physical attributes of a poem, alludes to a wide range of sound aspects and techniques, from vowel and consonant selection; to **alliteration, assonance** and **consonance;** to rhyming and off-rhyming; to the orchestration of **sound systems;** and to the larger consideration of conversational phrasing and **sentence sounds.** In the largest sense of sound, Stanley Plumly called the music of free verse, "speech barking back at song." The study of sonics builds an appreciation for the shape and feeling of words, their physicality. Just as an accomplished pianist frees himself from having to pay attention to the placement of his fingers, a poet refines and develops his "ear" and becomes accomplished by practicing the selection of words with apt sound values until he doesn't have to pay much attention to them while in the process of writing. Here's what Dylan Thomas, a master at orchestrating sound systems, wrote about his life-long, intense relationship to the sound of words:

> I should say I wanted to write poetry in the beginning because I had fallen in love with words. The first poems I knew were nursery rhymes, and before I could read them for myself I had come to love the words of them, the words alone. What the words stood for, symbolized, or meant, was of very secondary importance; what mattered was the *sound* of them as I heard them for the first time on the lips of the remote and incomprehensible grown-ups who seemed, for some reason, to be living in my world. And these words were, to me, as the notes of bells, the sound of musical instruments, the noise of wind, sea, and rain, and the rattle of milkcarts, the clopping of hooves on cobbles, the fingering of branches on a window pane, might be to someone, deaf from birth, who has miraculously found his hearing. I did not care what the words said, overmuch, nor for what happened to Jack & Jill & the Mother Goose rest of them; I cared for the shapes of sound that their names, and the words describing their actions, made in my ears; I cared for the colours the words cast in my eyes. . . . There they [words] were, seemingly lifeless, made only of black and white, but out of them, out of their own being, came love and terror and pity and pain and wonder and all the other vague abstractions that make our ephemeral lives dangerous, great, and bearable. Out of them came the gusts and grunts and hiccups and hee-haws of the common fun of the earth; and though what the words meant was, in its own way, often deliciously funny enough, so much funnier seemed to me, at that almost forgotten time, the shape and shade and size and noise of the words as they hummed, strummed, jigged and galloped along.

Sound Systems

A **sound system** is a passage that displays a conscious or intuitive arrangement of various consonant and vowel groupings. Like the notes in a chord, or the images in an **emblem,** the artful arrangement of sound values creates both a cohesion and an expressive meaning separate from the denotative meaning of a work. Dylan Thomas, who it is said worked each morning to compose his quota of three lines a day, laying down sound values reminiscent of the heavy hand of Beethoven, would create mosaics of orchestrated sound systems that expressed the mood or emotion of an experience about which he was writing. Here are the first fifteen lines of his poem, "After the Funeral," which is a block (**strophic**) poem, but, which, for the purposes of illustration, has been broken up into sonic and stanzaic units that isolate its different sound systems.

After the funeral, mule praises, brays,
Windshake of sailshaped ears, muffle toed tap
Tap happily of one peg in the thick
Grave's foot,blinds down the lids, the teeth in black,
The spittled eyes, the salt ponds in the sleeves,
Morning smack of the spade that wakes up sleep,
Shakes a desolate boy who slits his throat
In the dark of the coffin and sheds dry leaves,
That breaks on bone to light with a judgment clout,
After the feast of tear-stuffed time and thistles
In a room with a stuffed fox and a stale fern,
I stand, for this memorial's sake, alone
In the snivelling hours with dead, humped Ann
Whose hooded, fountain heart once fell in puddles
Round the parched worlds of Wales and drowned each sun
(Dylan Thomas, "After the Funeral")

Internal and Slant Rhyme

As mentioned earlier, most free verse moved its sonic controls inside its lines, and so with full **end-rhyme** abandoned by many poets, rhyme, repetition, **slant rhyme, consonance, assonance,** and **alliteration** work internally—and often in the middle of syntactical units, as opposed to the ends—for a less conspicuous, subtler effect. Here are nine lines from the poem "Prodigal" by Bob Hicock that display a good amount of sonic density and rhythmic syncopation. The harmonic sonic effects have been set in boldface and, when necessary, separated by a **virgule** (/) for illustration.

You c**oul**d d**rive ou**t **of this cou**/ntry
and attack the **world** with **you**r **amb/**ition**,**
in**vent wond**er pl**asmas,**
be/come an **artist of the** pro**voc**a**tive gest/ure,**
the sug**gestive nod, you** could **leav**e
want/ing the **world and re/turn**
carry/**ing** it, a noisy b**un/dle**
of s**team** and l**ibid**o, a **ball of fire**
balanced on **your tongue**
(Bob Hicock, "Prodigal")

Sentence Sounds

Another aspect in considering sound in poetry that is important for conversationally written free verse is what Robert Frost, in a letter to John T. Bartlett, termed **sentence sounds,** by which he meant the nonlexical, rhythmic, and sonic effects that the sound-form of a sentence may feature. He said:

> I give you a new definition of a sentence:
>
> A sentence is a sound in itself on which other sounds called words may be strung.
>
> You may string words together without a sentence-sound to string them on just as you may tie clothes together by the sleeves and stretch them without a clothes line between two trees, but—it is bad for the clothes.
>
> The number of words you may string on one sentence-sound is not fixed by there is always danger of over loading.
>
> The sentence-sounds are very definite entities (This is no literary mysticism I am preaching.) They are as definite as words. It is not impossible that they could be collected in a book though I don't at present see on what system they would be catalogued.
>
> They are apprehended by the ear. They are gathered by the ear from the vernacular and brought into books. I think no writer invents them. The most original writer only catches them fresh from talk, where they grow spontaneously.
>
> A man is all a writer if all his words are strung on definite recognizable sentences sounds. The voice of the imagination, the speaking voice must know certainly how to behave how to posture in every sentence he offers.
>
> A man is a marked writer if his words are largely strung on the more striking sentence sounds.
>
> A word about recognition: In literature it is our business to give people the thing that will make them say, "Oh yes I know what you mean." It is never to tell them something they don't know, but something they know and hadn't thought of saying. It must be something they recognize.

In other words, Frost erases the words of a sentence and listens to the sort of sine-wave signature that the inflections or nonverbal "gestures" of a sentence makes. This is not the same, as in the section on syntax, as listening to the rhythmic patterns that sentences, taken singly or in combinations, make. Frost is calling attention to the "sound-form" a sentence exhibits, and thinks of that as a unit of intelligence or meaning, in and of itself, in the poem.

Following are some examples of full and partial sentence sounds taken from the spoken language that inherently carry their own musical meanings. There may be different inflections one might use in speaking these conversational units, but the general effect should be demonstrable.

Why did you do that?

* * *

Every once in a while . . .

* * *

Well, I never!

* * *

And that was that.

* * *

No matter what I say and do . . .

* * *

Now, here's a little something you're all going to like . . .

* * *

Who in the world do you think you are?

* * *

What in the world do you think you're doing?!

* * *

I just can't keep it up.

* * *

Is anybody home?

SONICS EXERCISE

Using a poem you have written, work on the following exercises.

1. **Alliteration, assonance, and consonance:** Throughout the poem, substitute word choices so that the poem becomes heavy with **alliteration, assonance,** and **consonance** (repeating and slant rhyming consonants and vowels).
2. **Sound systems:** Create two distinctly different SOUND SYSTEMS by using the following combinations.

   heavy: lines using words with low plosives (d, b, k, g) and low vowels (o, u, y)

   light: lines using words with high plosives and fricatives (p, t, s, f, h, v, z)
3. **Sentence sounds:** See if you can create more musicality and inherent meaning with the use of colloquially based sentences and fragments carry certain implicit assumptions in their "form."

SCALE OF TEXTURES

Texture is the tactile aspect of poetry. One can't "touch" a poem, but the mind's inner senses can evoke a sense of how dense, cluttered, smooth, clear, rough, spiky, or forcefully paced the **aesthetic surface** of a poem (sonics, rhythm, imagery, lineation, typography, syntax, rhetorical devices, tropes, etc.) may be. Generally speaking, texture is composed of the elements of a poem that cannot be paraphrased—the aesthetic effects beyond semantic meaning—but which in and of themselves are "intelligences" or units of nonverbal meaning in the poem: sonics, rhythm, imagery, types and arrangements of syntax and sentencing, lineation and typographical arrangement, etc. For instance, in painting, the paint and colors of a Van Gogh are laid down in thick textures and saturated colors, while those of Matisse and Dali give the impression of being spread out flatly and thinly. In poetry, one could say that Dylan Thomas, Gerard Manley Hopkins, John Milton, and Seamus Heaney use thick, dense, and rough textures, while William Blake, William Carlos Williams, Mark Strand, and Jelaluddin Rumi use more delicate and clearer textures. Here is a scale of textures, followed by examples that range from transparent to dense:

← transparent light medium heavy dense abstract →

Transparent Texture

This term indicates a poem that has an extremely light, lyrical quality, almost absent of texture in the way that a watercolor is still a painting but exhibits little of the density of an oil painting. The aesthetic of the poem with a transparent texture is simplicity, clarity, and lightness. The example below exhibits these qualities and depends only upon lineation, the rhetoric of a moral lesson, parallel syntactical structures of balance, and a few elements of repetition.

Vacancy

If you want to make a difference
go to an empty place,
fill it up with yourself,
then let go of that
until the place is emptied again.
Bring all of you with you.
What you leave behind will make a difference.

An allied device to the textureless poem is the **flat statement** (pp. 183–189), an occasionally applied line or two that stands out in high relief against lines composed with heavy imagery, sonics, rhythm, and syntax.

Light Texture

Moving a third up the scale, we begin to see more forceful images, a light lyric-narrative story, and the definite musical effects of imagery, tropes (similes and metaphors), and light sonics and rhythm. Here is a short lyric by Jelaluddin Rumi. Even though it's in translation from the Persian and we can't access its original music, as a translation it still stands as a good example of light texture.

Some souls flow like clear water.
They pour into our veins
and feel like wine.

I give in to that. I fall flat.
We can sail this boat lying down!
(Jelaluddin Rumi, "Some Souls Flow . . .," trans., Coleman Barks)

Medium Texture

In this medial area of the texture scale, Kimiko Hahn's poem displays a delicate narrative pacing, a wistful **tone color,** and subtle sonic and rhythmic effects, which give the poem a good deal of its weight and "feel."

When You Leave

This sadness could only be a color
if we call it *momoiro,* Japanese

for peach-color, as in the first story
Mother told us: It is the color of the hero's skin

when the barren woman discovered him
inside a peach floating down the river.

And of the banner and gloves she sewed
when he left her to battle the horsemen, then found himself

torn, like fruit off a tree. Even when he met a monkey,
dog, and bird he could not release

the color he saw when he closed his eyes. In his boat
the lap of the waves against the hold

was too intimate as he leaned back to sleep. He wanted
to leave all thoughts of peach behind him—

the fruit that brought him to her
and she, the one who opened the color forever.
(Kimiko Hahn, "When You Leave")

Heavy Texture

This far up the texture scale, the sound effects, images, semantic inventiveness, rhythm, and rhetorical density begins to become more of a strategy and signature than a feature; they become substance rather than a quality. Here are some stanzas from Pattiann Rogers' "The Hummingbird: A Seduction."

If I were a female hummingbird perched still
And quiet on an upper myrtle branch
In the spring afternoon and if you were a male
Alone in the whole heavens before me, having parted
Yourself, for me, from cedar top and honeysuckle stem
And earth-down, your body hovering in mid-air
Far away from jewelweed, thistle and beebalm;

And if I watched how you fell, plummeting before me,
And how you rose again and fell, with such mastery
That I believed for a moment *you* were the sky
And the red-marked bird diving inside your circumference
Was just the physical revelation of the light's
Most perfect desire;
(Pattiann Rogers, "The Hummingbird: A Seduction")

Dense Texture

Gerard Manley Hopkins, known for his style of plastering on thick consonants, alliteration, rhyming, impacted **sprung rhythm,** exultant voice, and high-stressed monosyllabics, is perhaps the epitome of dense texturists. On the next page, in full, is a well-known poem of his.

The Windhover

To Christ our lord

I caught this morning morning's minion, king-
dom of daylight's dauphin, dapple-dawn-drawn Falcon, in his riding
Of the rolling level underneath him stead air, and striding
High there, how he rung upon the rein of a wimpling wing
In his ecstasy! then off, off forth on swing,
As a skate's heel sweeps smooth on a bow-bend: the hurl and gliding
Rebuffed the big wind. My heart in hiding
Stirred for a bird,—the achieve of, the mastery of the thing!

Brute beauty and valour act, oh, air, pride, plume, here
Buckle! AND the fire that breaks from thee then, a billion
Times told lovelier, more dangerous, O my chevalier!

No wonder of it: shéer plód makes plough down sillion
Shine, and blue-bleak embers, ah my dear,
fall, gall themselves, and gash gold-vermilion.

(Gerard Manley Hopkins, "The Windhover")

Abstract Texture

Beyond this point at the high end of the texture scale, we leave the denotative, semantic aspect of language behind and encounter a poetry that is composed of pure abstract sound values whose rhythms and sonic—**melopoetics**—are the only elements that suggest or evoke any meaning. This genre is equivalent to the works of the Abstract Expressionists in painting. Forms of it can be found in children's nonsense verse, snatches from songs (Julie Andrews' "Supercalifragalistic-expialidoshus"), Lewis Carroll's poem "Jabberwocky," the bulk of Gertrude Stein's experimental poetry, and the work of the Futurists, an early twentieth-century Russian school of poetry who wrote **trans-sense verse.** Here is an imitation of abstract verse:

The Bee's Day

Zon krazztit stit zont stanisfrukasch
chit grombel druk, grombel druk, zanchuker.
Shtangel ind choprat chondult,
zeetershuk franticri omberskuptak

TEXTURE EXERCISE

1. **Degrees of sonic density:** Here is a three-part scale that shows increasing degrees of density in the use of sound. The words in brackets are possible alternatives. Select which words sound most apt and effective to your ear or add your own.

   Light
   There was moonlight on the ocean.
   Medium
   The full moon shone on the sea.
   [fell asleep] [deep]

Heavy

The harvest moon scattered its trail of yellow crystals over the
[blue] [showered] [wake] [topaz] [seeds]
[spilled] [veil]
[splintered]
[fertilized]

2. Using one of your poems, try to create the following four different sonic versions of it.

   Transparent lyric: Describe the images, feelings, tropes, and events of the poem in a nonsubjective way so that there is no "personality" of a speaker—no filtering personality or character between the reader and the experience, and very light sonic effects.

   Light texture: Use images and tropes sparingly, and select or create only those that have a light and lyrical feel to them.

   Medium texture: Use more images, actions and tropes, and select wording for them that has a heavier sonic density and a somewhat more weighty and intense feel.

   Heavy texture: Pack in the images, actions, and tropes densely, selecting and creating those with very dense sound values and highly stressed syllables, those that have impact, weight, and force to them in terms of their meaning and sonics.

   Abstract texture: Imagine a subject with high energy, color, and rhythms, and then create thickly laid down sound and rhythm patterns to evoke the feel of your subject.

THE FLAT STATEMENT

The **flat** or bald **statement** is a phrase, line, or sentence that, because of its lack of imagery, sonics, rhythm, aesthetic surface effects, or other poetic attributes, stands in heightened contrast to its surrounding context and therefore, paradoxically, like a gem in a well-designed setting, has a striking effect.

Having just discussed the scale of textures in poetry, where craftsman such as Thomas and Hopkins, the Russian Futurists, the new Language Poets, and others have pushed the decorative, expressionistic, and logical effects of language to its fullest, it is appropriate that we now go to the other extreme and discuss unadorned, and seemingly "unpoetic" kinds of language. The Postmodernist movement, breaking the Modernist rules of compression, efficiency, distillation, and heightened poetic language, has found a way to make the flat statement work.

As a Contrast to Textured Language

The flat statement stands out and is highly effective as a contrast to highly textured language. It attains a powerful and dramatic starkness in Marianne Moore's poem that follows, where the baroque elegance and fifteenth-century excess of ornate settings is a perfect foil to the flat statement in the concluding line.

No Swan So Fine

"No water so still as the
dead fountains of Versailles." No swan,
with swart blind look askance
and gondoliering legs, so fine
as the chintz china one with fawn-
brown eyes and toothed gold
collar on to show whose bird it was.

Lodged in the Louis Fifteenth
candelabrum-tree of cockscomb-
tinted buttons, dahlias,
sea-urchins, and everlastings,
it perches on the branching foam
of polished sculptured
flowers—at ease and tall. The king is dead.

(Marianne Moore, "No Swan So Fine")

As a Contrast to Imagery

In James Wright's poem below, he has packed all but the last line with rich, softly surreal, beautiful, natural images that imply idleness and waste. The last line creates a strong sense of drama and surprise by reversing the speaker's seeming sense of peace when he abruptly shifts from the external world of nature to his troubled insight, from rich imagery to an unexpected statement, which, in fact, has been artfully prepared by the implications of the previous imagery.

Lying in a Hammock at William Duffy's Farm in Pine Island, Minnesota

Over my head, I see the bronze butterfly,
Asleep on a black trunk,
Blowing like a leaf in green shadow.
Down the ravine behind the empty house,
The cowbells follow one another
Into the distances of the afternoon.
To my right,
In a field of sunlight between two pines,
The droppings of last year's horses
Blaze up into golden stones.
I lean back, as evening darkens and comes on.
A chicken hawk floats over, looking for home.
I have wasted my life.

(James Wright, "Lying in a Hammock at William Duffy's Farm in Pine Island, Minnesota")

As a Thematic Statement

The flat statement can also function as a thesis sentence, as in John Skoyles' poem, "Burlesque," in which the line "The lights go on and go off" appears several times in modified form as a repeating symbolic refrain, and thus becomes a central structural element of the poem.

Burlesque

after Weldon Kees

The day the dancer in the loud red dress
tossed her hair and said "What else is there to do?"
I remembered what my father told me.
She looked into the mirror applying makeup
while the traffic lights went on and off outside.
What my father told me was this:
women look into mirrors looking for men:
blondes toss their hair indifferently all night
but finally settle down; changes of heart

flicker like the traffic lights.

We fall in and out of love in rooms
where women wearing makeup
reflect our fantasies and lust:
so we're to blame for whatever they become.
And looking back, how could we

have taken that dancer so seriously?
But the way to forget
how she stepped out of her dress
was something our fathers couldn't tell us.
The lights go on and go off.
(John Skoyles, "Burlesque")

As a Focusing Device

Here the flat statement "so that is what I am" (in boldface) functions as a point of focus, a place toward which the poem's content and drama funnel. In W. S. Merwin's poem below, the flat statement is the pivoting point of the poem. It knits the external narrative and feelings of the speaker together.

Fly

I have been cruel to a fat pigeon
Because he would not fly
All he wanted was to live like a friendly old man
He had let himself become a wreck filthy and confiding
Wild for his food beating the cat off the garbage
Ignoring his mate perpetually snotty at the beak
Smelling waddling having to be
Carried up the ladder at night content

Fly I said throwing him into the air
But he would drop and run back expecting to be fed
I said it again and again throwing him up
As he got worse
He let himself be picked up every time
Until I found him in the dovecote dead
Of the needless efforts.

So that is what I am

Pondering his eye that could not
Conceive that I was a creature to run from

I who have always believed too much in words
(W. S. Merwin, "Fly")

As a Stylistic Device

It is also possible to use a number of flat statements in a poem to form a style of writing and yet still maintain the requisite tension typical of poetry. In William Stafford's "Passing Remark," his use of the flat statement becomes not only the style of the poem but also its strategy and its theme: that opposites attract. The repetition of parallel prepositional phrases in the first three lines, the predominance of unstressed words, and the feminine line endings are all elements that downplay the poem's language.

Passing Remark

In scenery I like flat country.
In life I don't like much to happen.

In personalities I like mild or colorless people.
And in colors I prefer gray and brown.

My wife, a vivid girl from the mountains,
says, "Then why did you choose me?"

Mildly I lower my brown eyes—
here are so many things admirable people do not understand.
(William Stafford, "Passing Remark")

As a Contrast to Syntax

An unusual use of the flat statement is when it acts as a contrast to the word order of the rest of the poem. In E. E. Cummings' poem "Me Up At Does," he wrenches, reverses, and delays the poem's syntax so that the final flat statement arrives as a relief to the bewildered reader and acts as a dramatic climax in terms of its message. Because of his act of empathy, the speaker changes places with a half-dead mouse, and this reversal, to Cummings' thinking, called for a reversal in both syntax and characters.

Me up at does

Me up at does

out of the floor
quietly stare

a poisoned mouse

still who alive

is asking What
have i done that

You wouldn't have

(E. E. Cummings, "Me up at does")

The Typographically Twisted Flat Statement

In another uncommon instance, D. J. Enright has comically played off his title's statement with a clever rearrangement of spellings, which appear to be typographical errors, in order to make the point that it's not the tool but the person behind the tool that's truly important.

The Typewriter Revolution

The trypewiter is cretin
a revulsion in peotry.

(D. J. Enright, "The Typewriter Revolution")

FLAT STATEMENT EXERCISE

Although the flat statement (a sentence devoid of imagery, musicality, tropes, and figures of thought) seems unpoetic, and is to the typical poem what the antihero is the movies, it can be a very effective focusing device in the same way that empty space surrounded by woodlands can be a strong focal point. Look at the following ways in which the flat statement can be employed, and then try your own versions of these types from the list of suggested flat statements.

1. **As a contrast to dense imagery and sonics**

So, Seth, sweating, sawed the log
and sweltered under the downpouring
ruthless sun, and when at last his strength

was lost, and the oblivion of night came on,
the day was won.

2. **As a dramatic focusing device**

At first I stole a chocolate bar that
turned into a purse; then after I hurt
a rich man merely for the fun of it,
I set ablaze the things I should've blessed.
Is this who I've become, a man who has to lose
everything he has to see what he loves best?

3. **Suggested flat statements**

I went to bed late.
You give your wife a kiss.
My mother calls collect.
I pay the rent on time.
What's wrong with eating alone?
As usual, I forgot what it was I came for.
There's a tiny crack in the glass.
I smile and bow and say goodbye.
I like my coffee black.
I think it's over.

CHAPTER

6

Types of Poems

This chapter surveys a representative sampling of generic, structural, and specific types of poems. It is not intended to be an exhausting and comprehensive catalogue, but more of a presentation of types.

GENERIC TYPES

Controlling Device Poems

Within free verse, the predominant mode of contemporary poetry writing, poets often turn to the use of various kinds of controlling devices that direct and make their poems coherent and unified. Often, what controls the poem does work beyond being a mere device, and acts as an **organizing principle** that might dictate not just the arrangement of the poem's logic but its underlying development as well. In other words, it acts as a device to generate content. The various forms of controlling devices include the controlling metaphor, the controlling symbol, abstract concepts, the controlling **figure of thought** (**hyperfigure**), an emblematic gesture, a state of consciousness, an analogue—in short, almost any element in a poem can act as a controlling device.

Most poems before the twentieth century that used these devices were commonly found in the lyric mode, by poets such as Shakespeare, Donne, and Dickinson, who set up the controlling device in the opening of the poem. Then, within the fairly narrow and somewhat artificial-feeling confines of the controlling device, the poet would relate the outside world's events and relationships back to the controlling device. Typically, the song or argument of the poem would be linear and tightly logical. No matter how complex, intricate, or ingenious it might be, there is, of course, a predictability to it whose effect is offset by the poem's grace, form, and manners.

Recent poets using the controlling device form have opted for a looser, rangier, more naturally discursive mode for their poems, and usually they have set the core controlling device deep inside the work. The new controlling device poems, for the most part, are set against the old models' rigidly systematic forms of logic (thesis, antithesis, synthesis; or induction and deduction), and are, typically, crossbred, hybrid forms of the lyric, narrative, and dramatic genres.

THE HYPO-FIGURE AND THE HYPER-FIGURE There are two simultaneous and seemingly opposite operations at work in balancing the poet's **location** while writing a poem: *holding on* (conscious, rational control of content, structure, and the conventions of language) and *letting go* (allowing the unconscious to dredge associations from the archetypal, cultural, and personal levels of stored experience). This requires repeated surfacing and diving between the unconscious and conscious areas of awareness. A dependable artifact for communicating the location of a poet is the controlling device poem, which can be composed from the unconscious, conscious, or any combination of these two areas. The **hypo-figure** poem indicates poems that are mostly derived from the unconscious realm of the psyche, while the **hyper-figure** poem denotes a poem derived mostly from the conscious realm of the psyche.

The most effective and authoritative controlling devices in poems are arrived at organically through a combination of the poet's conscious and subconscious thinking. The diagram on the next page, admittedly overly simplistic, is meant to show two extreme **locations** (the perspective of consciousness or mental stance a poet assumes in the initial stages of a work, ranging from the unconscious origination of a controlling device to a fully conscious origination and manipulation of a controlling device.

Here are some recent examples of controlling device poems. Make up your own mind as to the relationship and proportions between consciously and unconsciously derived content.

CONTROLLING METAPHOR Below, a direct comparison between the speaker's life and that of the moles is made just at the midpoint in the poem.

Moles

Every day that their sky droops down,
they shrug before it can harden
and root for life, rumpling along
toward the green part of the garden.

Every day the moles' dirt sky
sags upon their shoulders,
and mine too sags on many a day,
pinned by heavy boulders.

We get tired, the moles and I,

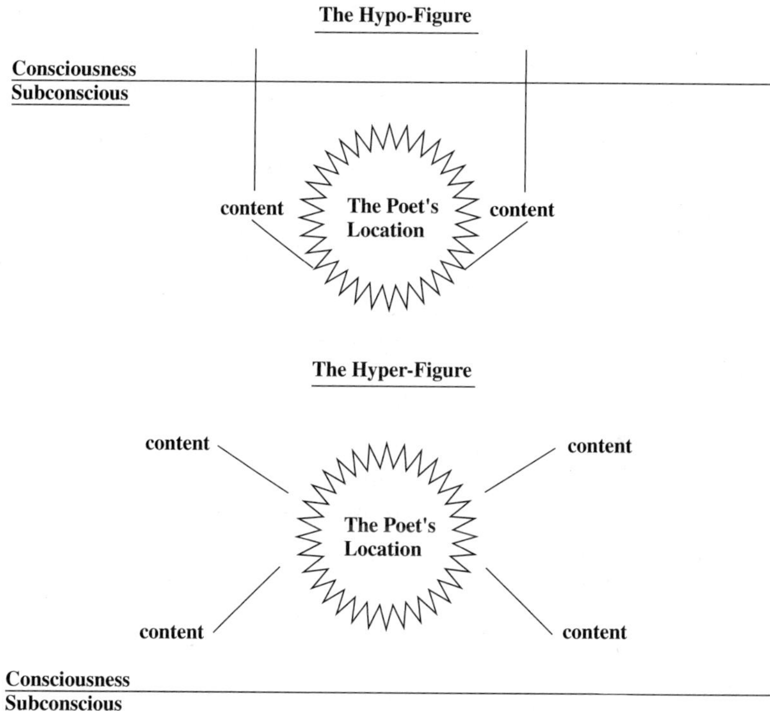

toiling down our burrows.
They shrug dirt along their way,
and I rumple on through sorrows.
(William Stafford, "Moles")

CONTROLLING SYMBOL In the following poem, a nettle tree is a **controlling image** that grows into becoming a symbol as the speaker attaches more and more personal context to its presence in his life:

The Nettle Tree

Mine was the nettle tree, the nettle tree.
It grew beside the garage and on the river
and I protected it from all destroyers.

I loved the hanging branches and the trunk
that grew like a pole. I loved the little crown
that waved like a feather. I sat for hours watching

the birds come in to eat the berries. I read
my Homer there—I wanted to stay forever
sleeping and dreaming. I put my head on the trunk

to hear my sounds. It was my connection for years,
half-hanging in the wind—half leaning, half standing.
It was my only link. It was my luxury.
(Gerald Stern, "The Nettle Tree")

CONTROLLING PROCESS Nancy Willard's very accurate, step-by-step description in her **process poem,** with the poet's eye toward connotative meaning, lifts itself out of the technical into a magical, new realm. Her Zen cooking instructions seem to have another, happier agenda in mind, which has little to do with cooking.

How to Stuff a Pepper

Now, said the cook, I will teach you
how to stuff a pepper with rice.

Take your pepper green, and gently,
for peppers are shy. No matter which side
you approach, it's always the backside.
Perched on green buttocks, the pepper sleeps.
In its silk tights, it dreams
of somersaults and parsley,
of the days when the sexes were one.

Slash open the sleeve
as if you were cutting a paper lantern,
and enter a moon, spilled like a melon,
a fever of pearls,
a conversation of glaciers.
It is a temple built to the worship
of morning light.

I have sat under the great globe
of seeds on the roof of that chamber,
too dazzled to gather the taste I came for.
I have taken the pepper in hand,
smooth and blind, a runt in the rich
evolution of roses and ferns.
You say I have not yet taught you

to stuff the pepper?
Cooking takes time.

Next time we'll consider the rice.
(Nancy Willard, "How to Stuff a Pepper")

CONTROLLING CONCEIT A **conceit** is basically an elaborated metaphor, a controlling device that more or less thoroughly investigates particular, literal aspects of the subject at hand, in this case writing, so that those elements develop connotative levels of meaning. Stanley Moss' poem is a wonderful example of the imaginatively striking and more elaborated form, termed a Petrarchan conceit.

The Lace Makers

Their last pages are transparent,
they choose to see a world behind the words
not the words, tatting not stitching, an open page
of knots, never a closed fabric stitched by needles.
They see from the apples and pears on their plates
out to the orchard, from their tatting
to a bird with a piece of straw in his beak.
From combings transferred onto a running thread,
they make a row of rings resembling a reef,
a chain of knots, hammocks, fish nets,
things found in the hands of sailors.
Without looms, with their fingers,
they make bridal objects, knotted hair nets
seen in certain Roman bronze female portraits,
the twisted threads and knotted fringes of dusty
Egyptian wrappings, something for the cuff,
the lapel, the drawing room, nothing to wear in the cold.
They care about scrolls and variations,
a handkerchief, a design on a pillow,
a completed leaf, four ovals with connecting chains
becoming four peacocks, part of a second leaf,
as if they were promised the world would not
be destroyed, with or without paradise.
Noting the French for tatting is *frivolité,*
they make false chains, things obsolete, improper,
in search of new forms. They carry a thread
to a distant point, eight measured peacocks
of equal size with an additional thread
and the ends cut off. It has the heartless advantage
of being decorative in itself.
They sit and work in the aging light
like Achilles, hiding from his pursuers
in a dress, tatting among the women,
discovered by Odysseus offering gifts:
the women picked hammered gold leaves and bracelets;

deserted by his gods, Achilles chose a sword.
In any fabric there are constant beginnings

and endings with cut threads
to be finished off and cut out of sight.
The lacemakers read their yellow lace,
washing and ironing it is a fine art—
beautiful a straw basket filled with laundry
and language. But shall we call gossip prophecy?
Who will turn the hearts of the fathers to the children
and the hearts of the children to their fathers?
They are unworthy of undoing the laces of their own shoes.
(Stanley Moss, "The Lace Makers")

CONTROLLING FIGURE OF THOUGHT In Naomi Shihab Nye's poem below, the themes of power and domination are developed and controlled by the idea and function of things that bind (a rope, leashes, "owning" a pet, clothing, forced labor, nooses of smoke, etc.), a device known as a **figure of thought,** which is similar in construction to a **conceit.** The figures and images of binding are in boldface.

Ropes

On the beach at Karachi, **a man tells his monkey**
to dance, to strut like Nehru, to bounce on his hands.
Behind us a camel pauses**: it has just walked**
six miles without a rope.
Tonight its owner will step outside
and become hysterical. **But the rope**
on Mister Potato's neck is firm.
He crosses his legs carefully,
placing huge sunglasses over his nose.
He beats a drum and swivels his head.
The terrified gaze says:
It is not happily a monkey does these things.

From the waves, women race**, wringing their dripping**
shalwar kameez. To be barer? **Unthinkable.**
They detest the foolishness a beach attracts,
magicians, snake charmers with exhausted mongoose
and swollen flutes. After hours of their music
it sounds like a movie where everyone goes mad.
We see best what we have never seen before;
horizon over this repetitious little act.

The man with the monkey sets it moving,
then looks away.

Yesterday at the airport in Dubai,
Pakistani laborers crouched together near the gate.
"You will rise!" shouted a hostess.
"You will please to sit in your seats!"
They crouched unmoving, **nooses of smoke**
sliding from their cigarettes.
A very old white-bearded one smiled so hard
you knew he knew what was going on.
The men had been heaving crates for months,
fingering their **tight passports,**
sleeping in the butcher's alley near the canal.
Now they were **going home with their envelopes**
and they wanted to sit on the floor.

For a moment the monkey is just a monkey.
You want to hold him there, where four paws
touched ground and stricken eyes darted,
where **the leash** went suddenly slack.
Down the beach the nuclear power plant
casts its **vaulted shadow** over the waves.

Tonight you'll learn **Afghanistan has no seacoast.**
A man will show **where a shark once bit him open,**
jagged seam across his thigh.
A magician will say he would be rich by now
had he only stayed in Hong Kong performing for
businessmen
who know how wonderful it is to **spring free from a rope**
after tying it very tightly around your own neck,
letting everyone check it to be sure.
(Naomi Shihab Nye, "Ropes")

CONTROLLING STATE OF CONSCIOUSNESS The speaker in the following poem by Robert Long experiences alternate states of reality and artificially tranquilized consciousness, which control the imagery and mood of the poem.

Chelsea

I'm comfortable here, on 50 mg. of Librium,
Two hundred bucks in my pocket
And a new job just a week away.
I can walk the streets in a calm haze,

My blood pressure down to where I'm almost human,
Make countless pay-phone calls from street corners:
Buzzing, they go by in near-neon trails,
People, people like me, headed for black bean soup,
For screams in alleyways, for the homey click
Of the front door's closing, heading home
Past all those faces you know you've seen before:
Like a rear-screen projection in an old movie,
The actors pacing a treadmill or pretending to steer,
And the same '56 Dodge weaving in the background.
It's like walking into a room
And suddenly realizing you've had sex with everyone there
At least once, watching your friends' lives
Tangling as you all grow somewhat older,
Somehow more resolute. Bookshelves grow, too,
And you notice your handwriting becoming more matter-of-fact.
It's as if all of that comic smartness we glided through in youth
Were somehow desperate. And now we come to terms
With the sidewalk's coruscating glamour,
The rows of dull but neat garbage cans,
Each with its own painted number,
The poodles and patrol cars, the moon rising high,
Like Aspirin, over Eighth Avenue.

I get some cigarettes on a corner,
Catch my reflection in the glass. I'm neatly tranquilized,
And strangely happy just to walk out near the traffic,
Consider the asphalt intersections where kids lean on lamp posts
    and fire alarms,
Where a man is shutting the iron gate on his ochre divans,
Where the beautiful taxis whizz and honk,
Clanking over sewer covers and smashing beer cans.
And windows light, one by one, like comic strip inspirations,
And me, here, on your streetcorner,
In my second-favorite neighborhood in the world,
My index finger in the hole marked "9,"
Ready for anything, finally, and finally ready.

(Robert Long, "Chelsea")

CONTROLLING GESTURE In Mark Cox's poem below, which is a **fractured narrative,** the implied and explicit **controlling gesture** of touching and not touching—in its various forms along an extended scale—is the controlling element behind the poem, and is in boldface.

Donald

When chimpanzees are threatened, they band together at first
and **touch their hands** to each other's mouths
as if to say, **"yes, I'm here."**

Something like the way a man might find himself
hurrying down the hall, **running**
a callused thumb over his kid's lips, saying,
"don't be afraid," again and again,
even after the child has leaned back into **the limbs of sleep.**

The chimps will then venture out, **away from the group—**
on land in the savannah,
across the tree, in the trees—
and **throw what they can** at their enemy in an underhanded motion,
or break off sticks and **approach it.**

Today at work, in the washroom mirror,
while I was trying to **get the water in my cupped hands to my face**
without spilling any,
I saw **little smears of paint** everywhere
and realized how **often I'd touched my own face** during the day:
a decision in front of the candy machine; **rubbing my eyes,**
the bridge of my nose. Though I didn't know,

it rained all morning and into afternoon while I painted
the superstructure of the ceiling of that factory, by which
means now, **strapped in** and idling next to the 7-11,
my hand inside a small paper bag,
listening to the new silence of a new exhaust system,
the almost evening summer light seems clean here on the parking lot.

From outside, **through the glass of the windshield**
and then the glass of the storefront,
half-clearly and half-convoluted by the reflection
of both bars across the street, I can see
a kid in a tuxedo, his hands two bulges in the
pockets of his pants, smiling at the counterman.

If I didn't know him, he could be any young guy holding his
head in such a way it's obvious **his shirt neck's too tight;**
but I do, and I know
the graft marks on the side of his face that isn't towards me
and I know the thick, kind speech that betrays brain damage.

His date is in there too, **fussing now and again with his chopped hair,**

a pretty woman, tall and with a sure walk when she parked the car
and got out a minute ago. And **I've found what I was looking for**
in the bag, and I'm in reverse now, **backing up from the window,**
trying
to enjoy one of those smiles one smiles **remembering something,**

when they appear wholly, carrying nothing,
while the **counterman neglects a customer** to watch them do so,
and as the boy walks along the sidewalk, across the entryway
he's swept and shoveled out a thousand times,
he turns the leathery, **gasoline-smeared left side of his face,**
and turning her attention once more to the hair above its ear,
she touches him briefly there.

I'm turning the wheel with the flat palm of one hand,
scratching (which is a sign of indecision in chimps)
my chest with the cold root beer in my other,
and hesitating at the exit, thinking I could so easily
get sad now, because I know it's his sister,
but when I look in the rearview mirror, look back, I can see
that **his friend, and probably his employer, has come out to**
wave,

and think instead of how always **the chimps return to touch**
and be touched again, that if you were here, you'd know
what I was about to say, as if you were here, **I feel, bringing**
the cool rim of that can to my lips, your fingers and **pull away.**
(Mark Cox, "Donald")

CONTROLLING CONCEPT OR ABSTRACT THOUGHT William Olsen's poem "Tomorrow" centripetally spirals in toward and centers upon our inability to synchronize time, meaning, and consciousness. The past impinges upon the present until we realize this, and then the present, which disappears when we think about the past, is being continually eroded by the future so that, as the poet says, the present in which we live serves merely as a conduit for possibility to become extinction, a trap that obliterates our consciousness of the unity of time. The developing strands of his "argument" are in boldface, while the argument's fire wall, a kind of no-exit circumstance, is in italics. The poem's energy focuses on describing an abstract process.

Tomorrow

A water sprinkler empties into parabolas
which, before **they collapse into the past,**
hang in air unencumbered by the ones before,

each as **irreplaceable** as the gauzy streetlights
blossoming above the electric leaves
of the tall clouds of elms staring across the street.
Though it's midnight and **the black material of being**
crumbles between the tendril tips of stars
that poke and rummage through the **compost of the summer sky,**
as late as it is the old cop is sweeping
our common driveway, **the sound of his labor**
wearing as thin as the sucking tide of cars.
And every tomorrow comes down to the next
moment like the first green sticky hand-grenade
bud of **spring about to explode into leaf.**
Soon the trees have crowns, and the blue rugs of their
shadows. Then the first leaf kisses the ground
and scuttles on its rusted tips across our driveway
until **the sycamores are bleached antlers in the sunlight.**
But this occurs gradually, this neat, bare ascent to absence.
As it happens, the old cop gets knocked off duty
many tomorrows ago, and many tomorrows later
it occurs to me I haven't seen him raking,
his bicycle tangled in the morning glory vines,
and still more tomorrows later I started this poem
one morning when I looked back at the bed
my sleep had messed, betraying me to the knowledge
that **we vacate the past by looking on it.**

Wasn't that you I saw slumming around there,
enjoying an hour by the pond, watching
the children fold up newspapers into boats and set them afloat?
The water took the tragic newsboats oh so lightly.
A big wind overturned them without looking back
and the geese pulling out from the marges
were leaving their Christmas-tree wakes intact
to ravel outward to possibility or was it
extinction? Yet in spite of everything
afternoons are everything while they are happening
and you are walking home by beef-red houses
drowning in blue sky till the extraordinary moments of dusk—
every night thins to the sucking tide of cars on the street,
a few mysterious sprinklers on manicured lawns,

the canners squeaking down the avenues their
shopping carts burdened like mules with bulging Glad Bags,
about to turn the corner toward whatever will
be the thing they have lost all track of.
Each tomorrow staggers by, like the steps
of the bum tottering giraffelike on two crutches,
a bottle of Thunderbird stuck in his crotch.
He swears at every hermetic car hissing by. But soon
he's a stick figure at the end of a tunnel of oaks,
too small and contemptible to worry over much,
even if part of what tomorrow slurs is true about us.

So the language of the past is too easy a sadness,
whereas we always generalize from within the cool,
spacious, eternal living room of the present.
And though our neighbors are deepened by autumn,
we don't even know what they do there in their windows.
And tomorrow seems entirely indifferent to charity,
so who can blame us if we watch an hour of TV
with the stars unnoticed overhead, raw papery buds
untouched by frost, and car lights swim through ink
and turn the trunks of sycamores into glowworms
and if it happens to be Christmas, archipelagoes of bulbs
celebrate a beautiful innocence, and by spring
the sprinklers turn out their parabolas
while the next century already mists in the trees.
But one day you fall backwards into a night that matters,
kamikaze into an armchair, and **all the people**
who ever sat there put their arms around you,
the lives that seek you out because you
can't betray them, and while pools of TV blue
make rings around your ankles, on comes
some thirty-second spot about some disaster
on the other side of the world, tonight's it's an earthquake,
German sheperds running in and out of the rubble
of a downtown Mexico City hospital, and outside
in an electronic ear, *a boy's faint heartbeat*
taps like a blind man's cane for a way out.

For a moment you look up and it's raining so hard
you can't even see the myrtles giving up their blossoms.

Tomorrow is a stone on the other side of the world
you can't move. It is the fact that a little boy
will die, out of the long, bright, slamming, hammering sunlight,
that the volunteers know it, and still they work.
Tomorrow has the one face of our television sets,
which are dumb enough to want to spend their whole
portable existences staring out at whoever
lives behind the other faces, the ones safely concerned,
our dumb, troubling, troubled faces staring into
tomorrow.

(William Olsen, "Tomorrow)

The Syllogism

A **syllogism** is a logical form of argument that adds up a major general statement and a more specific minor statement to form an airtight logical conclusion. For example:

(MAJOR PREMISE) All nuns are female.
(MINOR PREMISE) Janet is a nun.
(CONCLUSION) Janet is female.

On the other hand, we could use the same logic, but exchange parts, and thereby arrive at a false conclusion:

(MAJOR PREMISE) All nuns are female.
(MINOR PREMISE) Janet is female.
(FALSE CONCLUSION) Janet is a nun.

The following poem by Richard Brautigan humorously masks the associative process of creating a symbol by way of what seems to be syllogistic reasoning.

The Net Wt. of Winter Is 6.75 Ozs.

The net weight of winter is 6.75 ozs.
and winter has a regular flavor
with Fluoristan to stop tooth decay.

A month ago I bought a huge tube
of Crest tooth paste and when I put it
in the bathroom, I looked at it
and said, "Winter."

(Richard Brautigan, "The Net Wt. of Winter Is 6.75 Ozs.")

The Memory Narrative

The **memory narrative** is a very popular contemporary type of story-poem that bases most, if not all, of its frame of reference on the past, some past event, relationship, emotion, character, etc. Typically, the form is triggered by something in the speaker's present state of mind or environment, but the narrative may just be a retelling of the past in the elaborate form of the **flashback.**

In Mark Doty's "The Pink Palace," a memory narrative, the speaker recaps trips to an old mansion-turned-museum that his father used to take him to on weekends. The speaker has come to understand that the story contains for him a significant rite of passage, perhaps triggered by the symbolic description of the roomful of tiny doors and the unreachable, seemingly paradisiacal life behind them.

The Pink Palace

My father would take me, Saturdays,
to an unfinished mansion: a rich eccentric
had built a few rooms and a façade
of pink granite before the money ran out
and the fragments became property of the state,
a museum for children. Of what
I'm not sure—I remember only one room,
a wall of tiny doors, some at floor level,
others all the way up to the ceiling.
I would open the lowest; he would hoist me
to others so I could stare inside until
he grew tired of holding me. Behind the doors,
behind glass, a tree, huge in memory,
hung with all the glory of taxidermy: robin
and jay, squirrels racing or paused, sitting upright,
everything that lived overhead.

Many windows: each would yield
a little. I thought if I could see it all
the tree would spread like a Sunday school story
of paradise, bearing up on its branches
all the finished houses of heaven. And these
were the citizens: openmouthed blackbird
fixed in the nest, incapable of change.
I know I magnified the tree.
Maybe if I'd seen it all at once
it could never have held so many—
the visible, the mostly hidden,

glowing feathers behind the leaves.
Were there leaves at all?

That summer the outings with my father ended.
The Pink Palace, and then nothing.
Whatever he intended, what he showed me
seemed a lesson—that no single view will hold.
As if he knew I'd need to tell myself
a story—one strong enough to carry me,
and not in his favor—and whatever I told myself
would be incomplete, that nothing will ever
be finished except the past, which is too large
to apprehend at once. All that changes
is the frame we choose. And so he said
as he clutched my waist between his two big hands, *See,*
look at this one, and held me higher.

(Mark Doty, "The Pink Palace")

The Meditation Poem

As its term indicates, this type of poem focuses upon and processes thought, **felt-thought,** and/or feelings, which usually set forth, articulate, and attempt to solve a problematic set of circumstances in an event, relationship, or state of being. In contrast to poems that have only a brief **meditative moment,** Leslie Ullman's poem "Desire" imagines, by way of a central underwater image, what at first feels like a calming self-guided meditation. But as she drives deeper and deeper into imagining her new world underwater, the reality of her memory of once catching a fish intersects violently with her fantasy, and she once again is faced with the difficulty of living in her natural element.

Desire

While the pulse in my neck
taps "trouble, trouble," I think about
deep sea fish—their calm gills,
eyes like iced flowers, cold hearts
pumping. I think, *tons of water*
could be holding me down, the vast
blue pressure shot with light that doesn't
break the darkness, but turns
whole fields of minnows into stars.
How slowly they move in the immense

privacy, while grasses wave in slow motion
as they have forever, fanning time,
not this fever, not tongues of flame
springing from this face. . . .

I imagine I breathe water,
suddenly skilled at drawing
what little air I need and sending
the rest back to its heavy world—
that's the miracle of fish, what I
envy—then I remember the striped bass
I once lifted from fresh water to my
natural element, this giddy vanishing
of all substance, that drowning.
(Leslie Ullman, "Desire")

The Definition Poem

The **definition poem,** as its name implies, is developed by and built upon defining something. It is a special form of the **fill-in-the-blanks poem** in that it also utilizes lists of attributes, conditions, actions, or other things that provide context for the subject being defined. One of the more original poets to use a dictionary entry form of the definition poem is the French Surreal poet Francis Ponge. Following is an American example of the definition poem in the straightforward form of a **list poem,** a small catalogue of attributes and actions.

American Poetry

Whatever it is, it must have
A stomach that can digest
Rubber, coal, uranium, moons, poems.

Like the shark, it contains a shoe.
It must swim for miles through the desert
Uttering cries that are almost human.
(Louis Simpson, "American Poetry")

The Proposition Poem

The **proposition poem** sets forth an idea or conditions under which other things may or may not occur. In one of the most time-honored examples of this subgenre, the sly speaker of Andrew Marvell's "To His Coy Mistress" attempts, through overly generous and complimentary exaggerations in the first half of the poem, to seduce his virgin mistress by arguing that if time weren't their enemy he'd take a world of time to court her. But, he argues in the second half of poem, they must seize the day now before it's too late.

To His Coy Mistress

Had we but world enough, and time,
This coyness, lady, were no crime.
We would sit down, and think which way
To walk, and pass our long love's day.
Thou by the Indian Ganges' side
Shouldst rubies find; I by the tide
Of Humber would complain. I would
Love you ten years before the flood,
And you should, if you please, refuse
Till the conversion of the Jews.
My vegetable love should grow
Vaster than empires and more slow;
An hundred years should go to praise
Thine eyes, and on thy forehead gaze;
Two hundred to adore each breast,
But thirty thousand to the rest;
An age at least to every part,
And the last age should show your heart.
For, lady, you deserve this state,
Nor would I love at lower rate.
But at my back I always hear
Time's wingéd chariot hurrying near;
And yonder all before us lie
Deserts of vast eternity.
Thy beauty shall no more be found;
Nor, in thy marble vault, shall sound
My echoing song; then worms shall try
That long-preserved virginity,
And your quaint honor turn to dust,
And into ashes all my lust:
The grave's a fine and private place,
But none, I think, do there embrace.
Now therefore, while the youthful hue
Sits on thy skin like morning glow,
And while thy willing soul transpires
At every pore with instant fires,
Now let us sport us while we may,

And now, like amorous birds of prey,
Rather at once our time devour
Than languish in his slow-chapped power.
Let us roll all our strength and all
Our sweetness up into one ball,
And tear our pleasures with rough strife
Through the iron gates of life:
Thus, though we cannot make our sun
Stand still, yet we will make him run.
(Andrew Marvell, "To His Coy Mistress")

Poetizations

A **poetization** is poetic treatment of a work borrowed from another genre, art form, document, myth, or piece of oral history, much like "novelizations" describe books that have been adapted to filmmaking. It is not known whether the following poem is newly imagined, but it seems to be based upon an Eastern religious myth; most certainly it is a Buddhist lesson.

Buddha's Parable of the Burning House

Gautama the Buddha taught
The doctrine of greed's wheel to which we are bound, and
advised
That we should shed all craving and thus
Undesiring enter the nothingness that he called Nirvana.
Then one day his pupils asked him:
What is it like, this nothingness, Master? Every one of us would
Shed all craving, as you advise, but tell us
Whether this nothingness which then we shall enter
Is perhaps like being one with all creation
When you lie in water, your body weightless, at noon,
Unthinking almost, lazily lie in water, or drowse,
Hardly knowing not that you straighten the blanket,
Going down fast—whether this nothingness, then,
Is a happy one of this kind, a pleasant nothingness, or
Whether this nothingness of yours is mere nothing, cold,
senseless and void.
Long the Buddha was silent, then said nonchalantly:
There is no answer to your question.
But in the evening, when they had gone,
The Buddha still sat under the bread-fruit tree, and to the
others,

To those who had not asked, addressed this parable:
Lately I saw a house. It was burning. The flame
Licked its roof. I went up close and observed
That there were people still inside. I opened the door and called
Out to them that the roof was ablaze, so exhorting them
To leave at once. But those people
Seemed in no hurry. One of them,
When the heat was already scorching his eyebrows,
Asked me what it was like outside, whether it wasn't raining,
Whether the wind wasn't blowing perhaps, whether there was
Another house for them, and more of this kind. Without
answering
I went out again. Those people, I thought,
Need to burn to death before they stop asking questions.
(Bertolt Brecht, "Buddha's Parable of the Burning House")

The Persona Poem

A **persona poem** uses an animal, inanimate object, or a character that is obviously someone or something other than the typical speaker of a poem. Technically speaking, the term **mask** denotes a human speaker in a poem not intended to be the poet, while "persona" denotes something not human. The **voiceless poem** or **transparent lyric** employs a disembodied or characterless voice. Following are examples of the three types.

ANIMAL PERSONA

Animals Are Passing from Our Lives

It's wonderful how I jog
on four honed-down ivory toes
my massive buttocks slipping
like oiled parts with each light step.

I'm to market. I can smell
the sour, grooved block, I can smell
the blade that opens the hole
and the pudgy white fingers

that shake out the intestines
like a hankie. In my dreams
the snouts drool on the marble,
suffering children, suffering flies,

suffering the consumers
who won't meet their steady eyes

for fear they could see. The boy
who drives me along believes

that any moment I'll fall
on my side and drum my toes
like a typewriter or squeal
and shit like a new housewife

discovering television,
or that I'll turn like a beast
cleverly to hook his teeth
with my teeth. No. Not this pig.

(Philip Levine, "Animals Are Passing From Our Lives")

INANIMATE OBJECT PERSONA Here is the voice of a flute from Jelaluddin Rumi's "The Reed Flute."

"Since I was cut from the reedbed,
I have made this crying sound.

Anyone separated from someone he loves
understands what I say.

Anyone pulled from a source
longs to go back.

At any gathering I am there, mingling
in the laughing and the grieving,

a friend to each, but few
will hear the secrets hidden

within the notes. No ears for that.
Body flowing out of spirit,

spirit up from body. We can't conceal
that mixing, but it's not given us

to see the soul."

(Jelaluddin Rumi, "The Reed Flute," trans., Coleman Barks)

THE SPEAKERLESS POEM This type of poem does not use a mediating speaker through which experience is perceived, filtered, and transformed by that character's personality. The **voiceless** or **speakerless poem** (which critic David Walker termed the **transparent lyric**) directly interfaces the reader with what is experienced, as in the following **haiku** by Gary Snyder.

Over the Mindanao Deep

Scrap brass
dumpt off the fantail
falling six miles
(Gary Snyder, "Hitch Haiku")

GENERIC TYPES EXERCISE

Try your hand at writing the following generic types of poems.

1. **Hypo-figure or hyper-figure:** Write a poem that is controlled and organized by an unstated and intuitive impulse arising from your unconscious (hypo-figure), or by an unstated, abstract idea you have consciously conceived (hyper-figure).
2. **Controlling metaphor:** Create a central metaphor and then develop a poem whose parts are derived from attributes of that metaphor.
3. **Controlling symbol:** Write a poem featuring a main symbolic image whose attributes are then salted selectively throughout the poem.
4. **Controlling process:** Write a poem whose content develops through an explanation of how something functions or the steps by which it is made.
5. **Controlling conceit:** Write a poem in which you elaborate in detail the characteristics and/or parts of a central metaphor.
6. **Controlling state of consciousness:** Write a poem from a particular feeling or psychological state, and then allow that state of being to generate and suffuse images, actions, and ideas throughout the rest of the poem.
7. **Controlling gesture:** Think of a physical gesture (such as waving goodbye) and then create as many variations of that gesture as you can to surface in different guises (actions, images, tropes, etc.) throughout the rest of the poem.
8. **Syllogism:** Write out a statement of opinion or a truism in the form of a major premise, and then, elaborating on the terms of the major premise, add a few subordinate statements to create and support some conclusion you draw.
9. **Memory narrative:** Write about a particularly vivid memory you have of a place or time in your life. Then imbue the literal details and images of that place or time with a metaphorical level of meaning that expresses your feeling and experience concerning the subject.

10. **Meditation:** Write about time or place in your past and allow the images that you conjure to generate thoughts about your experiences about that time or in that place.
11. **Definition:** Choose a concrete object or an abstract idea and form a definition of your topic according to its particular characteristics, condition, function, or effects.
12. **Proposition:** Set forth a proposition in which something may or may not happen, and then form an argument as to why events may or may not occur as your proposition had predicted.
13. **Poetization:** Think of a well-known story, myth, or historical event and write a poetic adaptation of your topic that puts it in an entirely new light or context, or explains it in unexpected ways.
14. **Persona:** Choose an inanimate object, an animal, or an idea and then speak directly and convincingly from that speaker's point of view about its ideas, intentions, state of being, etc.
15. **Speakerless poem:** Write a poem that does not exhibit any discernible speaker or personality through which it filters its experience.

STRUCTURAL TYPES

The Fractured Narrative

The **fractured narrative** describes a narrative structure in which the linear storyline of a narrative (elements of time frames, places, events, and characters) is fragmented and reorganized back into a nonlinear arrangement, a method very common in film editing, which is achieved through various **jump cuts** and **cross cuts** (see Cinematic Techniques, pp. 74–83). The form is used to mirror how the writer (and thus the viewer) perceives a different-than-linear congruency in the relationship and importance of the elements of story and its thematic buildup, and it is left to the reader to reconstruct the fragmented narrative into a coherent, "straight" storyline.

There are three major types of fractured narratives: (1) the **episodic structure,** which relates by way of small vignettes, anecdotes, or scenes out of sync in time, place, events, or characters, and is held together by some sharing of common elements among the discrete parts; (2) the **associational structure,** whose coherence and unity are supplied through an implied threading of **associational logic;** and (3) the **retake,** a term borrowed from film, in which an event is retold from multiple perspectives.

EPISODIC STRUCTURE This type of fractured or fragmented narrative keeps switching its attention from one aspect of a subject to another, whether those elements are chosen from among different scenes, characters, images, or time frames. In other words, the subject is narratively explored by way of flashing upon various and disparate mini-episodes that are held together by mood, theme, or tone. Belle Waring's poem below, "Baby Random," is an example of a small fractured narrative, written in an almost stenographic style of voice, which moves from focusing on a premature, anonymous newborn, to newspaper headlines, to a young doctor, to the baby's mother, to questions about birds, to Pablo Neruda, back to the baby, to a pigeon outside, to the speaker's friends, and back to the hospital scene.

Baby Random
                    tries a nosedive, kamikaze,
when the intern flings open the isolette.

The kid almost hits the floor. I can see the headline:
DOC DUMPS AIDS TOT. Nice save, nurse,

Why thanks. Young physician: "We have to change
his tube." His voice trembles, six weeks

out of school. I tell him: "Keep it to a handshake,
you'll be OK." Our team resuscitated

this Baby Random, birth weight
one pound, eyelids still fused. Mother's

a junkie with HIV. Never named him.
Where I work we bring back terminal preemies,

No Fetus Can Beat Us. That's our motto. I have
a friend who was thrown into prison. Where do birds

go when they die? Neruda wanted to know. Crows
eat them. Bird heaven? Imagine the racket.

When Random cries, petit fish on shore, nothing
squeaks past the tube down his pipe. His ventilator's

a high-tech bellows that kicks in & out. Not
up to the nurses. Quiet: a pigeon's outside,

color of graham crackers, throat oil on a wet street,
wings splattered white, perched out of the rain.

I have friends who were thrown into prison, Latin
American. Tortured. Exiled. Some people have

courage. Some people have heart. *Corazon.*
After a shift like tonight, I have the usual

bad dreams. Some days I avoid my reflection in store
windows. I just don't want anyone to look at me.
(Belle Waring, "Baby Random")

ASSOCIATIONAL STRUCTURE The fractured narrative that uses the associational structure employs slanting forms of logic among imagery, characters, scenes, time frames, and musical effects and is held together and associated by what the poet Hart Crane termed the **logic of the metaphor** (comparison, substitution, or identity) in order to coherently fuse disparate entities. It is similar to the episodic structure in that it also uses associative logic, but where the former juxtaposes small vignettes, the associative type uses fast segues within and between lines from one image to another. In the following stanza from Albert Goldbarth's "How the World Works: An Essay," there is an almost dizzying march of inter-reflecting associations that, while seemingly disparate, actually form an all-inclusive view of how things in this world are connected: from a satellite image of clouds flowing over the earth that "coincidentally" mirrors the pattern of tiles in The Alhambra, from tassels rippling on Turkish hats, to slivery, blind cave fish entering fissures in Mexico, to a poacher in Nepal spooning musk (for perfume) from a deer, to a cologne-drenched Manhattan pimp and his charges.

That's my topic. How complex, Alhambran arabesques of
weather
(seen computer-screened by satellites); and the weathering
eddies on tiles
in the courtyards and intimate tryst-rooms and policy chambers
of The Alhambra itself: construe a grander pattern.
How the west wind whipples the osiers. How the slivery,
eyeless
cave fish in Mexico slip through their fissures unerring.
In Nepal, a poacher reams a spoonful of musk
from that orifice near the urethra, holding—with his other
gloved hand—the deer's small death-kicks steady; and in
mid-Manhattan at 3 a.m., at Chico's place, the Pimp Prince
enters swimming in coke, with one new frou-frou-cunted
acolyte on each eelskin sleeve, and he reeks of a vial
of musk. I'm singing the rings-in-rings song of the planet,
its milks, its furnaces, its chlorophyll links.
(Albert Goldbarth, "How the World Works: An Essay")

THE RETAKE A third type of fractured narrative is the **retake,** a term borrowed from cinema's method of reshooting scenes. It was used as a film technique in the classic Japanese movie *Rashomon,* which presented multiple versions of an event as told by several witnesses, each of whom testified from a contradictory **point of view** (see **synchronicity**). It is also a technique that the media routinely employs to give a fuller account of an event. In the example poem below concerning the battle of the sexes, one or both of the characters' memory of their first meeting is colored by their negative subjectivity.

When we first met

you wore soiled jeans, and acted tipsy.
Whatever was I thinking?

No, I was dressed to the nines
and sharp enough to see past
your smile that let me know
you thought I was a catch.

No, what I thought was here was a man
who might commit if I could change him,
when you should have been committed.

Yes, I should have been committed
for being taken by your girlish charm
and that walk you walked.

And I should've gone to a home
for the deaf and blind
where no one can see or talk.

The Cut-and-Shuffle Poem

The cut-and-shuffle format features lines or stanzas from two or more disparate scenes, events, characters, and moods more or less alternately shuffled together. An interesting effect of this structuring of content is that the separate situations and descriptions take on a third level of meaning that becomes implied through triangulation, much in the way that a ship can obtain its position (equivalent to a third kind of meaning) by receiving reports from two other ships in its area. In other words, two random and mutually exclusive situations, when shuffled together, will often form a previously nonexistent relationship through the implication of their juxtaposed parts. Following is an example from two short scenes originally composed separately.

scene 1

She sits in class.
She idly twists a curl.
She flips through the pages of a book.
She closes her eyes and sighs.
She concentrates on what the teacher says.

scene 2

A boy flexes one of his biceps.
He thinks of yesterday's scrimmage.
The smell of perfumed hair wafts toward him.
He thinks he'd like to have a girlfriend.

scenes 1 and 2 shuffled together

She sits in class.
A boy flexes one of his biceps.
She idly twists a curl.
He thinks of yesterday's scrimmage.
She flips through the pages of a book.
The smell of perfumed hair wafts toward him.
She closes her eyes and sighs.
He thinks he'd like to have a girlfriend.
She concentrates on what the teacher says.

By alternating the actions and characters of each scene, an implied relationship and some unintentional plays on words are built in the synthesized version, and the reader assumes that there is a tacit understanding built up between the two characters.

The most common implied effects that the cut-and-shuffle can create are:

1. a doubling of the perspective in which two points of view record the same scene;
2. a simultaneous layering or "double exposure" in which inner and outer states of being (real and imagined, or psychological and objective) are portrayed;
3. a third, implied relationship between events or characters, triangulated from the two original scenarios;
4. an ironic, paradoxical, or humorous intersecting of two different events.

The List Poem

The **list poem** is a contemporary version of the ancient, Biblical catalogue form. Its basic content is an extended listing of a subject's characteristics, actions, conditions, or effects. The challenge of the form, if it is to be successful, is to be highly imaginative and selective in the contents of the list. Mexican poet Jaime Sabines' "The Moon" bases its list (a variety of medicinal forms such as capsule, amulet, eye drops, etc.) upon the moon's being prescribed as a cure-all for those who are stricken by not being romantic.

While, as is often the case, entire poems may not be composed in the list form, many poems do include parts that are lists. Here, as an example, is a passage from Maura Stanton's "The Grocery Store."

Every week the garish headlines
Insist there is another world
That ordinary people see—
Spaceships in backyards;
A baby cures a multitude;
An angry ghost destroys the china
To the amazement of a waitress;
A dentist shouts from his coffin—
(Maura Stanton, "The Grocery Store")

The Fill-in-the-Blanks Poem

The **fill-in-the-blanks poem** is a more limited form of the **list poem** in that it is more closely constrained by the characteristics of its subject. Its simple structural form begins by stating its subject and then continues by filling in a number of the subject's attributes, which take on symbolic resonance.

(TITLE AND SUBJECT)	The Door
(GENERAL CONDITION)	The door you choose will make a statement.
(LIST OF	You may choose it close an opening
CHARACTERISTICS)	or block the view; others can be seen
	right through. It can open outward
	to the world or inward. It can lock others out
	and keep others in. It can be strong or vulnerable.
	When houses are razed, they save the doors.

The "IF . . . THEN" Poem

The "if . . . then" poem is a poem based upon a rhetorical structure whose content is strung between the poles of the cause-and-effect setup of its **syntax.** Following, in her typically celebratory mode of nature, is a Pattiann Rogers' *tour de force* of this construction.

The Hummingbird: A Seduction

If I were a female hummingbird perched still
And quiet on an upper myrtle branch
In the spring afternoon and if you were a male
Alone in the whole heavens before me, having parted

Yourself, for me, from cedar top and honeysuckle stem
And earth-down, your body hovering in mid-air
Far away from jewelweed, thistle and beebalm;
And if I watched how you fell, plummeting before me,
And how you rose again and fell, with such mastery
That I believed for a moment *you* were the sky
And the red-marked bird diving inside your circumference
Was just the physical revelation of the light's
Most perfect desire;

And if I saw your sweeping and sucking
Performance of swirling egg and semen in the air,
The weaving, twisting vision of red petal
And nectar and soaring rump, the rush of your wing
In its grand confusion of arcing and splitting
Created completely out of nothing just for me,

Then when you came down to me, I would call you
My own spinning bloom of ruby sage, my funneling
Storm of sunlit sperm and pollen, my only breathless
Piece of scarlet sky, and I would bless the base
Of each of your feathers and touch the tine
Of string muscles binding your wings and taste
The odor of your glistening oils and hunt
The honey in your crimson flare
And I would take you and take you and take you
Deep into any kind of nest you ever wanted.

(Pattiann Rogers, "The Hummingbird: A Seduction")

The Montage

The **montage** is a structural technique in which disparate but closely associated contents are brought into a coherent and unified whole. Adrienne Rich's three-part series of ghazals, "Ghazals: Homage to Ghalib," is a montage of self-contained and independent couplets whose disparate parts are linked by the theme of personal growth within the socio-political revolution of the feminist movement. For the purposes of illustration, we could create a montage by forming a cluster of associated images having to do with light: stars hung high and clear, a billion single-socket light bulbs, glowing cigarettes, car headlights, lights reflected in your eyes, etc.

Under a crystal star,
past a thousand miles of streetlights,
behind my lowered headlights,
by the glow of my cigarette
your eyes reflected all that in mine.

The Collage

The **collage** is a construction similar to the montage, except that its contents are much more disparate and widely gathered from various sources. Rather than the closely implied association and interrelationship among its parts, as in the montage, the collage depends more upon its overall effect for coherence, as if the reader were squinting at disparate objects to bring them into a harmonic and coherent frame. Robert Francis' "Silent Poem" offers a "patchwork quilt" of "fragmented surfaces" held together by sound, emotional thrust, setting, and a seemingly implied walk that moves the reader from the front of the farmhouse to its back.

Silent Poem

backroad leafmold stonewall chipmunk
underbrush grapevine woodchuck shadblow
woodsmoke cowbarn honeysuckle woodpile
sawhorse bucksaw outhouse wellsweep
backdoor flagstone bulkhead buttermilk
candlestick ragrug firedog brownbread
hilltop outcrop cowbell buttercup
whetstone thunderstorm pitchfork steeplebush
gristmill millstone cornmeal waterwheel
watercress buckwheat firefly jewelweed
gravestone groundpine windbreak bedrock
weathercock snowfall starlight cockcrow

(Robert Francis, "Silent Poem")

The Prose Poem

The **prose poem** is a poetic form that contains any of the devices of poetry except the line break. The form is commonly used to instruct or entertain, and, because of its lack of lineation, is a good form for wild content, narrative, descriptive, or associative strategies, and large syntactical structures. In the bittersweet mien of Charlie Chaplin, James Tate's protagonist becomes hopelessly entangled in an impossible situation because of his innocence, awkwardness, and simple wonderment.

Deaf Girl Playing

This is where I once saw a deaf girl playing in a field. Because I did not know how to approach her without startling her, or how I would explain my presence, I hid. I felt so disgusting, I might as well have raped the child, a grown man on his belly

in a field watching a deaf girl play. My suit was stained by the grass and I was an hour late for dinner. I was forced to discard my suit for lack of a reasonable explanation to my wife, a hundred dollar suit! We're not rich people, not at all. So there I was, left to my wool suit in the heat of summer, soaked through by noon each day. I was an embarrassment to the entire firm: it is not good for the morale of the fellow worker to flaunt one's poverty. After several weeks of crippling tension, my superior finally called me into his office. Rather than humiliate myself by telling him the truth, I told him I would wear whatever damned suit I pleased, a suit of armor if I fancied. It was the first time I had challenged his authority. And it was the last. I was dismissed. Given my pay. On my way home I thought, I'll tell her the truth, yes, why not! Tell her the simple truth, she'll love me for it. What a touching story. Well, I didn't. I don't know what happened, a loss of courage, I suppose. I told her a mistake I had made had cost the company several thousand dollars, and that, not only was I dismissed, I would also have to find the money to repay them the sum of my error. She wept, she beat me, she accused me of everything from malice to impotency. I helped her pack and drove her to the bus station. It was too late to explain. She would never believe me now. How cold the house was without her. How silent. Each plate I dropped was like tearing the very flesh from a living animal. When all were shattered, I knelt in a corner and tried to imagine what I would say to her, the girl in the field.
(James Tate, "Deaf Girl Playing")

Poems of Addition and Subtraction

Here is a class of thematic shapes that build wholeness out of an implied set of opposing, self-balanced figures of addition and subtraction, a narrative or argument whose cycle seems archetypal. In the following poem by Donald Hall, that story tells of a way of life that is rich in its earthiness and values but poor in its worldly rewards.

Ox Cart Man

In October of the year,
he counts potatoes dug from the brown field,
counting the seed, counting
the cellar's portion out,

and bags the rest on the cart's floor.

He packs wool sheared in April, honey
in combs, linen, leather
tanned from deerhide, and vinegar in a barrel
hooped by hand at the forge's fire.

He walks by his ox's head, ten days
to Portsmouth Market, and sells potatoes,
and the bag that carried potatoes,
flaxseed, birch brooms, maple sugar, goose
feathers, yarn.

When the cart is empty he sells the cart.
When the cart is sold he sells the ox,
harness and yoke, and walks
home, his pockets heavy
with the year's coin for salt and taxes,

and at home by fire's light in November cold
stitches new harness
for next year's ox in the barn,
and carves the yoke, and saws planks
building the cart again.
(Donald Hall, "Ox Cart Man")

Poems of Absence and Presence

Another class of poems, similar to the one above, goes through its changes only to arrive in spiral fashion back where it started, but, on a deeper level, in a new condition. In the following poem by Raymond Carver, the speaker gets a life full of what he wished for when he experienced a lustful taste for it when he was young.

Luck

I was nine years old.
I had been around liquor
all my life. My friends
drank too, but they
could handle it.
We'd take cigarettes, beer,
a couple of girls
and go out to the fort.
We'd act silly.
Sometimes you'd pretend

to pass out so the girls
could examine you.
They'd put their hands
down your pants while
you lay there trying
not to laugh, or else
they would lean back,
close their eyes, and
let you feel them all over.
Once at a party my dad
came to the back porch
to take a leak.
We could hear voices
over the record player,
see people standing around
laughing and drinking.
When my dad finished,
he zipped up, stared a while
at the starry sky—
it was always starry then
on summer nights—
and went back inside.
The girls had to go home.
I slept all night in the fort
with my best friend.
We kissed on the lips
and touched each other.
I saw the stars fade
toward morning,
I saw a woman sleeping on our lawn.
I looked up her dress,
then I had a beer
and a cigarette.
Friends, I thought this
was living.
Indoors, someone
had put out a cigarette
in a jar of mustard.
I had a straight shot
from the bottle, then
a drink of warm collins mix,

then another whiskey.
And though I went from room
to room, nobody was home.
What luck I thought.
Years later,
I still wanted to give up
friends, love, starry skies,
for a house where nobody
was home, and all I could drink.
(Raymond Carver, "Luck")

The Refrain Poems

There are many formal types of poems that use a **refrain** device, the repetition of words, phrases, lines, or sentences (the sestina, villanelle, ballad, etc.). Building on a variation of this tradition and capitalizing upon the emphatic power inherent in repetition, free verse poets have used refrain extensively in their work. Note in John Skoyles' poem below how the refrain changes in meaning and **tone color** as it occurs in different parts of the poem.

Conviction

I feel most alone when someone
calls me by name. Even though
there are times I'm completely withdrawn:
when the woman beside me,
as she's speaking abstractly,
seems more alive than in bed;
and although her breathing reminds me
we'll be on our own sooner or later,
I feel most alone
when someone calls me by name.

When someone calls me by name
I want to turn myself in
for bearing my fingertips
and a whole family's blood;
my hands twitch like the couple downstairs
swearing again they were better off alone;
and I remember hearing it sighed so often
"I love so-and-so dearly, but . . ."
I'm ashamed to be near you
while having mixed feelings.

When someone calls me by name I remember
the people who thought twice about me,
who repeat to themselves the names
they're attached to, from pleasure
or heartbreak, and I think of myself
only as proof of two people's love,
that took them beyond the reach
of their bodies and settled here somehow,
where I feel most alone
when someone calls me by name.
(John Skoyles, "Conviction")

STRUCTURAL TYPES EXERCISE

Try your hand at writing the following structural types of poems.

1. **Fractured narrative:** Write a nonlinear narrative poem whose stanzas or sections jump from one time frame to another, from one place to another, from one event to another, and from character's point of view to another.
2. **Episodic structure:** Select an event or experience and then write about it in discrete stanzas that each describe a separate action, image, or perspective concerning that event.
3. **Associational structure:** Write about the same event or experience you chose for the episodic structure above, but this time use one block stanza whose lines quickly connect various parts and aspects of that event by way of associational logic.
4. **Retake structure:** Write about that same event (from item 3 above) from widely different points of view or perspectives that are stacked upon one another.
5. **Cut-and-shuffle:** Now write a brief version (about six lines) of that same event. Then write another six lines about an opposite kind of event or experience. Now alternately shuffle the two six-line stanzas together into one poem.
6. **Montage:** Quickly write a series of associated images in a cluster. Then build a line or two out of each image so that you develop about a twenty-line poem.
7. **Collage:** Think of a particularly memorable place, person, or event and quickly create a list of anything that comes to mind, such as salient images within the topic and any associations outside of it that

come to mind. Then strategically place these images in some sort of order that creates either an implied narrative or theme.

8. **Prose poem:** Write down something you feel strongly about and, allowing yourself to be wild, entertaining, or didactic, use any poetic device that naturally comes to mind. Make each sentence do an interesting and different kind of work than what comes before and after it.
9. **Addition and subtraction:** Create a story in which the depletion of something results in the completion of something else; or, as in the opposite, the completion of something results in the depletion of something else.
10. **Absence and presence:** Write a circular poem in which a condition, event, or experience that you first thought would be positive turns out to be something negative, although on the surface it looks the same as you first imagined it.
11. **Refrain:** Write a poem in which the same repeated line or phrase changes its meaning slightly according to the different context of the lines around it.

SPECIFIC TYPES OF POEMS

This section offers free verse models of types of poems that have become "standards" in contemporary poetry.

The Childhood Poem

The following poem by Bill Tremblay is a wonderfully conceived creation myth as seen phenomenologically through the eyes of a child.

Creation

In school the nuns taught God
made the heavens and earth in six
days. Duhamel never believed it.
He saw his mother and father make it
in one day.
                    At first it *was* dark.
His mother lifted the curtain and made
light shine through the glass windows

and the wooden crossbars, making their
children, the shadows.
His mother
carried him and created the kitchen,
the bathroom, talcum, pleasure. She
made the air, the smell of hot toast.
His father walked him with both hands
and created doors, the world outside,
angel clouds, and telephone wires strung
above streets were how things're connected.
He created motion in a maroon Packard,
and colors for go, stop, and maybe.

They created smokestacks, steeples, and silos
to mark the different kinds of work.
They created Revere Beach and, for
everything without end, the Atlantic,
with waves rushing toward him saying,
"Reverse. Everything in reverse."

Darkness came: laughter in reverse.
Shouting came: laughter in reverse.
Duhamel invented more uses for darkness,
the pleasures of making the world over.
Bathrobe sky. Melted tar night. Packard wind.
He hummed as his eyes opened in reverse.
(Bill Tremblay, "Creation")

The Fable

A **fable** is a short work written in a plain style, which uses animals as characters that symbolize various human traits of folly and nobility. In the following prose-poem fable by Russell Edson, the strangeness of human sexual attraction is powerfully brought home by a reversal in perspective.

The Rat's Legs

I met a rat under a bridge. And we sat there in the mud discussing the rat's loveliness.

I asked, what it is about you that has caused men to write odes?

My legs, said the rat, for it has always been that men
have liked to run their hands up my legs to my secret parts;
it's nature . . .
(Russell Edson, "The Rat's Legs")

The Myth

The **myth** is an apocryphal story (of unknown origin) that seeks to explain how certain things in nature or in the nature of man or animals came to be. William Stafford's mesmerizing renewal myth, in its time-honored tradition, warns us not to take what we have for granted.

The Animal That Drank Up Sound

1

One day across the lake where echoes come now
an animal that needed sound came down. He gazed
enormously, and instead of making any, he took
away from, sound: the lake and all the land
went dumb. A fish that jumped went back like a knife,
and the water died. In all the wilderness around he
drained the rustle from the leaves into the mountainside
and folded a quilt over the rocks, getting ready
to store everything the place had known; he buried—
thousands of autumns deep—the noise that used to come there.

Then that animal wandered on and began to drink
the sound out of all the valleys—the croak of toads,
and all the little shiny noise grass blades make.
He drank till winter, and then looked out one night
at the stilled places guaranteed around by frozen
peaks and held in the shallow pools of starlight.
It was finally tall and still, and he stopped on the highest
ridge, just where the cold sky fell away
like a perpetual curve, and from there he walked on silently,
and began to starve.

When the moon drifted over that night the whole world lay
just like the moon, shining back that still
silver, and the moon saw its own animal dead
on the snow, its dark absorbent paws and quiet
muzzle, and thick, velvet, deep fur.

2
After the animal that drank up sound died, the world
lay still and cold for months, and the moon yearned
and explored, letting its dead light float down
the west walls of canyons and then climb its delighted
soundless way up the east side. The moon
owned the earth its animal had faithfully explored.
The sun disregarded the life it used to warm.

But on the north side of the mountain, deep in some rocks,
a cricket slept. It had been hiding when that animal
passed, and as spring came again this cricket waited,
afraid to crawl out into the heavy stillness.
Think how deep the cricket felt, lost there
in such a silence—the grass, the leaves, the water,
the stilled animals all depending on such a little
thing. But softly it tried—"Cricket!"—and back like a river
from one act flowed the kind of world we know,
first whisperings, then moves in the grass and leaves;
the water splashed, and a big night bird screamed.

It all returned, our precious world with its life and sound,
where sometimes loud over the hill the moon,
wild again, looks for its animal to roam, still,
down out of the hills, any time.
But somewhere a cricket waits.

It listens now, and practices at night.

(William Stafford, "The Animal That Drank Up Sound")

The Folktale

The **folktale** is a narrative passed down orally through generations, which attempts to explain the origin of events, aspects of human nature, or ideals in super- or nonhuman forms. In Marcia Southwick's poem on the following page, the dilemma the character faces, which the speaker uses as a springboard to her own personal musings, is another cautionary tale that takes to task the aphorism "opposites attract."

The Rain's Marriage

In an African folktale, the rain
falls in love with a blacksmith.
At the wedding, the downpour dies out

to a single stream, a column of water.
As the first drop touches soil,
feet appear, then legs, a torso, arms . . .
The woman, waves of transparent hair
falling over her shoulders, is called
the *Water Bride* and doesn't fully lose
her identity as rain. Once,
I was certain of the boundaries of my body
and whatever it touched, as if
touch itself were a way of defining exactly where *I* stopped
and the rest of the world began.
Then I lost the sense that I was hemmed in
by skin. My body felt like something loaned to me—
it might break, or dissolve to ashes,
leaving me stranded,
a pure thought without a skull to inhabit—
like rain falling into any shape that accepts it,
every hollow place made equal by its touch.
The mind of rain
contemplates even the smallest crack in the parched dirt
where nothing will grow.
Why can't I fall effortlessly in love?
If I knew the exact place where my body stops
and everything else begins, I'd marry.
Like the *Water Bride,* I'd be unafraid,
though surely trouble would exist, as between rain
and a blacksmith's fire.
(Marcia Southwick, "The Rain's Marriage")

The Classic Syndrome Poem

A **classic syndrome** poem is one that examines an occurrence so common in a culture that it has become a cultural cliché. In Louis Simpson's poem on the next page, ostensibly about a routine breakdown on a freeway, his portrait takes a satirical potshot at the way our inner identity is so connected closely to our material possessions.

American Classic

It's a classic American scene—
a car stopped off the road
and a man trying to repair it.

The woman who stays in the car
in the classic American scene
stares back at the freeway traffic.

They look surprised, and ashamed
to be so helpless . . .
let down in the middle of the road!

To think that their car would do this!
They look like mountain people
whose son has gone against the law.

But every night they set out food
and the robber goes skulking back to the trees.
That's how it is with the car . . .

it's theirs, they're stuck with it.
Now they know what it's like to sit
and see the world go whizzing by.

In the fume of carbon monoxide and soot
they are not such good Americans
as they thought they were.

The feeling of being left out
through no fault of your own, is common.
That's why I say, an American classic.
(Louis Simpson, "American Classic")

The Fairy Tale Poem

Many poets have turned toward fairy tales for new perspectives and interpretations of well-known children's stories. In the poem below, Doug Mailman plays off the *Jack and the Beanstalk* fairy tale in a humorous vein.

Jack Has No Choice

So now we know, there was a girl up there, a real Princess.
You ditched the golden goose at home, slurped a bowl of barley soup
and went back up to free her.

But the giant knew what you were up to. He knew
all you could do
was make him chase you out of those clouds.

And as he's sliding down the stalk he's thinking
I'll squeeze that guy's kishkas out

in one hand and chew him like a stringy bean.

The giant with the black-bristle face was
always with the girl you couldn't have,
and isn't that

the way it must be? And you, with the last bit
of strength you had left
started hacking down your only way back up.

And now she's princess on a cloud somewhere you don't know
and you're in Jersey, looking for a job,
a wife, someone to tell your story to, your life.

The golden goose? For you, it was nothing,
having your hands free to hack the beanstalk down
which had grown so suddenly into a tree;

the golden goose is that you know
she's gone, forever,
the perfect love that can never be.

(Doug Mailman, "Jack Has No Choice")

The Cultural Icon Poem

Millions of Americans grew up in the 1930s, '40s and '50s reading *Dick and Jane* primer books in the first grade. In the poem below, Judith Kroll's excoriating and satirical play off America's prefeminist notions of sex and gender roles as depicted in the primer books announces a new order of things.

Dick and Jane

Dick is the one with the weenie
who gets to be doctor
and never cries,
in love with mechanics and motion.

Jane is the one with nothing under her skirt,
so soft and weepy,
in love with the rulers of earth.

Dick gulps his soup and burns his tongue.
Jane blows and blows to cool hers,
it takes so long
she has ages to see

that Dick is just a boy
with a rubber jiggler.

She can take his tongue on hers and cool it off.
She can cut his thing off at the root.
She can tuck him in bed and sing him to sleep.
She can leave him alone.
(Judith Kroll, "Dick and Jane")

The Political Poem

One of the most powerful and exciting advents in contemporary American poetry has been its revival of sociopolitical content brought into the arena of art by poets whose values and identities of ethnicity, race, gender, and sexual preference are other than those of middle-class, white, mainstream America. The best **political poems** derive from specific, concrete images from personal experience, set in lyric form. Below, Adrian Louis, a Sioux Indian poet, addresses his tribe's ruin by describing the state of their "welfare."

The First of the Month

Undeodorized and radiant in rags
she squats sullenly
upon the crooked earth
and pokes her brown finger
at fat, red ants
dragging a dead fly home.
My reflection in her eyes
dazzles the air from my lungs.
I shrivel inside
the vacuum of formic arms.
Now's hourglass is frozen.
The bubbling brook is foetid
and the ancient, wondrous
songbirds are chancrous.
Against my dark void
of memories
of blood upon blood
White Clay, Nebraska, explodes
with a thousand faces
of my drunken race
cashing their welfare checks.
(Adrian Louis, "The First of the Month")

The Photograph Poem

The photograph poem offers a great deal of leveraging power because it can hold images and time itself in stasis, as opposed to the fluidity of the poet's memory, so that the poet can concentrate on selecting the literal-*cum*-metaphorical aspects the photo is addressing, as in the repetitive mentioning of the literal and figurative grays in the photograph Richard Hugo is using as a biographical springboard.

Burn this shot. That gray is what it is.
Gray gravel in the street and gray hearts
tired of trying love. Your house,
that ominous gray shake alone on the right,
pear tree bent in what must have been wind
and gray boy playing. The wind had a way
of saying The Lord is My Shepherd high
in electric wires. That blur could be
a bitter wren or a girl named May Jane
running away from a prehistoric father.
(Richard Hugo, "A Snapshot of 15th S.W.")

The Painting Poem

The painting poem, a precursor of and similar to the characteristics of the photograph poem, has a long tradition and is a good example of how one art can piggyback upon another. Usually, there is an overt and conscious melding of the poet's perceptions and thoughts with those originally expressed by the painter, so that through this synthesis a new work of art is produced. In a larger sense, there's an interesting cyclical process going on: the painter puts into concrete images what has been previously locked up in thought, feeling, and language. The poet then reverses that process by decoding the painted images back into language. The best painting poems, even given the poet's added perceptions and thoughts, seem to be those that make paintings and their values come alive. In the poem below, Seamus Heaney delves into the mind and character of Cézanne, and honors the ethos of the artist-as-archetype by referencing images from his painting.

An Artist

I love the thought of his anger.
His obstinacy against the rock, his coercion
of the substance from green apples.

The way he was a dog barking
at the image of himself barking.
And his hatred of his own embrace
of working as the only thing that worked— . . .

The way his fortitude held and hardened
because he did what he knew.
His forehead like a hurled boule
travelling unpainted space
behind the apple and behind the mountain.
(Seamus Heaney, "An Artist")

The Letter Poem

The **letter poem,** which crossbreeds the devices of poetry with the conventions of letter writing, has the intimate connecting power of working off an established relationship in which the speaker addresses a "you." It offers an inherent, safe intimacy for the writer because it will be received at a removed time and distance by the addressee. Yet it can also offer, if the poet so chooses, all the formal freedoms from preciosity that the **prose poem** allows. Richard Hugo's book, *31 Letters and 13 Dreams,* offers a number of poems in this subgenre. Below, Philip Schultz's poem employs the intimate, indeed, confessional conventions of letter writing; yet the poem also maintains its heart-breaking distance.

A Letter Found on a January Night in Front of the Public Theatre

Dear Emily Permutter,

Today I read how good you are as Nina
and even Chekov couldn't be so proud
but hearing from me must be a shock
since your grandma said I died from TB
on Ellis Island (if she was alive she'd spit
three times!) but better you should know
the truth and maybe forgive me. I had TB
but my brother Izzy was the one who died.
They wouldn't let him in (imagine after
all our grief being sent back to Russia!)
and after weeks in detention he cut his wrists
on a sardine can (others did the same but used
fancier methods). I'm not making excuses but
life on the Lower East Side was no piknic.
Thousands on each block ate herring and crackers

without a cracked pot to piss in and I wasn't
twenty (and so green my first banana I ate peel
and all and was insulted to eat corn—in Russia
we fed it to pigs!) when grandma had your mother
and day and night we sewed crotches for pennies
the uptown Germans paid (may they eat steak in Hell!).
My cousin Sam broke hands—two bits a knuckle—
and put his own sister on the street (where she didn't
sell pickles!) so maybe it's better not to judge
what you haven't suffered . . .

Your photo in the *Times* shows your grandma's eyes
but I'm afraid you have my mouth that made me
so much trouble always insulting the wrong person.
Like you I was an actor but maybe my most famous role
is wife-deserter. After two years in the Yiddish Theatre
I went to Hollywood but with my bad English (a Campbell
soup can I couldn't read without stuttering) got only
extra work and ended up selling plastic legs
after I lost my left one making bombs against Hitler
(one mistook me for a Nazi?). But never I stopped
writing tho your grandma sent back only fishhooks
(not that I blame her—she wiped the blood I coughed
in steerage and fed me her rations eight months pregnant!)
but believe me I've been punished. God put me in this
welfare home for retired actors where each night
lights-out means an encore. When they're not singing Sinatra
they're dancing on my head like Fred Astaire—at least
they keep trying! But failure can be a demanding mistress
and now that you know success early I pray you remember
Nina's lines—"What matters is not fame, not glory . . .
but knowing how to have faith." Talent isn't always
sympathetic so please don't make TV commercials or
hide behind your beauty. Emily, I've written you
maybe a thousand letters but shame isn't postage
and even if you can't forgive me I hope you won't mind
if I'm always in the front row clapping. Be strong
and honest (thank God you didn't change your name!)
and there's nothing you can't accomplish. Darling,
your black hair is so outspoken I break glasses.
With respectful admiration,
Lewis Pearlmutter

(Philip Schultz, "A Letter Found on a January Night in Front of the Public Theatre")

The Dream Poem

The dream poem deals directly or indirectly with the content of dreams, and often uses surreal images (odd under- and oversized objects, unexpected contexts, and odd juxtapositions of images) and associative modes of logic. The three main formatting methods of presenting dream poems are: (1) a literal recording of the dream itself; (2) referencing selected elements of the dream as content for a conventional poem; and (3) using the images from a dream that are "translated up" from their unconscious symbolism into a more conscious awareness of the dream's meaning, which is then incorporated into everyday life. In Jean Valentine's poem "The Second Dream," she seems to be using actual dream material summarized from a dream she had. The title lends more than a bit of mystery to the poem, since we are not able to ascertain the message of the first dream her speaker must have had. And that feeling is substantially increased in the poem about this second dream, with its atmosphere charged with fear, the characters who seem helpless in the face of the catastrophic fate that is about to befall them, and the surrealistic images salted throughout the poem that lend a striking and authenticating air to the poem.

The Second Dream

We all heard the alarm. The planes were out
And coming, from a friendly country. You, I thought,
Would know what to do. But you said,
"There is nothing to do. Last time
The bodies were like charred trees.'

We had so many minutes. The leaves
Over the street left the light silver as dimes.
The children hung around in slow motion, loud,
Liquid as butterflies, with nothing to do.

(Jean Valentine, "The Second Dream")

The Rite of Initiation Poem

The **rite of initiation** poem lays out the ritualistic trials and tribulations one must undergo to become part of some new group or order of experience. Meant as tests, these supposedly honorific rituals and hazings sometimes devolve into mere sadistic abuse, as in the following ordeal by Gary Gildner.

First Practice

After the doctor checked to see
we weren't ruptured,
the man with the short cigar took us

under the grade school,
where we went in case of attack
or storm, and said
he was Clifford Hill, he was
a man who believed dogs
ate dogs, he had once killed
for his country, and if
there were any girls present
for them to leave now.

No one
left. OK, he said, he said I take
that to mean you are hungry
men who hate to lose as much
as I do. OK. Then
he made two lines of us
facing each other,
and across the way, he said,
is the man you hate most
in the world,
and if we are to win
that title I want to see how.
But I don't want to see
any marks when you're dressed,
he said. He said, *Now.*

(Gary Gildner, "First Practice")

The Rite of Passage Poem

The **rite of passage poem** is a poem that focuses on encountering the inner feelings attending the outer events, characters, emotions, and ambiance of a traumatic, major life experience, such as the ambivalence and ambiguity of first love, the grief over the death of a loved one, leaving home and being on one's own, the advent of middle or old age, marriage, the birth of a child, etc. It is a time-honored and important subject in poetry, in which we can see how others have felt about and handled these watershed experiences. In the poem by Philip Levine that follows, a child steals his way over a transom and drops into a rite of passage in the form of a closed barber shop and, suffering his first major bouts with guilt and the certainty of being caught, has created for himself a terrible, no-exit situation.

To a Child Trapped in a Barber Shop

You've gotten in through the transom
   and you can't get out
till Monday morning or, worse,
   till the cops come.

That six-year-old red face
  calling for mama
is yours; it won't help
  because your case

is closed forever, hopeless.
  So don't drink
the Lucky Tiger, don't
  fill up on grease

because that makes it a lot worse,
  that makes it a crime
against property and the state
  and that costs time.

We've all been here before,
  we took our turn
under the electric storm
  of the vibrator

and stiffened our wills to meet
  the close clippers
and heard the true blade mowing
  back and forth

on a strip of dead skin,
  and we stopped crying.
You think your life is over?
  It's just begun.

(Philip Levine, "To a Child Trapped in a Barber Shop")

The Special Moment Poem

Countless times throughout life, we experience ineffable kinds of "special moments" that often are opposite in kind and quality to the clichéd snapshots of formal occasions we keep in our photo albums. These moments are usually very brief, but full of great and resonant human meaning. Here's an example of one of those moments captured by Tess Gallagher.

The Hug

A woman is reading a poem on the street
and another woman stops to listen. We stop too,
with our arms around each other. The poem
is being read and listened to out here
in the open. Behind us
no one is entering or leaving the houses.

Suddenly a hug comes over me and I'm
giving it to you, like a variable star shooting light
off to make itself comfortable, then
subsiding. I finish but keep on holding
you. A man walks up to us and we know he hasn't
come out of nowhere, but if he could, he
would have. He looks homeless because of how
he needs. "Can I have one of those?" he asks you,
and I feel you nod. I'm surprised,
surprised you don't tell him how
it is—that I'm yours, only
yours, etc., exclusive as a nose to
its face. Love—that's what we're talking about, love
that nabs you with "for me
only" and holds on.

So I walk over to him and put my
arms around him and try to
hug him like I mean it. He's got an overcoat on
so thick I can't feel
him past it. I'm starting the hug
and thinking, "How big a hug is this supposed to be?
How long shall I hold this hug?" Already
we could be eternal, his arms falling over my
shoulders, my hands not
meeting behind his back, he is so big!

I put my head into his chest and snuggle
in. I lean into him. I lean my blood and my wishes
into him. He stands for it. This is his
and he's starting to give it back so well I know he's
getting it. This hug. So truly, so tenderly
we stop having arms and I don't know if
my lover has walked away or what, or
if the woman is still reading the poem, or the houses—
what about them?—the houses.

Clearly, a little permission is a dangerous thing.
But when you hug someone you want it
to be a masterpiece of connection, the way the button
on his coat will leave the imprint of
a planet in my cheek
when I walk away. When I try to find some place
to go back to.

(Tess Gallagher, "The Hug")

The Split-Self Poem

Either by accessing memory and imagination, or perhaps by using photographs from early and recent periods in one's life, this is an excellent method by which to see the difference in character and values between who one was and who one has become. Here is a poem by Jon Anderson in which he looks at a black-and-white childhood photograph of himself and addresses that child he was.

The Photograph of Myself

Surely in my eyes that light is now lost,
or has deepened; and my hand, which
in the photograph seems tense
and strong, is less sure.

It is
the right hand? Yes, it is still
lean, and larger now;

enough to hold this small boy's hand
within it, like a son's,

perhaps to reassure him, as I do not
my own sons, who are not yet born.
Across the grey garden

stand some men; I do not know them.

Nor, I think, does he. But they stand firm,
a terrible simplicity
which will disappear. So, too, the other,
unknown, as far from him

as my living self, who again
clicks the shutter.

He did not know it would reach this far.

But it's not real, the boy,
myself, looking out at me but not seeing,

and the garden, which never grows.
Good friend, believe me,
here I am, perhaps your best intention;

my hand can hold now your entirely small body.
I can love you;
you are the friend's son, myself,

to whom I speak and listen.

(Jon Anderson, "The Photograph of Myself")

The Father/Mother Poem

It seems that every poet, at one time or another, has had cause to look back at his or her origins in the form of parents, upbringing, and environment, and written a father/mother poem. There's probably more blame than praise in this subgenre of poem that comes in all forms. In Robert Mezey's poem below he uses the **letter poem** form (from the mother to her son) to portray what his speaker has to put up with in terms of the stereotypical Jewish mother.

My Mother

My mother writes from Trenton,
a comedian to the bone
but underneath serious
and all heart. 'Honey,' she says,
'be a mensch and Mary too,
its no good, to worry, you
are doing the best you can
your Dad and everyone
thinks you turned out very well
as long as you pay your bills
nobody can say a word
you can tell them, to drop dead
so save a dollar it can't
hurt—remember Frank you went
to highschool with? he still lives
with his wife's mother, his wife
works while he writes his books and
did he ever sell a one
the four kids run around naked
36, and he's never had
you'll forgive my expression
even a pot to piss in
or a window to throw it,
such a smart boy he couldn't
read the footprints on the wall
honey you think you know all
the answers you don't, please, try
to put some money away
believe me it wouldn't hurt
artist shmartist life's too short
for that kind of, forgive me,
horseshit, I know what you want

better than you, all that counts
is to make a good living
and the best of everything,
as Sholem Aleichem said,
he was a great writer did
you ever read his books dear,
you should make what he makes a year
anyway he says some place
Poverty is no disgrace
but its no honor either
that's what I say,
love, Mother'

(Robert Mezey, "My Mother")

The Erotic Poem

From the ancient Indian book on sexual positions and technique, the *Karma Sutra,* to today's explicit art shows, films, and literature, poems of erotica have held a time-honored, if often censored, place in the history of art. In the following poem by Thea Temple, she creates an inventive tension between, on the one hand, very contemporary language-slinging, puns, jumpy rhythms, and subject matter and, on the other hand, the decorative, rhyming sonnet form.

Modern Love

Tonight, we swig tequila shots and smoke
Hawaiian, playing sperm roulette. Two days
from now, I zoom above Ohio Hills,
and leave behind "La Belle de Rivières,"
that curvey, corkscrew path to New Orleans.
We argue, voices rising jazz-like, scenes
that whine for sax-play . . . but we put on airs.
I'm drunk. And sad. I talk about the bills
of platypuses, slurring into ways
they copulate. We're both drunk, so you joke,
not knowing what this means to me. I stroke
your penis, changing subjects. "Monotremes
don't mate for life?" you say, parting my limbs;
they're limp. From gills to girls, love's based on whims.

(Thea Temple, "Modern Love")

The Work Poem

Most work poems describe blue-collar work as opposed to office work, maybe because of the more concrete, interesting, and physical nature of the workplace and its tools and machines. Typically in these poems, the poet uses physical detail in service to some higher thematic purpose, such as the inhuman conditions, the ruthless efficiency and scale of the machinery, or the driving forces behind capitalism. Yusef Komunyakaa's poem below selects imagery from the saw mill that make it seem to the child-speaker's mind like a vision of hell.

Temples of Smoke

Fire shimmied & reached up
From the iron furnace & grabbed
Sawdust from the pitchfork
Before I could make it across
The floor or take a half step
Back, as the boiler room sung
About what trees were before
Men & money. Those nights
Smelled of greenness & sweat
As steam moved through miles
Of winding pipes to turn wheels
That pushed blades & rotated
Man-high saws. It leaped
Like tigers out of a pit,
Singeing the hair on my head,
While Daddy made his rounds
Turning large brass keys
In his night-watchman's clock,
Out among columns of lumber & paths
Where a man & woman might meet.
I daydreamed some freighter
Across a midnight ocean,
Leaving Taipei & headed
For Tripoli. I saw myself fall
Through a tumbling inferno
As if hell was where a boy
Shoveled clouds of sawdust
Into the wide mouth of doubt.

(Yusef Komunyakaa, "Temples of Smoke")

The Place Poem

Richard Hugo, who invented a term called the **triggering town,** often uses places that he would visit once. After absorbing selected details, he would pretend he was a long-time inhabitant of the place and describe details of it in order to get at an inner, psychological state by way of external environs. He felt using too well-known places couldn't allow the imagination to free itself. Here is one of Hugo's place poems that illustrates his method.

Degrees of Gray in Phillipsburg

You might come here Sunday on a whim.
Say your life broke down. The last good kiss
you had was years ago. You walk these streets
laid out by the insane, past hotels
that didn't last, bars that did, the tortured try
of local drivers to accelerate their lives.
Only churches are kept up. The jail
turned 70 this year. The only prisoner
is always in, not knowing what he's done.

The principal supporting business now
is rage. Hatred of the various grays
the mountain sends, hatred of the mill,
The Silver Bill repeal, the best liked girls
who leave each year for Butte. One good
restaurant and bars can't wipe the boredom out.
The 1907 boom, eight going silver mines,
a dance floor built on springs—
all memory resolves itself in gaze,
in panoramic green you know the cattle eat
or two stacks high above the town,
two dead kilns, the huge mill in collapse
for fifty years that won't fall finally down.

Isn't this your life? That ancient kiss
still burning out your eyes? Isn't this defeat
so accurate, the church bell simply seems
a pure announcement: ring and no one comes?
Don't empty houses ring? Are magnesium
and scorn sufficient to support a town,
not just Phillipsburg, but towns

of towering blondes, good jazz and booze
the world will never let you have
until the town you come from dies inside?

Say no to yourself. The old man, twenty
when the jail was built, still laughs
although his lips collapse. Someday soon,
he says, I'll go to sleep and not wake up.
You tell him no. You're talking to yourself.
The car that brought you here still runs.
The money you buy lunch with,
no matter where it's mined, is silver
and the girl who served you food
is slender and her red hair lights the wall.

(Richard Hugo, "Degrees of Gray in Phillipsburg")

The Object Poem

The object poem, similar to the place poem (except in scale), requires careful looking at and into the characteristics of an object, and then thinking about associated ideas behind the making or use of the object. In Louis Simpson's poem below, the technical advances made to a common and innocuous object in the name of convenience turn out to have a false bottom in our hallowed vision of human progress.

The Ice Cube Maker

Once the ice was in a tray.
You would hold it under a faucet
till the cubes came unstuck, in a block.
Then you had to run more water over it
until, finally, the cubes came loose.

Later on, there was a handle you lifted,
breaking out the ice cubes.
But still it was nuisance—
in order to get at one ice cube
you had to melt the whole tray.

Then they invented the ice cube maker
which makes cubes individually,
letting them fall in a container

until it is full, when it stops.
You can just reach in and take ice cubes.

When her husband came home he saw that she was drunk.
He changed into an old shirt and slacks.
He stared at the screen door in the kitchen . . .
the screen had to be replaced.
He wondered what he was doing. Why fix it?
(Louis Simpson, "The Ice Cube Maker")

SPECIFIC TYPES OF POEMS EXERCISE

Try your hand at writing the following specific types of poems.

1. **Childhood poem:** Write a poem that features vivid images, events, people, and experiences that you remember from your childhood. Don't be afraid to mix in imagination and felt-thought.
2. **Fable:** Using animals as characters to soften your didacticism, write a morally instructive tale that makes an incisive point about human nature.
3. **Myth:** Thinking about the origin or creation of things, or of how things in the world came to be the way they are, create a colorful story that explains this and that employs extraordinary settings and characters with special powers.
4. **Folktale:** Write a narrative poem about some bit of oral folk wisdom passed down by your family or community in which some aspect of human nature or behavior is explained or cautioned against.
5. **Classic syndrome:** Think of one of the many snafus typical in our modern culture and write a poem that explores the ethical and moral aspects of that situation.
6. **Fairy tale:** Write a contemporary version of a well-known fairy tale that incorporates, in disguised form, your own personal experience.
7. **Cultural icon:** Think of a cultural icon (such as Uncle Sam, G. I. Joe, or a Barbie doll) and see if you can subvert its usual symbolic meaning by creating a new context and perspective from which it is viewed.
8. **Political poem:** Write a poem that contains a political or social message, but one that is couched in concrete imagery and personal experience.

9. **Photograph/split-self:** Take an old photo of yourself, and then:
   a. Write down what is *objectively* there in the photo (who's there, where it is, why you're there, when it was, etc.). You might also include any physical characteristics of the photograph itself (its borders, sepia tone, scalloped edges, general square or rectangular shape, etc.).
   b. Allow in personal, *subjective* material accessed from memory, associations, ambiance of the age or time of day, and anecdotes, fantasies, and any flashbacks that come to mind.
   c. Then take a more recent photo of yourself and go through the same two-step process. When this is done, you can either act as an omniscient narrator between the two selves in the photo, or have one photo speak to the other.
10. **Painting:** Using a painting as your subject matter, write a poem that either explains or completely changes the original artist's vision and meaning.
11. **Letter:** Write a prose poem to someone you know well, using the conventions of the letter form, that tries to explain or express something that would be very difficult to express in person.
12. **Dream:** Write a poem that uses the imagery, irrational logic, and heightened emotion of a dream, and in the poem see if you can grasp some new insight into the dream.
13. **Rite of initiation:** Think of an initiation ceremony (formal or informal) that someone made you go through in order for you to become part of some group, and then write a poem about it that addresses its purpose, its excesses, or some other aspect of the ritual.
14. **Rite of passage:** Think of some event or experience (formal or informal) that, looking back upon it, seems to have been a doorway to a new stage in your life, and then write a poem about it that expresses what it felt like for you.
15. **Special moment:** Think of a moment or fleeting experience from your past that has come to represent something ineffable and yet emotionally indelible for you, and then write a poem that expresses that.
16. **Father/mother:** Write a poem that portrays some aspect of your mother or father and that employs a good deal of his or her phrasings, imagery, and tone.
17. **The erotic:** Write a poem whose purpose is to evoke some sensual or erotic moment you have experienced or can imagine.

18. **Work:** Write a poem that portrays some kind of work or workplace and that uses lots of concrete imagery and sense details.
19. **Place:** Write a poem about a specific place that has come to have symbolic and/or psychological meaning for you. Use this place to stand in for the state of mind or attitude you've ascribed to it.
20. **Object:** Write a poem that carefully describes selective aspects and/or functions of some object, and then for your closure leap away from the object and make a conclusive statement about the human condition.

CHAPTER

7

Opening, Closing, Titling

OPENINGS

"Making it interesting" should be, if not an overriding rule, at least a primary consideration when opening a poem. The beginning of a poem, like anything in life that has the power to grab and hold our attention, should somehow earn our attention through the effects it creates, the way it's structured, or how and what it says. The opening, occupying the position that it does, is the second most important part of a poem, the closure or ending being the first. An opening should have the force of interest that a first impression has when meeting someone new. It might contain suspense, a striking image or **juxtaposition,** a spring-bound rhetorical or syntactical construction, a compelling insight, a fascinating or outrageous viewpoint or **tone,** a paradoxical or enigmatic set of ideas, or a conclusive bit of wisdom. Whether the logic and **thematic shape** of a poem move in an inductive, deductive, circular, dendritic, litany-like, centripetal, or centrifugal way—whether or not the opening lines set up the subsequent strategy—the opening should somehow at least make us want to read the poem.

In recent times, the advent and preeminence of the lyric-narrative or story-poem tends to have slacked off in this regard, probably because the burden of having to carry the baggage of time, place, setting, character, and plot have made interest and economy secondary considerations. On the other hand, the lyric and dramatic forms, by their very nature, inherently tend to escape the problem of boredom or supplying mere information.

Since good openings, as opposed to endings, are easier to discern without having to read the entire poem, it's a good idea to peruse the openings of poems or the first lines index in a few good anthologies for ideas. Simply put, what will interest you as a writer will interest your reader.

The poet Michael Waters, in an essay from *The Practice of Poetry,* comments on the generating power opening lines have stored in them as potential energy, when he says:

> A good opening line triggers a series of responses, additional lines that surge forward like ocean swells, unstoppable. Suddenly the poet is swimming with possibilities, anxious to chart each direction. Working alone, the poet might free-associate, jotting down line after line without regard for narrative continuity, logic, or craft. Simply allow whatever comes to mind to find its way onto the page. Then consider each line—its evocations, its particular music. Which line crooks its finger to beckon? In which line have you already begun to immerse yourself?

Types of Openings

THE OUTRAGEOUS OPENING

When mother died
I thought: now I'll have a death poem.
(Stephen Dunn, "The Routine Things around the House")

THE FANTASTICAL OPENING

Today, the angels are all writing postcards,
Or talking on the telephone.
(Robert Long, "Saying One Thing")

THE RHETORICAL OPENING These kinds of openings are basically **fill-in-the-blanks** units in which the rhetorical structure of the sentence supplies the "clothesline" from which you hang words and ideas. The following are examples of the "if . . . then" or "As if . . ." construction (see p. 237).

If Freud was right and dreams of falling are
dreams of having fallen **then** you must have been
the beautiful declivity of that hill, Raoul. . . .
(Lynn Emanuel, "On Waking after Dreaming of Raoul")

* * *

As if my answering machine were a rejection,
you'd leave your forlorn message.
(Gail Mazur, "Phonic")

PARALLEL AND BALANCED AND SYNTAX

I know a little
about it: I know
if you contemplate suicide
long enough, it
begins to contemplate you—
(Franz Wright, "Certain Tall Buildings")

CAMERA SHOTS AND ANGLES

Red-and-green leather helmeted
maniacally grinning motorcyclists
crash at all angles
on Lev Smith's pajama top
(Michael Ryan, "TV Room at the Children's Hospice")

THE CONCLUSIVE OPENING

About suffering, they were never wrong,
The Old Masters: how well they understood
Its human position
(W. H. Auden, "Musée des Beaux Arts")

FOCUS ON SUBJECT

I think continually of those who were truly great.
(Stephen Spender, "I Think Continually of Those Who Were Truly Great")

DIALOGUE

"Terrence, this is stupid stuff:
You eat your victuals fast enough . . ."
(A.E. Housman, "Terrence, This Is Stupid Stuff")

THE DRAMATIC SITUATION OPENING

I heard a Fly buzz—when I died –
(Emily Dickinson, poem # 465)

THE INDEFINITE REFERENCE OPENING

Not while, but long after he had told me,
I thought of him, washing his mother, his
bending over the bed and taking back
the covers.
(Tess Gallagher, "Each Bird Walking")

CONTRARIES

My son asks
why he should go to sleep
just to wake up.

THE PARADOXICAL (OR OXYMORONIC) OPENING

What does not change
is the will to change
(Charles Olson, "Maximus")

THE TRADITIONAL FORM OPENING

THE LIMERICK:	There once was a lady from Kent.
THE FABLE:	Once upon a time
THE ALLUSION:	In the Beginning, there was the Word.

THE IMAGISTIC OPENING

Whatever they said, those ten foot lips pouting across
the screen at the Den Rock Park Drive-In . . .
(Richard Jackson, "A Violation")

THE TONAL OPENING

The holy light of loneliness
shines within a single cell
(Cynthia Huntington, "Breaking")

THE COMPARATIVE OPENING

Simile

Suddenly seeing you again was
like the time you dumped ice down my back.

Metaphor

Language was any
funny money I was playing with
(Heather McHugh, "Inflation")

THE DESCRIPTIVE OPENING

Undeodorized and radiant in rags
she squats sullenly
(Adrian Louis, "The First of the Month")

THE HYPERBOLIC (EXAGGERATED) OPENING

Bulldoze the bed where we made
(Heather McHugh, "Earthmoving Malediction")

THE STATE-OF-BEING OPENING

I wanted to die so I walked
the streets. Dead night,
black iris, cold as the toes
on a barefoot drunk
(Lorna Dee Cervantes, "Colorado Blvd.")

OPENINGS EXERCISE

Practice creating a series of interesting openings to a poem you've already written by making its opening, by turns, 1) one that is outrageous, 2) one that is fantastical, 3) one that poses a contradiction or paradox, and 4) one that employs balanced and parallel syntax. In other words, try imitating the various model openings in this chapter.

CLOSINGS

Closure as Foundation

Without a doubt, the most important part of a poem is its closure (and the same holds true for the end-word in a line). It is the foundation, intersection, and place of confluence where all the narrative, expositional, descriptive, argumentative, dramatic, and/or lyric elements previously prepared by the poem converge. Its quality or character, depending upon the needs of the poem, can be static, fluid, resonant, epiphanic, or transformational. This—aside from the blank white page—seems to be one of the most feared parts of the compositional process, probably because of what student-poets sense is the ambition, scope, and achievement of its task. But practiced poets have been able to hone their "ear," in this case, the kind of poetic sense that is skilled in the simultaneous and delicate job of firmly controlling the direction and flow of theme and content, on the one hand, while, on the other hand, relaxing control and letting go to allow the poem itself, as if it were a living, multiconscious probe, to generate its own direction, content, shape, and conclusion.

The complementary qualities that most practitioners try to arrive at in forming a closure are surprise and a sense of inevitability. The surprise in the content or insight should be organically arrived at through the **discovery mode,** the "How-Do-I-Know-What-I-Think-Until-I've-Said-It" method of impromptu exploration. The sense of inevitability isn't the quality of predictability, but the apprehension of an order of inner and outer perfected form which our senses of aesthetics, intuition, and logic make us feel when something has been organically and fully completed. It goes without saying that unlike openings, in order to judge whether or not a closure is effective, one must read the entire poem.

Closure Supplying Resonance

Resonance is a quality of interpretive richness that arrives as a constellation of levels of meaning, sense impressions, and emotional, linguistic, and intellectual associations in a work of art. Its lends depth, a sense of inner spaciousness, and the altered sense of time that capital "T" Truth creates. Although it's not the one and only kind of closure that good poems feature—sometimes one wants a simple, refreshing piece of fruit instead of a French meal—it is prized for its harmonic complexities and richness. Let's look at some common types of resonant endings.

EASTERN AND WESTERN ENDINGS Generally speaking, there are two opposite, yin/yang qualities of closure that probably relate more to a poet's aesthetic sense and character than to anything technical in nature, although a poem's subject and theme will have a bearing on the style of closure chosen. One could easily think of them as being masculine and feminine in character: the active, external, aggressive, linear **Western ending;** and the receptive, curvilinear, inward-directed **Eastern ending.** The story about the Roman general and the Persian general meeting before they do battle is illustrative of the difference. The Roman general, with a great show of force, threatened his enemy by unsheathing his broad sword and smashing a chair into pieces with it. "We will crush you like that!" the Roman general roared. In reply, the Persian general simply smiled, unsheathed his razor-sharp scimitar, took a silk scarf, threw it up into the air, and let the piece of silk cut itself in two as it fell over the sword. In terms of closure, the up-front power and brute force of the Roman general is called the **Western ending,** because cultures of the West tend to use this kind of overtly dramatic ending, often relying on artistic use of hyperbole, overstatement, striking imagery, the clash of ironies, and other devices and rhetorical strategies that lend a sense of drama, impact, and finality to the poem. Poems that employ this style of dramatic closure are completed when the last word in the poem has been read. Former Poet Laureate Robert Hass, in writing about listening to language, said:

> In *A Zen Wave,* Robert Aitken's book about [the great Japanese poet] Basho, he observes that the Japanese customarily wave until a departing guest has disappeared from sight. We [Westerners] are more likely to turn away before that happens, not so much erasing the other person as turning inward, toward our own separateness, and getting on with it. [The Japanese poet] Buson doesn't do that; he lets the moment define itself, lets distance speak.

One could well argue to what degree a closure is representative of the Western or Eastern sensibility, but the categories are useful touchstones in thinking about the affective qualities of closure.

WESTERN ENDINGS All of the following Western endings, whether simply or complexly fashioned, feature the offering of a knowledge made available by way of the poet who has gone considerably more than halfway in preparing explicit and accessible material for the reader.

Slam Bang Ending

I want to dig you up and say, look,
it's like the time, remember,
when I ran into our living room naked
to get rid of that fire inspector.

See what you miss by being dead?
(Ruth Stone, "Curtains")

Focuses a Question Rhetorically speaking, concluding a poem by asking a question is a very dramatic and effective means of forcing focus on an issue. In Mark Halliday's poem below, the warring struggle between the flesh and the spirit, between what is given and what is sought, between ordinariness and specialness, converges sardonically in the final line's questions.

Seventh Avenue

Late Tuesday afternoon the romantic self weaves
up Seventh Avenue amid too many lookers, too many
feelers: romance hates democracy;

how can *you* be so great and golden inside
if your trunk is shouldered among other trunks
block after block, block after block—

you can't help glimpsing an otherness in others
that is not just surface: they ache,
their aches ache away north and south all Tuesday

in murmurous torsos like yours . . .
What apprehension blossoms even now in Manuel
shifting steaks at the ten-foot grill of Charley O's

beneath the towering chef's hat they make him wear?
When I was twenty I'd have written
that he was only thinking of Cadillacs and sex;

now I'm afraid he's just as worried as I am
about love vs. lesser things and the point of it all.
Manuel, stay there at the sizzling grill till midnight

and then just drink or sleep, man,
don't write poems—
do me that favor. It's loud enough already

out here on Seventh Avenue with the cat's boombox
and these three giggle girls being Madonna together
and that guy hawking wind-up titans wielding laser lances.
Who's Wordsworth for any extended period on Seventh Ave?
In this predusk traffic you catch the hint
that Manuel and thou if seers at all are seers only

for seconds—now the steak, taxi, buttocks, headline
and wallet resume their charismatic claim to be what counts.
Soul on Seventh is a sometime on-off quick-flip thing. . .

What I want is a poem long as Seventh Avenue
to sprinkle gold on every oppressed minority,
every young woman's subtly female hips,
every sad and suspicious American face
and the quiddity of every mud-tracked pizza shop;
proving, block after block, stanza by stanza
that I'm not just one skinny nervous pedestrian
but the one who matters because he sees and says.
I want that. The Avenue grins and says
"You want that? How does it feel to want?"
(Mark Halliday, "Seventh Avenue")

Resolves an Argument In Andrew Marvell's time-honored **proposition poem** "To His Coy Mistress," he enjoins his mistress to seize the day by not giving into propriety but exploiting their brief time of youth together by making love while the bloom of youth's sexual vitality urges them on. Following are the opening four and closing fourteen lines of the poem (see the entire poem on p. 207). The **heroic couplet** of the last two lines holds the resolution and rationalization of his argument.

Had we but world enough, and time,
This coyness, lady, were no crime.
We would sit down, and think which way
To walk, and pass our love's long day.

* * *

Now therefore, while the youthful hue
Sits on thy skin like morning dew,
And while thy willing soul transpires
At every pore with instant fires,

Now let us sport while we may,
And now, like amorous birds of prey,
Rather at once our time devour
Than languish in his slow-chapped power.
Let us roll all our strength and all
Our sweetness up into one ball,
And tear our pleasures with rough strife
Through the iron gates of life:
Thus, though we cannot make our sun
Stand still, yet we will make him run.
(Andrew Marvell, "To His Coy Mistress")

Offers a Final Knowledge In Larry Levis' title poem to his book *Winter Stars,* he addresses the seemingly irreconcilable distance between a father and his son. In the last seven lines of the poem, he speaks of this impasse in relation to his sense of the inhuman, mocking distance and emptiness of the cosmos and eternity. And so, safely by the indirection of objective logic, he offers to make peace with his father. The last section begins:

When I left home at seventeen, I left for good.

That pale haze of stars goes on & on.
Like laughter that has found a final, silent shape
On a black sky. It means everything
It cannot say. Look, it's empty out there, & cold.
Cold enough to reconcile
Even a father, even a son.
(Larry Levis, "Winter Stars")

Enriched Restatement A very common kind of Western closure concludes by making an enhanced or enriched restatement on another level of what the poem's content has already said in a variety of other ways. Michael Decker's poem below, a version of the **list poem** whose strategy of the **retake** performs variations on a situation or condition, is a strong example of this type of closure.

The Tour Guide

Take me, they say, to see the impossible,
        The faraway falls,
Those raining voices of hush beyond

The highest groan of a tour bus, see
        Some magic obelisk,
A worn dictionary of words which fully

Decline meaning, or some grove of Buddhas
    Sitting fatly on one
Big secret. They all want lunch too

Early: nouvelle unseen up the Seine, or
    To be hotelled back
By two and dream of some imaginary

City where love is served in bed by
    A divine waiter. No
Wonder they're even hungry

In the presence of a Tiepolo or Fuseli,
    And tea time some
Give me that look, a Guide whose

Every door opens the way to more
    Of less, relentlessly
Turning foreign corners in white pursuit

Of a hot thought escaping like a rabbit.
    They *are* the impossible —
The single girl still urgently so,

The agnostic dressed with nowhere up
    To go, a burnt-out
Linguist translated into lost,

The pure gleamers whose compromise
    Is to grasp my arm
Hard like this and say Take me.

(Michael Decker, "The Tour Guide")

Self-revealing This is a very common kind of closure in contemporary poetry, although it wasn't so, not in such an intimate manner, before the breakthrough in the arts in the 1950s. In Bruce Weigl's poem "A Romance," the insomniac, macho speaker is willing to risk a brawl, self-delusion, and the clichés of trying to pick up a woman in a bar in order not to feel alone. In the poem's closure, we see that speaker, helpless and unconscious as he appears, is not at all unaware of the plight he has put himself into, like men everywhere. Here are the last, revealing seven lines.

I don't sleep anyway so I go to bars
and tell my giant lies to women
who have heard them from me,
from the thousands of me
out on the town with our impossible strategies
for no good reason but our selves,
who are holy.

(Bruce Weigl, "A Romance")

Completes a Trope Very common in poetry throughout the ages is the closure that explores and manipulates an apt **trope,** whether it's a **controlling metaphor, extended metaphor, hyperfigure,** ***idée fixe,*** or, as in the following example, a **symbol.** Barry Goldensohn's speaker imagines, with at first a refreshing guiltlessness and later with a degree of high apprehension, the rarefied atmosphere of purity and truth in an afterlife in which the former civilized restraints of sexual, cultural, psychological, and biological proprieties have been erased. In their stead, we will find ourselves, as true and cold as mathematics, "Buried with open eyes in a dreamless order."

Post Mortem as Angels

When we meet then after death we will merge
easily, without the forced reserve
of our betraying bodies, the great routine
or the restraint with which we kept ourselves, alive.
There will be no husband then, or wife.
We will be all truth. Nothing to defend,
not one boundary. We will be one great friend.
No drama of discovery, nothing left to find.

We'll be so bored. Dissolved, the high theatre,
costumes, spooky music, uncovered letters,
devoted love jealous of him or her,
the reassuring masks we tried to wear
flung together in the backstage mirror.
We're buried with open eyes in dreamless order.

(Barry Goldensohn, "Post Mortem as Angels")

The Ironic Comment **Irony,** a play on words in which reality is poised against the appearance of reality, is as staple a device in poetry as bread and butter is to a meal. It deals with the nature of contraries, **paradoxes,** opposites, and duality, qualities of life that are fundamental to our experience of the world. While the strength of irony is its conveyance of surprise, revelation, and complexity, its weakness as a device for the poet lies in replacing profundity with merely being clever. In Gerard Manley Hopkins' "Spring and Fall," its wise and ironic closure arrives in the form of a psychological truism (concerning the Jungian principle of "projection") quite ahead of its time.

Spring and Fall

TO A YOUNG CHILD

Margaret, are you grieving
Over Goldenrod unleaving?
Leaves, like the things of man, you

With your fresh thoughts care for, can you?
Ah! as the heart grows older
It will come to such sights colder
By and by, nor spare a sigh
Though worlds of wanwood leafmeal lie;
And yet you *will* weep and know why.
Now no matter, child, the name:
Sorrow's springs are the same.
Nor mouth had, no nor mind, expressed
What heart heard of, ghost guessed:
It is the blight man was born for,
It is Margaret you mourn for.
(Gerard Manley Hopkins, "Spring and Fall")

The Double Dilemma Based upon the rhetorical model of the double dilemma, this kind of "Catch-22," "lose-lose" situation lends itself very well to the compact, epigrammatic style. Here's a particularly intriguing example from Jack Gilbert, who uses the famous Indian cautionary tale of "The White Elephant" (see **poetization**, p. 208) to warn against the "gift" of being a poet.

In Dispraise of Poetry

When the King of Siam disliked a courtier,
he gave him a beautiful white elephant.
The miracle beast deserved such ritual
that to care for him properly meant ruin.
Yet to care for him improperly was worse.
It appears the gift could not be refused.
(Jack Gilbert, "In Dispraise of Poetry")

The Reversal An example of reversal can be found in Tomas Tranströmer's poem "Allegro," where he constructs a metaphorical definition of the effects of music as a house of glass on a hill where stones fly, but the glass house of music, because of its eternal and transcendent quality, remains unbroken.

The Misdirecting Ending This type of closure seems to come as a surprise out of the background of the poem, and yet for all its nonsequitur-like feel, is appropriate because it touches the thematic horizon line of the poem. Here is an example from Stephen McNally.

Mysteries

The child in the well
wasn't saved, despite their floodlights

and their pulleys, their tears, every effort
was in vain. I kneel by the spot, now covered
and circled with flowers. What do I want here,
why did I drive five hours out of my way
to stare at this tragedy—no, this circle of flowers?
Tragedy is something we feel, it's in us,
not in the ground, or the clouds which float by
giving the same look to everything. I walk
around the other side of the circle,
hoping no one's seen me. And what would they care?
They've seen it all, have nothing else to say,
especially to a stranger. In the lunchroom
the waitress's face is a blank and the locals talk low.
They know why I came, as I knock over my water
and a farmer shoots me a look. The waitress touches
her white rag to the table and wipes it up with a smile
and not one damn word about the little girl who died.
(Stephen McNally, "Mysteries")

The Throwaway Ending The throwaway ending, like a shaggy-dog story, begins with the promise that something of interest will develop, but then just sort of drops off or slams into a brick wall. Here's an example poem that illustrates the closing gesture.

Before we arrived in the Arctic
I bet my friend the first thing we'd see
would be vast tracts of ice and snow,
but, of course, there was a blizzard and
we couldn't see a foot ahead
so that was that.

The Double Ending The double ending differs from a closure with repeating lines (see p. 271) in that it has two separate endings, as in Stanley Kunitz's poem "The Portrait," which creates a double, reflected ending. The first ending, a **plot point,** occurs when the speaker is slapped in the face by his mother, and the second ending occurs when the speaker closes the poem with the comment that he can still feel his cheek burning.

EASTERN ENDINGS Obversely, the **Eastern ending,** characteristic of Asian, African, and some other non-Western cultures, employs the subtler effects of understatement, restraint, nuance, and implication, and is completed in the reader's mind after the last word in the poem has been read. Following is a good example of the reverberating, meditative quality of the Eastern ending.

Sometimes I go around pitying myself
and all the while
I am being carried on a great wind.
(anonymous Ojibway poem)

Inward Folding One of the subtler kinds of "moving" closures is one that folds inward and back into the poem and requires the reader to partner with the poet in completing its content by having to connect up strategically placed implications in the poem. In Naomi Shihab Nye's beautiful and compassionate poem, "Rain," a criticism on a common kind of rigidity and narrow-mindedness in secondary education, the closure in the last three lines begins with an image originated in an earlier simile and completes itself in the reader's mind in the form of symbolic prophecy.

Rain

A teacher asked Paul
what he would remember
from third grade, and he sat
a long time before writing
"this year sumbody tutched me
on the sholder"
and turned his paper in.
Later she showed it to me
as an example of her wasted life.
The words he wrote were large
as houses in a landscape.
He wanted to go inside them
and live, he could fill in
the windows of "o" and "d"
and be safe while outside
birds building nests in drainpipes
knew nothing of the coming rain.
(Naomi Shihab Nye, "Rain")

The Description The aim of this kind of poem is simply to accurately and acutely describe something. In the example on the following page by Kate Daniels, the post-coital scene is described, purposefully and ironically, in the unblinking, concrete terms of sensual override. The closure does not move away from but further into the poem's **hyperfigure** of cleanliness that splits the two characters into opposite states of mind, after having made a kind of loveless physical love making.

Bathing

He always bathed afterwards,
slipping his fine and sticky
genitals over the cool rim
of the porcelain sink.
She lay in the other room
smoking and staring tiredly
out the window. The tiny sounds
of the suds came to her
worrisomely. The *suck-suck*
sound of his hand lathering
soap into his tight, dark curls.
Then the farewell groan of the drain.
The energetic flap of the towel.
When he was before her again,
his teeth covered by a smile,
the sweat and stench removed,
she studied him from the crushed
bed, admiring his cruel
beauty, her body still marked
and odorous. His, clean
and unstained, amnesiac
already.

(Kate Daniels, "Bathing")

The Definition The aim of this subcategory of endings is to define or name a condition, state of being, event, or experience. Again, the challenge inherent in this kind of straightforward strategy is to transform the closure so that its mode of perception differs in quality from that of the body of the poem. Consider the reverberating ending of Morton Marcus' narrative in his **prose poem** about the relationship between a boy and his grandfather.

The Moment for Which There Is No Name

On the sixteenth floor of one of the tall old buildings in the north end of the city, the windows of a vacant apartment look out over the bay. The apartment is empty, the floors and walls bare. There is only a chalked circle on the living room floor. The circle traces the spot where an armchair once stood, an armchair in which an old man regularly sat watching the smokestacks come and go in the harbor in the same way he had watched the swaying forests of masts when he was a boy, years before he became a bookkeeper for one of the city's three tool and die works.

The circle was drawn by the old man's grandson, while the child's parents were supervising the movers.

Tomorrow the new occupants will arrive, and preparatory to moving in they will clean the apartment. In the course of their cleaning, they will erase the chalk.

That is the moment for which there is no name.
(Morton Marcus, "The Moment for Which There Is No Name")

The Paradox One of the great, memorable "tiny" poems of the last half of the twentieth century has to be W. S. Merwin's "The Room," in which he is able to portray the soul and its character.

The Room

I think all this is somewhere in myself
The cold room unlit before dawn
Containing a stillness such as attends death
And from a corner the sounds of a small bird trying
From time to time to fly a few beats in the dark
You would say it was dying it is immortal
(W. S. Merwin, "The Room")

The Symbolic Image This sort of closure, very common in Eastern poetry, ends with a symbolic image that holds psychological, spiritual, emotional, and/or intellectual levels of meaning inside it. While the danger of its use, as is true of almost all "easy" kinds of techniques and forms, is the relative ease with which almost any poem can employ this kind of closure, its real achievement, when accompanied by authentic insight, is that of creating an indelible image that holds a rich emotional complex inside it. Michael Ryan's poem, below, has just such a discovered image in its closure.

TV Room at the Children's Hospice

Red-and-green leather-helmeted
maniacally grinning motorcyclists
crash at all angles
on Lev Smith's pajama top

and when his chocolate ice cream
dumps like a mud slide down its front
he smiles, not maniacally, still nauseous
from chemotherapy and bald already.
Lev is six but sat still four hours

all afternoon with IVs in his arms,
his grandma tells everyone. Marcie
is nine and was born with no face.

One profile has been built in increments
with surgical plastic and skin grafts
and the other looks like fudge.
Tomorrow she's having an eye moved.

She finds a hand-mirror in the toy box
and maybe for the minute I watch
she sees nothing she doesn't expect.
Ruth Borthnott's son, Richard,

cracked his second vertebra
at diving practice eight weeks ago,
and as Ruth describes getting the news
by telephone (shampoo suds plopped

all over the notepad she tried
to write on) she smiles like Lev Smith
at his ice cream, smiles also saying
Richard's on a breathing machine,

if he makes it he'll be quadriplegic,
she's there in intensive care every day
at dawn. The gameshow-shrill details
of a Hawaiian vacation for two

and surf teasing the ankles
of the couple on a moonlit beachwalk
keep drawing her attention
away from our conversation.

I say it's amazing how life can change
from one second to the next,
and with no apparent disdain
for this dismal platitude,

she nods yes, and yes again
at the gameshow's svelte assistant
petting a dinette set, and yes
to Lev Smith's grandma

who has appeared beside her
with microwaved popcorn
blooming like a huge
cauliflower from its tin.

(Michael Ryan, "TV Room at the Children's Hospice")

The Conclusive Statement As a type of effective closure, the typical, slam-bang **conclusive statement** is familiar to readers of Western poetry from Roman to contemporary times, although this kind of didactic certainty is becoming less common in contemporary poetry. Here's an example of closure with a conclusive statement, from the last seven lines of Bruce Weigl's "The Confusion of Planes We Must Wander in Sleep," in which the rhetorical thrust of the closure rings with a sense of finality but because the closure is composed of an implied summary of previous content, some complex insight, a bit of philosophy, and the authority of a final irony offered as instructive wisdom, the poem continues on in the Eastern fashion for some time in the reader's mind.

and something makes sense for once in my head,
the way that what we pass on is not always a gift,
not always grace or strength or music, but sometimes
a burden and that we have no choice but to live as
hard as we can inside the storm of our years and
that even the weaknesses are a kind of beauty
for the way they bind us into what love, finally, must be.
(Bruce Weigl, "The Confusion of Planes We Must Wander in Sleep")

The Narrative Spiral This is the kind of spiral movement literally ends up where it began, only on another level, and is the sort of plotted trick of meaning for which *The Twilight Zone* was famous. There's a limited kind of resonance achieved through a kind of double understanding or consciousness, so that although beginning and end are exactly the same, David Lehman has made sure his *film noir* narrative below provides two different levels of knowledge in them, one a Chaplinesque innocence, the other the knowledge of hell. The spanish word *perfidia* means "lost."

Perfidia

You don't know who these people are, or what
They'll do to you if you're caught, but you can't
Back out now: it seems you agreed to carry
A briefcase into Germany, and here you are,
Glass in hand, as instructed. You rise to dance
With the woman with garnet earrings, who is,
Of course, the agent you're supposed to seduce
And betray within the hour. Who would have known
You'd fall in love with her? Elsewhere the day
Is as gray as a newsreel, full of stripes and dots
Of rain, a blurred windshield picture of Pittsburgh,
But on the screen where your real life is happening

It is always 1938, you are always dancing
With the same blonde woman with the bloodshot eyes
Who slips the forged passport into your pocket
And says she knows you've been sent to betray her,
Or else it is seventy degrees and holding
In California, where you see yourself unscathed
From the car crash that wiped out your memory,
Your past, as you walk into a gambler's hangout
On Sunset Boulevard, in a suit one size too large,
And the piano player plays "Perfidia" in your honor
And the redhead at the bar lets you buy her a drink.
(David Lehman, "Perfidia")

The Circular Closure Nature's favorite form seems to be the circle, the return; and in literature the narrative, theme, or argument that curves back full circle to where it began is also a favorite form. Mark Strand's metaphysical understanding of the human condition, below, is a rarefied example of a subject in flashback returning to itself by way of definition-by-narration.

The Idea

For us, too, there was a wish to possess
Something beyond the world we knew, beyond ourselves,
Beyond our power to imagine, something nevertheless
In which we might see ourselves; and this desire
Came always in passing, in waning light, and in such cold
That ice on the valley's lakes cracked and rolled, . . .
And blowing snow covered what earth we saw,
And scenes from the past, when they surfaced again,
Looked not as they had, but ghostly and white
Among the false curves and hidden erasures;
And never once did we feel we were close
Until the night wind said, "Why do this,
Especially now? Go back to the place you belong;"
And there appeared, with its windows glowing, small,
In the distance, in the frozen reaches, a cabin;
And we stood before it, amazed at its being there,
And would have gone forward and opened the door,
And stepped into the glow and warmed ourselves there,
But that it was ours by not being ours,
And should remain empty. That was the idea.
(Mark Strand, "The Idea")

The Revelatory Plot Point Ending Just as in the convention of detective- genre fiction and film, oftentimes the work ends by supplying a missing, reshaped, or revealing piece of plot. Here is a particularly striking example of this from Jack Gilbert.

Married

I came back from the funeral and crawled
around the apartment, crying hard,
searching for my wife's hair.
For two months got them from the drain,
from the vacuum cleaner, under the refrigerator,
and off the clothes in the closet.
But after other Japanese women came,
there was no way to be sure which were
repotting Michiko's avocado, I find
a long black hair tangled in the dirt.
(Jack Gilbert, "Married")

In Medias Res* Ending** The conventional application of the term ***in medias res usually refers to a literary work that begins in the middle of the action. But in categorizing closures, there's a definite place for the literary work that ends in the middle of an action in order to make a point. In the instance below, Tess Gallagher leaves off her poem with the speaker in the middle of an unusual action accompanied by an unresolved, emotional dislocation.

The Hug

A woman is reading a poem on the street
and another woman stops to listen. We stop too,
with our arms around each other. The poem
is being read and listened to out here
in the open. Behind us
no one is entering or leaving the houses.

Suddenly a hug comes over me and I'm
giving it to you, like a variable star shooting light
off to make itself comfortable, then
subsiding. I finish but keep on holding
you. A man walks up to us and we know he hasn't
come out of nowhere, but if he could, he
would have. He looks homeless because of how
he needs. "Can I have one of those?" he asks you,

and I feel you nod. I'm surprised,
surprised you don't tell him how
it is—that I'm yours, only
yours, etc., exclusive as a nose to
its face. Love—that's what we're talking about, love
that nabs you with "for me
only" and holds on.

So I walk over to him and put my
arms around him and try to
hug him like I mean it. He's got an overcoat on
so thick I can't feel
him past it. I'm starting the hug
and thinking, "How big a hug is this supposed to be?
How long shall I hold this hug?" Already
we could be eternal, his arms falling over my
shoulders, my hands not
meeting behind his back, he is so big!

I put my head into his chest and snuggle
in. I lean into him. I lean my blood and my wishes
into him. He stands for it. This is his
and he's starting to give it back so well I know he's
getting it. This hug. So truly, so tenderly
we stop having arms and I don't know if
my lover has walked away or what, or
if the woman is still reading the poem, or the houses—
what about them?—the houses.

Clearly, a little permission is a dangerous thing.
But when you hug someone you want it
to be a masterpiece of connection, the way the button
on his coat will leave the imprint of
a planet in my cheek
when I walk away. When I try to find some place
to go back to.

(Tess Gallagher, "The Hug")

The Leaping Closure Robert Bly describes **leaping poetry** as quick movements from one level of consciousness to another and back again without the aid of explicit context or transitions. In the following poem by James Wright, notice how the last line of the poem leaps levels of consciousness and shifts in rhetorical tactics from surreal imagery to flat statement.

Lying in a Hammock at William Duffy's Farm in Pine Island, Minnesota

Over my head, I see the bronze butterfly,
Asleep on a black trunk,
Blowing like a leaf in green shadow.
Down the ravine behind the empty house,
The cowbells follow one another
Into the distances of the afternoon.
To my right,
In a field of sunlight between two pines,
The droppings of last year's horses
Blaze up into golden stones.
I lean back, as evening darkens and comes on.
A chicken hawk floats over, looking for home.
I have wasted my life.

(James Wright, "Lying in a Hammock at William Duffy's Farm in Pine Island, Minnesota")

The Broken-off Ending This kind of Eastern ending is an "open" ending, or, basically, a non-ending. It is meant to function in the way that the punctuation of ellipses dots indicates an ongoingness, a missing conclusion or **plot point,** or, as in the example below by Mark Spencer, an aspect of character.

Detenshun

Inkblot, interesting
500 written questions, boring.

Hi my name is Elizabeth
I used to go to Vial Elementary
Do you remember me? That girl
Michele is in here too, and Chip's x-girl.

Angela's dad won't tell me where she lives.
You have her pager number, which I think
Is turned off.

I should get out of here real soon
Cause I'm being real good now.

I've been thinking of a poem:

Do you think of me as much
As I think of you?
Just out of the blue?
We have gone different ways

But soon it will be different.

Well, it was better when I thought of it
But I couldn't write it down.

How do you like Mr. Berry's comb-over?
(Mark Spencer, "Detenshun")

The Plunging Closure The experience of abruptly falling down to the thematic "bottom line" in a poem can be as aesthetically exhilarating as its physical equivalent. Louis Simpson recapitulates "progress" in the history of the invention of the ice cube maker in order to make an unexpected and profound point.

The Ice Cube Maker

Once the ice was in a tray.
You would hold it under a faucet
till the cubes came unstuck, in a block.
Then you had to run more water over it
until, finally, the cubes came loose.

Later on, there was a handle you lifted,
breaking out the ice cubes.
But still it was a nuisance—
in order to get at one ice cube
you had to melt the whole tray.

Then they invented the ice cube maker
which makes cubes individually,
letting them fall into a container
until it is full, when it stops.
You can just reach in and take ice cubes.

———

When her husband came home he saw that she was drunk.
He changed into an old shirt and slacks.
He stared at the screen door in the kitchen . . .
the screen had to be replaced.
He wondered what he was doing. Why fix it?
(Louis Simpson, "The Ice Cube Maker")

The Repeated Line Closure The repeated line closure is not meant as a mere repetition of the same words and meaning, but, ironically, as a repetition of the same words with new levels and domains of meaning. In Robert Frost's perhaps most famous poem, "Stopping by Woods on a Snowy Evening," the repeated last two lines have literal and figurative, factual and spiritual levels in them.

Stopping by Woods on a Snowy Evening

Whose woods these are I think I know.
His house is in the village though;
He will not see me stopping here
To watch his woods fill up with snow.

My little horse must think it queer
To stop without a farmhouse near
Between the woods and frozen lake
The darkest evening of the year.

He gives his harness bells a shake
To ask if there is some mistake.
The only other sound's the sweep
Of easy wind and downy flake.

The woods are lovely, dark and deep,
But I have promises to keep,
And miles to go before I sleep,
And miles to go before I sleep.
(Robert Frost, "Stopping by Woods on a Snowy Evening")

Entrance to New Domain In William Hathaway's pastoral poem below, an idyllic and innocent scene suddenly opens onto whole new territory in its closure.

Oh, Oh

My girl and I amble a country lane,
moo cows and chomping daisies, our own
sweet saliva green with grass stems.
"Look, look," she says at the crossing,
"the choo-choo's light is on." And sure
enough, right smack dab in the middle
of maple dappled summer sunlight
is the lit headlight—so funny.
An arm waves to us from the black window.
We wave gaily to the arm. "When I hear
trains at night I dream of being president,"
I say dreamily. "And me first lady," she
says loyally. So when the last boxcars,
named after wonderful, faraway places,
and the caboose chuckle by we look
eagerly to the road ahead. And there
poised and growling are fifty Hell's Angels.
(William Hathaway, "Oh, Oh")

CLOSINGS EXERCISE

Here is a poem whose closing four lines have been deleted. Through close and careful reading, see if you can anticipate the general direction and content of the closures (given below). Also, go on to other poems you haven't read and see if you can guess their closures.

Word-Game

by Betty Adcock

A child watching a moonrise
might play a game of saying,
might hold the word moon in his mouth
and push it out over and over.

To make a sound like a fruit
repeat itself in the tongue's tree
is to forget what you know.
The word will grow, will cease
to be saying, will turn by itself
into tears into flesh into burning.

What rides in the sky will be free
of any name that the earth has heard
as though someone had severed a string.

[closing four lines are missing]

Answer

"Word-Game":

In a net of sound like the body's
own singing web, a child
will be rising
with light for language.

TITLING

Aspects of Titles

Titles aren't just names. This section is called "the act of titling" because giving a poem a title doesn't merely name it, but involves the same creative, thinking-through process that the body of the poem itself requires. Many poems use the title as a unit of meaning that functions in terms of naming the subject and, possibly, implying the plot of what follows within the body of the poem; but these are only two very limited functions within the arena of uses and types of titles that poets use (or sometimes, with reason, purposely ignore). In fact, because of the often freighted, resonant, multileveled connotative meanings subtly embedded in and around titles, this topic might well be considered last in this book, since only the body of a poem is what creates, elaborates, makes resonant and apparent the imaginative thinking that's embedded inside a title's surface meaning.

The basic functions of titles are to orient the reader and highlight some aspect of content. Titles can be created, pondered toward, or simply "arrived" at before, during, or after the composing process. Typically, most titles are conceived after a poem has been written because from this vantage point, as if the writer had secured the high ground, he or she has the best view from which to survey the work that the poem has done.

Titles point our attention toward or away from the poem, and on, above, or below its surface meaning. The character of its expression can be literal, denotative, figurative, or abstract in nature. Any of these can occur in combination.

General Types of Titles

1. **TAKING IT EASY.** The following kinds of titles don't require much invention.
   - **The self-evident title:** While most poets agree that a poem without a title is like a body without a head, traditionally, many poets have opted to forego the potential of adding meaning by creating a title and have simply entitled their work what it obviously is, as if you named your dog "Dog." Charles Bukowski has a poem entitled "What's the Use of a Title?" Emily Dickinson and Shakespeare simply numbered their poems. The poet Alan Dugan has so many poems entitled "Poem" that one wonders if in his labeling there isn't something more than meets the eye. So, in keeping with this kind of rebellious or noncommittal spirit, you could call any poem you wrote, "Poem."
   - **The literal title:** These titles merely name the subject or generally call attention to some obvious aspect within their subject matter. Some poets feel this is sufficient enough as a title, and opt to let the poem be and do the work. Other poets feel this is a lazy way to entitle a poem, that an

opportunity to apply further creativity has been lost in not treating the title with as much respect and attention as the poem itself receives. At the risk of belaboring the obvious, examples of this kind of title are (from well-known poets): Ben Jonson's "On My First Son," Gerard Manley Hopkins' "God's Grandeur," Wallace Stevens' "Sunday Morning," Langston Hughes' "The Weary Blues," and William Wordsworth's "Lines Composed a Few Miles above Tintern Abbey."

Another common form of the literal title is the **occasional** title, which announces its reason for composition, as in Robert Bly's ungainly but exacting "After Drinking All Night with a Friend, We Go out in a Boat at Dawn to See Who Can Write the Best Poem," or James Wright's well-known "Lying in a Hammock at William Duffey's Farm in Pine Island, Minnesota."

- **Titles taken from lines in the poem:** Poems are often titled after one of their lines, often the poem's last line. Sometimes there are particularly resonant, memorable, or deeply implicating lines or phrases in the body of the poem, lines that will give enriched meaning to returned readings of the title.
- **The formal title:** This names the form or genre of the poem, as in Federico García Lorca's great poem in honor of the slain Spanish matador Ignacio Sanchez Mejia, "Lament for the Death of a Bullfighter," and Allen Tate's "Ode to the Confederate Dead."

2. **SERVICEABLE TITLES.** This kind of title requires only a moderate amount of creativity and thinking.
   - **The naming title:** This is the sort of title that states the theme of a work, as in Charles Bukowski's volume of poems about his autobiographical tribulations called *War All the Time,* and Stephen Spender's "I Think Continually of Those Who Were Truly Great."
   - **Titles that capture a character or quality:** These focus on a particular trait that is highlighted, as in the movie *The Untouchables,* which is about the incorruptibility of Elliott Ness and his FBI men. Literary examples include Frost's famous poem, "For Once, Then Something," which combines both the poem's last line and the focus on an **epiphany;** W. H. Auden's ironic title for the twentieth century's anonymous man, "Who's Who"; Ralph Ellison's political work on being black in America, *Invisible Man;* Richard Hugo's "Degrees of Gray in Phillipsburgh"; Allen Ginsberg's *Howl;* and Etheridge Knight's *Copacetic.*
   - **The symbolic title:** Because of their prominent position at the head of the poem, these titles raise what may be a literal image to the connotative level of a symbol, as in Frost's "The Road Not Taken," Eliot's "The Wasteland," W. S. Merwin's "The Room," Sylvia Plath's "The Colossus," William Carlos Williams' "The Yachts," and Robinson Jeffers' "The Purse-Seine."

- **The apostrophe (or address) title:** These titles address someone or something, or dedicate themselves. Examples are Denise Levertov's *O Taste and See,* Andrew Marvell's "To His Coy Mistress," and Robert Burns' "To a Mouse."

3. **INVENTIVE TITLES.** This kind of title has obviously had a good deal of creativity and thought put into it, and the process of arriving at it requires much the same kind of inventive energy involved in working out the poem.
   - **The associative title:** This kind of title "thinks off the page" or "outside the box" in that it's meant to add to the poem a new dimension in meaning, tone, imagery, or a completely different domain of thought. It is often tangential or oblique in its angle of intersection to the body of the poem. It is a challenging title to derive and interesting for the reader who will make the connection, cross the associational space, or **leap** between what implied work the title and poem do. For instance, if a poem is about your love of your old car, it might be titled from the realms of slang and cliché, as in "If It Ain't Broke, Don't Fix It." Or a title could be taken from the announcement that flight attendants make when a plane is about to go on to its next connection, as in Maxine Kumin's "Our Ground Time Here Will Be Brief."
   - **The layered title:** This is the kind of poem whose title at first seems to be an almost simplistic naming, but takes on multiple levels of meaning after one reads through the poem. In Linda Pastan's poem "A Real Story," her title alludes to six kinds of stories being told: (1) the flashback to the days when the grandfather told his stories; (2) the story in the present of the grandfather's declining years; (3) the biblical past of the analogy to King David and Abishag; (4) the future life-after-death story of the chickens; (5) the story of the grandfather's refusal to tell the hard truth about death; and (6) the poem itself as a story.

A Real Story

Sucking on hard candy
to sweeten the taste
of old age,
grandpa told us stories
about chickens,
city chickens sold
for Sabbath soup
but rescued at the end
by some chicken-loving
providence.

Now at ninety-five,
sucked down
to nothing himself,
he says he feels
a coldness;
perhaps the coldness David felt
even with Abishag
in his bed
to warm
his chicken-thin bones.

But when we say
you'll soon get well,
grandpa pulls the sheet
over his face,
raising it between us
the way he used to raise
the Yiddish paper
when we said
enough chickens
tell us a real story.
(Linda Pastan, "A Real Story")

- **The plot title:** In the following poem by Philip Schultz, the title plays an integral and surprising part in completing the poem and supplying full closure to it.

**A Letter Found on a January Night
in Front of the Public Theatre**

Dear Emily Permutter,

Today I read how good you are as Nina
and even Chekov couldn't be so proud
but hearing from me must be a shock
since your grandma said I died from TB
on Ellis Island (if she was alive she'd spit
three times!) but better you should know
the truth and maybe forgive me. I had TB
but my brother Izzy was the one who died.
They wouldn't let him in (imagine after
all our grief being sent back to Russia!)
and after weeks in detention he cut his wrists

on a sardine can (others did the same but used
fancier methods). I'm not making excuses but
life on the Lower East Side was no piknic.
Thousands on each block ate herring and crackers
without a cracked pot to piss in and I wasn't
twenty (and so green my first banana I ate peel
and all and was insulted to eat corn—in Russia
we fed it to pigs!) when grandma had your mother
and day and night we sewed crotches for pennies
the uptown Germans paid (may they eat steak in Hell!).
My cousin Sam broke hands—two bits a knuckle—
and put his own sister on the street (where she didn't
sell pickles!) so maybe it's better not to judge
what you haven't suffered . . .

Your photo in the *Times* shows your grandma's eyes
but I'm afraid you have my mouth that made me
so much trouble always insulting the wrong person.
Like you I was an actor but maybe my most famous role
is wife-deserter. After two years in the Yiddish Theatre
I went to Hollywood but with my bad English (a Campbell
soup can I couldn't read without stuttering) got only
extra work and ended up selling plastic legs
after I lost my left one making bombs against Hitler
(one mistook me for a Nazi?). But never I stopped
writing tho your grandma sent back only fishhooks
(not that I blame her—she wiped the blood I coughed
in steerage and fed me her rations eight months pregnant!)
but believe me I've been punished. God put me in this
welfare home for retired actors where each night
lights-out means an encore. When they're not singing Sinatra
they're dancing on my head like Fred Astaire—at least
they keep trying! But failure can be a demanding mistress
and now that you know success early I pray you remember
Nina's lines—"What matters is not fame, not glory . . .
but knowing how to have faith." Talent isn't always
sympathetic so please don't make TV commercials or
hide behind your beauty. Emily, I've written you
maybe a thousand letters but shame isn't postage
and even if you can't forgive me I hope you won't mind
if I'm always in the front row clapping. Be strong

and honest (thank God you didn't change your name!)
and there's nothing you can't accomplish. Darling,
your black hair is so outspoken I break glasses.

With respectful admiration,
Lewis Pearlmutter

(Philip Schultz, "A Letter Found on a January Night in Front of the Public Theatre")

TITLING EXERCISE

1. **The symbolic title:** Locate in one of your poems an image, object, action, figure of speech, or abstraction that could contain and stand for multiple aspects of your poem's theme.
2. **The associative title:** Holding in mind the general subject matter and theme of one of your poems, think associatively away from its specific content and see if you can come up with a new domain from which you can create an interesting title which, upon first glance, seems at a great distance from the poem at hand.
3. **The layered title:** Go back through several poems you have written and find one that contains a phrase that at first glance appears to simply name the subject or theme of the poem but which, in light of the poem's content and upon further reflection, gathers much deeper significance and more complex levels of reference.

CHAPTER

8

Revision

Without a doubt, the most common attitude of inexperienced poets is the notion that revision, as opposed to the inspired headiness of composing the first draft, is work: proofreading, substituting vocabulary, re-ordering plot elements, etc. Perhaps that idea stems from the old adage: "Writing is 1% inspiration, 99% perspiration." Aside from some cultures and schools (such as Native American and some Eastern traditions, and adherents to the Surrealists' **automatic writing,** in which the act of focused attention in revision is seen as a violation of a sacred gift or an operation that violates the workings of the unconscious), 99.9% of all poets revise either on the page or in their head. As the name implies, revision means to "re-vision," to see again, and that can and should be as engaging, creative, and richly rewarding as drafting the first version of a poem. On the subject of practice, on the other hand, here's a well-known anecdote about the great golfer Jack Nicklaus that Richard Hugo builds advice on.

> Once a spectator said, after Jack Nicklaus had chipped a shot in from a sand trap, "That's pretty lucky." Nicklaus is supposed to have replied, "Right. But I notice the more I practice, the luckier I get." If you write often, perhaps every day, you will stay in shape and will be better able to receive those good poems, which are finally a matter of luck, and get them down. Lucky accidents seldom happen to writers who don't work. You will find that you may rewrite and rewrite a poem and it never seems quite right. Then a much better poem may come rather fast and you wonder why you bothered with all that work on the earlier poem. Actually, the hard work on the first poem is responsible for the sudden ease of the second. If you just sit around waiting for the easy ones, nothing will come. Get to work.

Just in terms of word choice, invention, and the task of naming, we don't have to look beyond our own bodies to consider the poverty of our language: for example, what is the name for the place where thigh meets belly; the name for the valley where your nose meets your face; is there a name for "the back of the knee"? What are the names for the difference between the silence of an empty attic and that of an empty stadium? Why don't we have names for different varieties of love—the love we feel for a grandparent as opposed to that for a puppy—for the different kinds of thrills: the thrill of a long fall vis à vis the thrill of opening a present? John Wisdom, in his *Paradox and Discovery,* said: "we are without means to refer to any state of affairs for which there is not a word." The poet can use time-honored tropes and cliches to refer to the intellectual and contextual meaning of something, but often the origins of these devices, which contained a level of richness beyond their meaning, is lost. For example, a distracting or misleading direction in any argument may be named a "red herring," but nowadays who knows why that image is apt? (Actually, it's derived from the practice of drawing a red herring across a trail in order to divert the attention of the hounds.) Creative revision continually invents and refreshes the language so that it's age-appropriate.

Generally speaking, there are two kinds of revision commonly used by poets. Poets who tend to overwrite in their early drafts use the **reductive revision** method, in which the content of the poem is reduced, distilled, and then made unified and coherent. Poets who tend to underwrite use **additive revision,** in which content, details, and lateral literal and figurative moves are added. And, of course, one can also revise from aspects of tone, point of view, persona, and more.

REDUCTIVE REVISION

Here's a combination of the first two, handwritten, original drafts of Sylvia Plath's poem "Thalidomide," which deals with the horrific fetal deformities produced by the anti–morning sickness pill thalidomide prescribed to and taken by pregnant mothers in the 1950s. In the drafts, with Plath's cross-outs and restarts, are the editor's guesses as to what she might have been thinking during the revision process. Looking over the drafts, it becomes apparent that her hallmark leaps of thought and imagery are as much a function of what she has deleted as they are symptoms of her vivacity of mind. By cutting out transitions, editorial comments, subordinate details, and the **laddering** of logical steps from one image to another, she creates a work with a great deal of verve and authority.

Half-Moon

	O half-brain luminosity! Negro, masked like a white,
	All night your dark
Already implied	Amputations crawl ~~sly,~~ & appal
	Spidery, unsafe,—
Lateral elaboration outside poem's domain	~~The zoo's bird-eater, that abortion~~ big

Deletes logical	~~That abortion!~~
development &	~~Hair-legged big man.~~
goes for a leap	~~As the man's hand—what glove~~
	What glove
	What leatheriness
	Has protected
	Me from that shadow!—
Reverse-overlap that	~~That absence, that turned back!~~
slows the poem down	The (?) buds
	Awful, indelible
	Knuckles at shoulder-blades
	And the flower faces
Adjustment in rhythm	~~Shoving~~ that shove into being, dragging
	The lopped
Too explicitly moral	Blood-caul of ~~guilt~~ absences.
	~~O Carpenter!~~
	I carpenter
Redundant	~~What~~ all night, ~~at my woodwork~~
Better sense	I ~~mark~~ make a place in the heart
Plodding,	For the thing I am given;~~ the (?) bloodclot~~
serial	
progression	~~The suicide, the idiot~~
	Two blue eyes and a screech,
	The wrong side of the moon & ~~The teeth that hurt~~
A series of attempts	~~And~~ the teeth that hurt
	The swell of perilous slumber.
to define,	
	~~The moon's backside,~~
describe,	~~The smell of perilous slumber.~~
and evaluate	Smiles, & perfections, ~~a slumber~~
	~~Perilous, thin—as an eyelid.~~
the accidental crime	A slumber of accident & indifference
	You turn & turn
and result	
	Perilous, ~~Thin as an eyelid.~~ Dark Fruit!
	~~An eyelid, a pane of ice~~
	~~leaf~~
	O unholy light,
	of accident & indifference
	~~Though it turns & turns~~

Child's eyelid,
Reversal ~~A leaf of ice!~~
White spit Nothingness! Black ox!

Half-Moon
The dark fruits revolve and fall.
Editorial comment ~~It is a sin that cries~~
~~Through the cracked glass~~

O moon smoke,

Unholy light!
Speeds up processed image The glass ~~warps & cracks across,~~

The image
Flees & aborts like dropped mercury.

Final version of "Thalidomide"

Thalidomide

O half moon—

Half-brain, luminosity—
Negro, masked like a white,

Your dark
Amputations crawl and appal—

Spidery, unsafe.
What glove

What leatheriness
Has protected

Me from that shadow—
The indelible buds,

Knuckles at the shoulder-blades, the
Faces that

Shove into being, dragging
The lopped

Blood-caul of absences.
All night I carpenter

A space for the thing I am given,
A love

Of two wet eyes and a screech.
White spit

Of indifference!
The dark fruits revolve and fall.

The glass cracks across,
The image

Flees and aborts like dropped mercury.
(Sylvia Plath, "Thalidomide")

REDUCTIVE REVISION EXERCISE

Take a poem you have written and, with an eye toward saying the same thing but using fewer words through implication, go through it carefully to weed out the following.

1. unnecessary modifiers
2. lazy or inactive verbs
3. overly obvious transitions
4. noncontributing narrative and plot elements
5. excessive uses of prepositional phrases
6. unnecessary editorial/authorial comments
7. aspects of overly obvious logical development

By paying close attention to these basic grammatical and structural aspects of the poem, larger and subtler ideas for editing the poem will come to mind.

ADDITIVE REVISION

This type of revision is typically more difficult because it requires generating new content in the form of tropes, analogies, and the opening up of larger frames of reference. Here are early and late versions of a poem. The early version attempts a pure cinematic presentation without commentary, interpretation, exposition, time/space frames, or other surrounding context.

Small Front Yard Scene

The child swirling face up
in her mother's arms
is pretending she's making

the clouds and sky
into a bowl of blue frosting.

Mother is making her long hair
fly around straight out
from her daughter's
squeal of glee.

Father seems to be heaping
dead leaves and laughter
into a barrel, but he is making more
and more room for more.

Here is a version some 20 drafts later in which the small family scene is (1) given both a specific time/space context; (2) supplied with a larger archetypal framework; and (3) has the previously absent or characterless speaker interact with the scene being observed.

Suburban Archetypes: A Miniature

I'm patiently waiting for my ex to drop off
my son for his weekly overnight, annoyed
at how the woman whose poems I'm reading
made her life into tangled clumps of abstract art.

It's interesting how boredom makes me look up
into this empty cliche of a Norman Rockwell still-life:
Small American Family Raking Leaves.

How, like Bugs, when I draw a trap-door in it
and pull the lever: Mother's a runaway merry-go-round
making her hair fly around her daughter's squeals of glee.
And Baby's whirling face-up, sky-high in her mother's arms
folding
pale blue food coloring and a meringue of clouds into a bowl of
blue
frosting. Father's heaping dead leaves and laughter into a barrel
he
jumps into and emerges pleased
he magically made room for more.

Then it dawns on me, these are archetypal symbols:
Mother twirling the child inside for lunch in little epicycles
like a skater; Father, bending down for a last armful of leaves,
instinctively glancing back to make sure they got in,

how if I weren't my own cartoon and had looked up just now,
I'd only see Father standing in a barrel of trash looking back

at a closed door I'd think was nothing; then me, projecting my
needs onto this day's blank screen, in commiseration at how
one time
long ago and far away that was me.

ADDITIVE REVISION EXERCISE

Take a poem you've written, which you sense could use further development and enrichment, and look for places of opportunity where you could create new content that does the following.

1. adds meaningful images, tropes, characterizations, and plot elements
2. supplies a larger narrative framework for the event
3. adds apt flashbacks or flashforwards
4. adds a telling anecdote that has a bearing upon the larger dramatic situation
5. adds commentary or statements that bring events to a higher level of meaning

DEEP REVISION

Bracing Yourself for Revision

The poet Lynn Emanuel wrote a wonderfully stringent and clarifying essay on revision entitled *In Praise of Malice: Thoughts on Revision.* Her perspective dealt with the necessity of being true to your real feelings, your imagination, and faithful to the rendering of the subject. Parts of it are included here because workshops, by their cooperative nature and semi-intellectual place in the writing of poetry, tend to smooth out the sometimes raw and rough edges of the retelling experience.

> I want to talk about the unacknowledged assumptions that inform our models of revision, to acknowledge that these assumptions make revision an almost impossible task.
>
> In revision we come face to face with ideology. If we imagine, in the initial composition of a poem, that we have free will, that we are saying what we want rather than what a culture both permits and demands, then it could be said that when we come to revision that illusion falls away. Most of us, I think, feel reprimanded. We have been unclear, sentimental, boring. And we have been. Mostly we've been boring. And orderly. And well mannered.

The first unacknowledged assumption from which we write is that of good manners. Good manners is the first thing to give up—at least in the imagination—in order to revise.

Here is a topic that we write about all the time—death. Let's say that grandmother has died. Good manners dictate that that one show grief and regret. In most of our poems death makes someone part of the great minority of the underprivileged. One does not speak ill of the disadvantaged. One does not make fun of those turned out of the home of flesh and sentience. And yet there are wonderful writers who do just that. Take for instance Nazim Hikmet's great poem *Human Landscapes.* It is a hugely rude work. It is breathtakingly un-Christian and profoundly uncharitable. It is also passionately compassionate. And wildly intelligent. Because in Hikmet's poem the poor are wicked, they are not worthy of our pity. They will not tolerate it. The poor are not the salt of the earth, they are not transformed by suffering, they persist in appalling human warty ugliness. They are hateful.

Human Landscapes is an indecorous and brilliant poem.

My suggestions for revising the poem that deals tenderly with grandmother's death might begin "This poem is not rude enough and, therefore, it is not smart enough." Because let's face it, this tender and pious poem doesn't really want for the human to swell up into palpability. It wants to be polite and get a B, even when it is written by oneself. It wants to go to the video arcade and hang out. And so it should.

That is why I think that most suggestions for revision—begin with the last stanza, write it as a *persona* poem, write it from a different point of view—are really evasions, ways of not thinking about what one is doing. Such recommendations are palliatives. I recommend brutality and simplicity. I recommend not loving one's own grief too much and, instead, having the courage and charity to put that old woman into the poem. That old woman who was cruel and sexual. That woman and her appalling and unbearable body and humanity, her bravery, her integrity, and her horrible prejudices and small-spiritedness toward the suffering of others. . . .

And so grandma has died. Generally, in the beginning of the poem, it will be raining. Let us say that we bring out from the dust cover of the clouds and polish with our tears a bare tree. We are now in desperate trouble. There is, in fact, no poem left to write. . . . The sun that enters the poem becomes a "contrast." It represents Hope. The sun is a hankie. . . .

At the bare tree, one could draw a line across the page and say "the poem ends here." I recommend that kind of act as a good way to begin a revision: amputate your ache, do not heal it. I recommend that one begin, instead, with a malicious celebration of grandma's death, telling every naughty secret one can invent. . . . I recommend lying and cheating one's way toward the finish line, tripping and elbowing all those dull runners in their costly gear—Love, Respect, Sorrow. . . .

As long as we try to be good, we cannot revise. . . .

(Lynn Emanuel, "In Praise of Malice: Thoughts on Revision")

Deep Revision

Elly Clay, a poet and former New York publishing house freelance copy editor, offers the following description of **deep revision** or **re-envisioning,** the type of revision that, in spirit and method, most closely resembles the original "green light session" of our first draft:

> A more radical kind of revision, sometimes called **deep revision** or **re-envisioning,** takes a different approach to the work than the standard, even extensive, revision practice this chapter covers. Re-envisioning is radical in two ways—it may result in a poem whose appearance on the page is so different that it is not immediately recognizable as revision of an earlier version; and, even more slippery for our linear, analytical, critical, minds, it may require a radical shift in thinking before the poet can allow the re-envisioned version to emerge. Re-envisioning asks that you stand far enough back that you cannot clearly see the poem in front of you—you must hold very lightly onto that version, with an almost conscious blindness or blurring (like squinting in order to see the forest and not the trees). In this state, you can return to a point in the process *after* you were aware of the urge to write the poem, but *before* you gave it particular shape, form, sound, and/or meaning on paper.
>
> Once you find that state, you can allow the poem, or the necessity of the poem, to develop a wholly different shape, form, sound, and/or meaning, one that may get closer to what it seems to want to say. The largest obstruction to the kind of revision is the resistance to letting go, at least temporarily, of the deeply embedded belief that the form a poem takes inside the words on paper has a sacredness, an audible heartbeat, that must be preserved. Re-envisioning requires a willingness, an eagerness, to throw away. As the poet Judith Skillman said in a 1999 lecture on revision: "It's not until you take the piece apart, cut out most of it, or throw it away altogether and attack your subject from a wholly different perspective, form, or point of view, that the deep process of revision has a chance to kick in."
>
> The often restricting Western mind's approach to revision, which often values product over process and likely views that poem as a word machine, tends to look solely for information, methods, actions, applications, practical advice, exercises, quick fixes like a cut-and-paste reorganization, something to *do*. But the often more liberating and organic Eastern approach to revision, which usually values process over product, asks the poet to remain open to listening to the poem itself, to what the *poem* (metaphorically as a living organism) is saying, to the poem as an open system and process that has the ability to *self-organize* while maintaining a stable state, much as our body over each seven-year period replaces all its cells.

Revising as Part of the Titling Process

The decision-making process that goes into creating titles can be as multifarious and self-selecting as the poems themselves. In some cases, the search for a title can cause the author to revise the poem extensively. Here it is useful to look at the worksheets of one poem and, by noting the types of revisions in each draft of the poem, resurrect the possible decisions that the author made in working toward his final title. As we will see in Robert Francis' poem, one of the major considerations in creating a title is the element of literary and interpretive balance. Does the title hold enough of the poem within itself? Does it focus its attention on the main thrust of the poem, or does it consider something minor in the poem? Reviewing Francis' poem "The Hawk" will shed some light on this delicate and difficult process.

In the first eight drafts of the poem, Francis doesn't concern himself with titling it. He concentrates on portraying the diving attack of a hawk with its eerie cry, and then begins a new theme by asking rhetorical questions: Why does the hawk scream? And whose scream is it, really?

Draft I April 5, 1946

Who is the hawk whose squeal
Is like a child's toy wound
And suddenly let loose in whirling wheels?
And why this warning sound
When silence would be deathlier?
But why ask why or whose

The last question in the poem appears to be an instance of the poem quarreling with itself, the poem thinking and sorting things out loud. In later drafts this question loses its direct function of asking the poet to answer, and becomes rhetorically oriented toward the reader.

Draft II (same day)

Who is the hawk whose squeal
Is like a child's toy wound
And suddenly let loose
In disengaging wheels?
And why this warning sound
When none would be deathlier?

And why? Why any sound
When none would be deathlier?

* * *

Who is the hawk whose squeal
Is like a child's toy wound
And suddenly let loose
In disengaging wheels?
And why the warning? Why
The silent wings, the cry?

Any

In the subsequent, third draft, Francis has a better grip on his argument; and then he begins to change the music of his poem by substituting new phrases for the death-dive of the hawk. At this point, he tentatively focuses on the second section of his poem, and titles it with the metaphysical questions, "Who? Why?"

Draft III (same day)

WHO? WHY?

Who is the hawk whose squeal
Is like a child's toy wound
Then
suddenly let loose

In disengaging wheels?
And why this warning cry?
          sound
Why any cry at all
since   in
When death does its best to fall ing

Silent if not unseen?

That evening, Francis makes some finer adjustments in the rhythm and sound of his poem, and tightens its organization. But at this point, he seems not to be concerned with titling the poem.

Draft IV (evening)

Who? Why?

Who is the hawk whose squeal
Is like the shivering sound
Of a too-tightly wound
Child's toy that slips a wheel?

And why the warning cry?
Why any sound at all
Since death does best to fall
Silently from the sky?

You may have noticed that the poet has imposed **end-rhyme** in an abba **rhyme scheme,** and that he has now identified the hawk as death or an agent of death so that it has become a **symbol** in the poem. In his fifth draft, a few minor changes are made: the word "sound" is substituted for "cry" in the second stanza, possibly so that it will echo the word "sound" in the first stanza and thereby relate the hawk more closely with death. And the word "the" is underlined in the second stanza, a reminder by the poet to himself that the word "a" might be a better choice. He also makes a few word changes in the seventh line.

Draft V (same evening)

Who? Why?

Who is the hawk whose squeal
Is like the shivering sound
Of a too-tightly wound
Child's toy that slips a wheel?

And why the warning cry?
sound
Why any ~~cry~~ at all
Since death has skill to fall
a
Silently from <u>the</u> sky?

Two days later, Francis scraps his title "Who? Why?" and leaves that place blank during the next few attempts. He substitutes the rhyme "wheel" for "reel," which cleverly implies both a wind-up reel in a child's toy and the concept of reeling in prey after it's hooked. In the second stanza, the first line is given more emphasis and momentum through word and sound changes so that the parallel theme of death is introduced dramatically.

Draft VI April 7, 1964
Suffern, N.Y.

Who is the hawk whose squeal
Is like the shivering sound
Of a too-tightly wound
Child's toy that slips a reel?

And since death
But Beyond the who is why?

Why any sounds at all
Since death has but to fall
a
Silently from <u>the</u> sky?
Soundlessly the

Who is the hawk whose squeal
Is like the shivering sound
Of a too-tightly wound
Child's toy that slips a reel?

Beyond who is why?
Why any cry at all

When death knows how to fall
Soundless from the sky?

In his seventh revision, Francis is caught between deciding which element of the poem he should focus on for his title: subject or theme. He uses both titles tentatively but later settles on the best one. Which of the following titles would you choose?

Draft VII **April 9, 1964**
Fort Juniper

The Hawk
and
~~Who? Why?~~

Who is the hawk whose squeal
Is like the shivering sound
Of a too-tightly wound
Child's toy that slips a reel?

But beyond who is why.
Why any cry at all
Since death knows how to fall
Soundlessly from the sky?

In his final revision of "The Hawk," Francis probably feels that his title contains everything he wants to get across: the subject of the poem, which acts as a symbol for the larger process of hunting and death. The formal organization of the poem into two four-line stanzas with an abba rhyme scheme seems straightforward and simple. But the metaphors and cross-identities underneath the poem's surface belie its seeming simplicity, which is summed up in the appropriately succinct title, "The Hawk."

Draft VIII

The Hawk

Who is the hawk whose squeal
Is like the shivering sound
Of a too-tightly wound
Child's toy that slips a reel?

But beyond who is why.
Why any cry at all
Since death knows how to fall
Soundlessly from the sky?

(Robert Francis, "The Hawk")

Revision Checklist

There are as many ways of approaching the process of revision and methods of applying it as there are types of poets: from the highly systematic, habitual, and ritualistic, to improvised *ad hoc* methods. And it probably should remain as mysterious as the creative process itself. When Hart Crane wrote his epic poem "The Bridge," he composed and revised while drinking Cutty Sark scotch and listening to Ravel's "Bolero"; John Keats, before writing, would bathe, powder, groom himself, and put on his best clothes, as if he were going out with a beautiful woman for a night on the town. And then there's the apocryphal story of W. H. Auden's having to have to have a shiny apple sitting on the left side of his desk before he felt comfortable. Each poet will develop whatever rituals and ceremonial accoutrements feel right for his or her purposes. Nevertheless, what follows are some suggestions, some common and some not so common, that go beyond the usual sort of basic and perfunctory considerations.

1. **Read the poem over and over** until you are patterned by what you have written, until you can just about memorize your poem. By locking yourself into the parameters of the world of your poem, you will gain the freedom (and lose the fear) to change what you have written. Also, snags and problems will appear more readily in contrast to the established overall flow of the poem. This paradox of imprisoning in order to free is the same principle of tension in a poem whereby a form, such as rhyming, creates a springboard toward generating wild content.
2. **Try not to complete a section** of the poem during the drafting and revising processes. Facing the formidable task of starting a new section or topic in the poem every time you sit down can be stultifying. Stop just before you know how you want to end a section and merely make notes toward possible options so you can freely pick up where you left off.
3. **Write early drafts in pen or pencil** until you gain a strong sense of the logical and aesthetic order of the poem. When it feels fairly formed, see what it looks like typed out. This way, you'll have allowed yourself maximum opportunity for invention before the form of the poem begins to assert its own control and close out creative options. Some poets, such as Richard Hugo, go so far as to suggest using a #2 pencil—because it has just the right amount of drag to keep in rhythm with one's thoughts. (Suggesting first using a pen or pencil to the computer generation might nowadays seem as atavistic and obsolete as suggesting using cuneiform tools. The point is to stage the formation of the poem through the drafting process.)

4. **View places where you get stuck as opportunities** to fall inside these sticking points and search that territory with questions and associative thinking. Sooner or later this will yield rich new directions and possibilities. The book *Zen and the Art of Motorcycle Maintenance* focuses on just this paradoxical concept.
5. **Examine the order and development of the logical relationships** between images and ideas (see **logopoetics,** pp. 52–59). In early drafts, these logical relationships will tend to be linear in nature. Begin to fuse and compress these serial elements into simultaneous and/or parallel orders so you create both richness and efficiency (see **recombinant syntax,** pp. 169–170).
6. **Notice that how after revising a line so it seems perfect,** the surrounding lines and even the shape of the whole poem will, by contrast, begin to show its flaws. Once you are conscious of these, the rest is just revising the work upward to the standard of that line.
7. **Beware of the orderly development of the poem,** because it tends to force and seduce you into clichéd and predictable types of endings. Check back with your original impulse for the poem, when you felt you "needed" to write it. This will help you break the poem's too stock and smoothed over surface so you can recapture the original impulse.
8. **Make a mental list of the function and content of each stanza** so that you have a sense of how they balance, design-wise and logically, with each other. This may result in a less creative, more consciously controlled kind of **additive revision,** but, at the same time, having given yourself the utmost freedom in your early drafts, your intuitive, creative side should be able to take orders from your more rational, reader-objective side.
9. **To create thematic endings,** pull back from the specifics of the poem in order to get a solid sense of its thematic strands, substrands, and **leitmotifs.** Then look at your line endings to see if you can more fully bring out, highlight, or nuance the poem's thematic content.
10. **Don't fall victim to old habits of voice, structure, or syntax.** Previous inventions may become fixed into "personal conventions," so you may end up imitating and limiting your own style. These routines of language, thought, and orders of logic tend to emerge from our ceremonial aspects of writing, and should at least be questioned.
11. **Put the poem in a drawer when you think you've finished** revising it. This is a way to become a new and objective reader of your own work, which is one of the most difficult perspectives to achieve for a writer. Then,

take it out when you've forgotten how it goes. Time (revision's sister) is the writer's second-best friend and one of the trade secrets in writing.

12. **Make sure you feel comfortable and at ease with your revising methods and mechanics.** You are the best and should be the sole judge of what feels right for you, even if it seems to take longer than "normal" amounts of time, or even if your rituals and methods might seem silly to others. Keep in mind that there are as many kinds, pacings, and stagings of revision as there are poets. Also keep in mind that although there certainly are aesthetic and craft standards and objectives, and technical means of ensuring a competent level of workmanship, the revising process is mostly empirical: if it works, then it's right.

DEEP REVISION EXERCISE

Take a poem you've already written and, in order to re-envision it in a new and more conscious light, try to follow the tips and guidelines.

1. Follow the **image narrative** (see pp. 67–70), rather than the usual linear logic or chronology of the "plot" narrative, looking and listening for an unexpected "story" or a tone different from what you have been working towards.
2. Track the pattern of Anglo-Saxon and Latinate words to discover whether there is unintentional conflict in your poem at the word level of etymology. If there is conflict, you may want to remove it *or* use it more fully.
3. Look and listen for what Richard Hugo, in his craft book *The Triggering Town,* called the "second" or "real" subject of the poem, and give it room in your re-envisioned poem.

> A poem can be said to have two subjects, the initiating or triggering subject, which starts the poem or "causes" the poem to be written, and the real or generated subject, which the poem comes to say or mean, and which is generated or discovered in the poem during the writing. That's not quite right because it suggests that the poet recognizes the real subject. The poet may not be aware of what the real subject is but only have some instinctive feeling that the poem is done.
>
> Young poets find it difficult to free themselves from the initiating subject. The poet puts down the title: "Autumn Rain." He finds two or three good lines about Autumn Rain. Then things start to break down. He cannot find anything more to say about Autumn Rain so he starts making up things, he strains, he goes abstract, he starts telling us the meaning of what he has

already said. The mistake he is making, of course, is that he feels obligated to go on talking about Autumn Rain, because that, he feels, is the subject. Well, it isn't the subject. You don't know what the subject is, and the moment you run out of things to say about Autumn Rain, start talking about something else. In fact, it's a good idea to talk about something else before you run out of things to say about Autumn Rain.

4. Try writing a completely new poem by keeping only a small fragment of the poem you are struggling with (only the title, the first line, the last line, a word or a phrase, etc.). Try writing with a different form, voice, speaker, etc.

CHAPTER

9

Troubleshooting and Workshops

Richard Hugo used to occasionally remind his students, "There are no problems in writing, there are only problems in writers." And if we consider the writer and what he or she writes as being mutually exclusive at some point, Hugo's point seems well taken. If there were only problems in writing, then given a thorough knowledge of craft, a strong heart and ego, and a gift for language, the poet should find his or her writing problem easy to solve. But there's a catch in this perspective: the poet is almost always blind to some of the faults in his or her own writing, even if he or she is an excellent critic of others' work.

A good deal of the problem is due to the overwhelming resonance of meanings that reverberate in the poet's mind when he or she interacts with that work. While writing out a scene or dramatic situation or lyric, the writer has a **gestalt** feeling for the subject and an intuitive sense of theme. Thousands of associations and facts crackle like static in the mind. Logic, memory, and imagination intertwine in an amorphous admixture, and yet, compared to how our minds perceive, we are constrained to use the relatively few and rigid forms of language to express this mindscape. To further complicate matters, oftentimes we believe that most of these complexes of attributes have spilled over onto the page, and there they are vibrating with all the intensity, freshness, and depth of the source-experience present in our imagination, when, in fact, our words on the page are only abbreviated codes of the colliding worlds inside us. The words we have written on the page may act as keys to unlock the resonance inside the writer, but for the reader the words may only hint at, mask, or miss entirely that experience. So, the most difficult part of solving this problem is that of the writer achieving an objective standpoint as to exactly what he or she has translated onto the page.

In order to examine what we have written, without the benefit of reader feedback, we should consider a few major aspects in the internal structure of the poem. To reverse Hugo's tongue-in-cheek aphorism, problems in the writer are really unsolved technical problems in craft whose symptoms are, finally, problems in expression. They are not problems inherent in the medium of language. This section of the book deals with major problems in controlling the poem: developing a useful literary strategy, delimiting the focus of a poem, eliminating editorial intrusions by the poet, and transcending the challenge of the poem.

TROUBLESHOOTING: TYPICAL PROBLEMS OF CONTROL

Strategy

A poetic **strategy** is a general plan of action that carries the poem from its opening through its closure. It usually forms the implied substructure of the poem in the same way the principles of engineering and physics express themselves in the form of, say, a suspension bridge or simple arch. It's bracing and revealing to ask yourself, "If this poem were a car, would I risk my life in it?"

From the original impulse to write, that vortex of undifferentiated energy in which the poem is inchoate and uncharacterized, when the poet doesn't yet have a theme or subject in mind, the energy begins to expand and emerge outward. As it emerges into full consciousness, it becomes colored by emotions, imagined sensations, and vague conceptual and logical structures. The poet now begins to ground him- or herself, to feel the thrust of the poem—the direction from which it is coming and the direction in which it is going. Then the poet begins to write from a particular perspective and level of consciousness, a "place" of initiation loosely termed the poet's **location.** He or she then begins to firm up, consciously or unconsciously, a strategy that will organize the previously inchoate feelings swirling inside the original need to write. At this point, whether or not the poet is aware of it, he or she is solving a formal technical problem, inventing a plan of attack that is most appropriate to and most efficient for the materials at hand.

Again, the poet may not decide upon the formulation of a specific strategy, but the poet may arrive at it circuitously or indirectly. For instance, maybe the poet feels bored with using the same old first-person point of view and resolves to use a second or third-person perspective, or a **masked pronoun.** That doesn't seem to have very far-reaching implications, but consider this: what is really happening is an objectification of the poet's inner reality, the creation of a greater leverage with which to lift the world inside. Thus this simple replacement exercise has become a strategy that can carry the poem through to completion because the poet has freed up his or her imagination, and now has the right **aesthetic distance** by which to discover theme.

Focus

It's difficult to write a poem even if you have a theme in mind, but it gets harder, obviously, when you don't know what you're going to say. Organically developed poetry (**organic composition,** see p. 10) presents us with the problem of uncertainty, which the poet Theodore Roethke, in addressing the nature of his spiritual quest, answered by saying: "What is there to know?/I learn by going where I have to go."

Interestingly, we can judge the achievement of a poem by employing the international standards for ice skating competition: Originality, Risk, and Excellence, the acronym ORE. To attain these goals a poem's focus, just as a superior skater's concentration, must maintain sharp control, whether consciously or unconsciously wrought. The language and form in the unfocused poem may be poetic, but most times what's on the page isn't a poem. Once the poem begins to be formed, the poet, like a jet fighter's automatic range finder locked onto its object, must keep the objective of the poem in focus. As with a bad foundation on a house, no amount of cosmetic or local tinkering can help if it is essentially unsound.

In order to keep an open attitude toward examining the aspect of focus, it's best to allow a poem time to develop, and to ask some very basic questions of it. Here is a list of questions the poet John Skoyles developed to help toward a fuller understanding of what is on the page and how it functions. It's a useful guide for getting back inside the poem.

1. Is the poem confused or obscure in places?
2. Do the lines and stanzas have solid logical relationships to one another, and are the references in the lines clear?
3. Is the tone of the speaker consistent throughout the poem, or does it arbitrarily switch or lose its attitude?
4. Are there unwarranted connotations in the images or phrases that might throw the reader and poem off track?
5. Is the poem so overloaded with abstractions that the reader has to supply his or her own **stock responses,** and the poem has no life of its own?
6. Does the poem contain clichés that don't work in a new way?
7. Can you hear the rhythms in the poem, or is it flat and lacking in musicality so that it seems like prose broken into lines?
8. Is its **diction** striking and fresh, or drab and routine?
9. Are the verbs charged, or do forms of the verb "to be" predominate? Is the passive voice used too much?
10. Does the poem say something in a new way, or do you simply imagine that it does?

THE MIXED MESSAGE The **mixed** (or confused) **message** is the most obvious way to lose focus in a poem. In the following example, the poem opens with dark imagery that suggests something negative and possibly menacing. But as the poem develops, it switches from a feeling of depression to the memory of good times, which is a natural enough reverse logical association but one that sends a mixed or confusing message to the reader, as it ends up stating something opposite of what seemed the original premise.

As the sun lowered itself
until it was even with the world,
shadows flew over one another
ike the threads of a cape, and
I thought of all the Thanksgivings
we had at grandmother's,
how happy those old times were.

If the poet were aware of his mixed message, he might have been able to make the turn in his thesis successfully by subordinating or processing the negative feelings in the first half in a more logical manner so that the positive vision in the second half of the poem didn't seem uncontrolled.

DIGRESSION Although digressions can be very interesting and effective devices for a kind of purposeful misdirection (see pp. 51–52), by definition, unless they serve some thematic purpose, they lead away from the poem. This happens a lot in conversations in which we end up wondering what our point was. The following negative example was designed as an extended digression based upon the appositive clause following the word "prayer." The poet may have found a nugget in the digressive riff off the word "prayer," but he's lost sight of the motherload.

St. Anselm, consumed by perfecting
his spirit, became consumed by prayer,
that long intoned leap of thought
arcing into who knows where, where
each syllable ripened as fallen fruit
released its needy seeds and crowded
space with clusters of redolent silence.

Overdecoration

Sometimes poets get too involved in feasting on the sensory details of an experience, to the point where this becomes an end in itself. Although there are certainly pleasures in indulging in richness, when it becomes a gorging self-indulgence the results are a poem with plenty of flash and sizzle but no substance. The clutter of musical effects and details become debris that suffocate whatever the original intention of the poem might have been and outweigh that substructure. The reader is left with a sagging, inert mass of description, as in the following example which, as Shakespeare said, is only "appetite eating itself up."

> Gloria glommed on swabs of costumed gee-gaws
> before her glamored mirror: faux onyx, malachite nuggets,
> day-glo saturated zircons, stalactites of pentacled
> golden triangles dangling from her glittered wrists
> to accent her neck's tangled mass of puce pearls.

Distracting Details

The following poem, written by Tracy Daugherty when he was a beginning writer, is basically sound and beautiful. But because it was conceived by depending upon specific details of setting, which was his original strategy, the thematic development is submerged and obscured. While the details of the poem were used as the vehicle to express its theme, those details needed to be weeded out in the final drafts. They distract the reader's attention from the smooth development of the poem's existential statements. The poet himself was not aware of their negative influence.

My Name

There are owls in old Dallas neighborhoods.
I've watched them. Perched on parked cars
or on nameless signs, they blink at my shape,
call to the dark. The sky with its elusive
center houses these birds.

These walls seem made of wings
when the wind blows and the wood creaks.
I've never seen an owl in this neighborhood
though I've listened for one, half-awake.
I strain and hear the sounds of my sleep.
The empty trees sink in the rain,
the wings in the walls hiss, twitching, uneasy. . . .

If I'm afraid, I'm not afraid of ghosts:
divorce and disownment, hatred
and need of a house; drunkenness
till you feel as if you're haunting the world.
I feel as if I'm haunting the world.

My name begins to lose its sense
like words repeated in a game. Still,

on solid Midwest nights I wrote
story fragments, hopeless chapters, a language
of hard impressions: birds
dead in the snow; edges in the sheets, this world
as unclaimed as a crime.
(Tracy Daugherty, "My Name")

Now, when we weed out the interrupting details, his theme of insubstantiality and alienation becomes more highly focused. A revised version of the draft above might read like this:

There are owls on nameless signs
that blink at my shape and call
to the dark elusive center of the sky.

They make the night a house
of wings where I've heard
the sounds of my own sleep
while the empty trees sink
in the rain and the wings
in the wall hiss, twitching, uneasy. . . .

If I'm afraid, I'm not afraid of ghosts:
disownment, yes, drunkenness until
you feel you're haunting the world.
I feel as if I'm haunting the world.

And my name begins to lose its sense
like words repeated in a child's game.
I write fragments, hopeless chapters
in a language of hard impressions,
and leave the world as unclaimed
as a crime.

OBSCURITY It's important to define specifically for yourself a general mood, feeling, or dramatic situation by anchoring it to specific details, appropriate **tropes,** and accurate statements. Rendering a vague feeling into abstract allusions or overly general "free floating" images will lead to a diffused focus and leave the reader with only suggestions and thin impressions, which is to say that the reader's experience of the poem will inevitably reflect the writer's approximated feelings. The example below makes sense, but is too slight a gesture and we have no idea what it's about.

Rimbaud exchanged Paris's absinthe
for a desert outpost so he could grow

wealthy like some inverted Siddhartha
who learned how to cross the river
of change in order to serve others.

OVERLY IMPRESSIONISTIC Some poems, like music, do succeed as mood pieces, impressions of a scene or event that summon an evocation of a special moment. But the poem must not lose focus, though the focus may be softened or allowed to wander undirected. The following poem is overly impressionistic and does not know what it wants to say. There seems to be a message beneath it, but the wispy images and pretty details pretend to be sufficient in themselves.

The old man in the top-floor window
viewed the world from this distance
of memory and smoke. The bellowing
barges and tug boats drew sunlight
to a fine point and the river slept
under a blanket of rolling fog.

Obviously, the piece is also too sentimental, which R. H. Blythe humorously defined thusly: "Sentimentality means having more tenderness for a thing than God has."

LACK OF REFERENCES In the previous example, we saw how a poem loses force and meaning by being overly general. In the example that follows, the poem suffers the opposite fate—that of being too specific and myopic. What the poem lacks is a frame of reference, in this case, a dramatic situation upon which the details can hang. The poet lives too far inside the experience for the reader to see what is happening and understand the poem's context.

Solid darkness. And everywhere doors
of space like a mountain of talus and scree
taunted him. "Use both hands!"
his father shouted out of his childhood.
His childhood of tinkling bells and
sycamores inched its way from its
husked chrysalis into the freezing air
of his trap.

OVER-INTELLECTUALIZED Contemporary workshoppers are familiar with the term "classical baggage," which indicates the defect that some scholarly, overly rational poets bring to their poems—a mountain of learned references and innuendo. This leads to the reader to decode a sagging and static mass of allusions, when the poet should have done the contextual work of the poem by fully absorbing and then processing this material.

Herr Wittgenstein's left turn
toward National Socialism
should have been Parsifal's
Red Knight, which is the way
St. Thomas Aquinas reaffirmed
by Descartes, modified by Leibniz,
rejected Kant, yet was revived by Hegel.
So he ate his artichoke whole.

OVERLY RHETORICAL **Rhetorical questions** in a poem should be used sparingly, either to introduce and focus on new material, or to point the reader to new levels of meaning. But too often rhetorical questions are used as a masking device that ironically shows up the writer's frustration at not being able to bring his theme to light. In the following example, the reader is attacked with accusing questions about an unstated subject and theme (a good defense is a strong offense). The force of the poem's language makes the reader feel uneasy and a bit guilty, but it is full of bombast and doesn't relate to anything. The reader finds himself trying to round up answers to questions with no frame of reference. It's as if he were being taken by surprise in the street by a maniac whose accusations are "full of sound and fury, signifying nothing."

Who comes with his axe of arrogance?
A new Ajax? Use the power of the flower
to surrender to the strength of your weakness!
What mountain doesn't remember its birth?
Do you think no bird flew over it?
Do you think force can force force itself?

IDIOSYNCRATIC SYMBOLS Almost anything can be made into a symbol if the poet takes the time to prepare its meaning by supplying the necessary context for it, or by processing it so its development seems logical. A symbol is, by its function, always defined by its context: the images, statements, actions, characterizations, and details that suffuse it with meaning. A mountain, typically, may stand for solidity, strength, and achievement in popular symbolism, but it can also be made to stand for piety, wealth, danger, or any other quality if it is surrounded by a different defining context. The following poem neglects to supply us with the information necessary in order to know how to decode or interpret the first line. We can only guess at some sort of negative meaning in the symbol, but we never know what it specifically means. The poet may have a special meaning in mind, but he has failed to impart that to us.

There is a hole in the lake
where an old couple sits like
crumpled newspaper on a day

when the last breath of winter
plays a harsh note on the pipes of spring.

Editorial Intrusions

AUTHORIAL INTRUSIONS An accomplished poet leaves his or her signature in the work through voice and style. This is desirable because the identifying hallmarks of a poet are not extraneous, disrupting elements in a poem, but the trace elements of vision and voice, qualities that make the work distinctive. But there are certain kinds of intrusions into the poem that are not desirable, such as emotional, editorial remarks that break the surface of the poem and thrust themselves at the reader in a didactic and wrenched manner. These types of intrusions reflect the writer's insecurity about his means of expression and his frustration in trying to succinctly express his ideas.

The bird has returned this spring.
He's perched on my neighbor's
rooftop singing his heart out
for a chance at love. He's no different
than any of us. We all sit on our own
rooftops calling out for love.

OVER-OBVIOUSNESS Similar to the authorial intrusion, the over-obvious statement is an attempt on the writer's part to summarize or explain what has already been stated in another way. The poet makes grand, vague, or abstract points about his subject to make sure the poem's message is getting across. The evocative power of the specific image and the connotations of language and tropes aren't being trusted. The poem tends to be too informational, prosy, and two-dimensional. In the following poem, the poet uses a fairly specific set of images and verbal metaphors in the first stanza, so that the reader can interpret his meaning. The second stanza uses a more generalized, prosaic, and less intense kind of language; and the third stanza falls into a sort of didactic cant in which the writing of poetry has been abandoned. The poet's message has overcome any possibility of making music with the words, and the reader's expectations are insulted by use of clichés.

The bag lady drags her garbage bag
of belongings into a filthy alley.

How would you like your own mother
to live like this? Expensive cars
whiz by her life like insults hurled
in an ostentatious display of wealth
and greed. This has become our America
lugging the burden of the American Dream.

Transcending the Challenge

CYCLICAL ENDING One of the most common types of compromises between all-out success and failure is the poem that features a **circular closure,** in which what was supposed to be an enriched restatement turns out to be just a repetition of something already said. Songs use this kind of repetitive refrain without entering new levels and nuances of meaning, without adding resonance or depth; but the accompanying music ameliorates what would be merely redundant on the page. In the following poem, the poet has failed to open up the poem with an elaboration of its content because he has simply restated the obvious situation (although there is a pun in the phrase "two at bedtime," which could refer both to the pills and lovers). But there is a sense of incompleteness to the poem that is the giveaway in determining whether or not the poem resolved and/or transcended the situational terms it set for itself.

relief comes
in blue green artificial
tranquility—two at bedtime
they soften the edges and smooth
the wrinkles in the winding sheets
slipping down into the bottom of sleep
there is only a vague dull ache for you
replaced by blue green chemical
warmth—two at bedtime.

MISDIRECTED ENDING The ending or **closure** of a poem must be able to support the whole poem in some way, through flat statement, an image or trope, dialogue, musical effects, word play, nuances of meaning, or plot element. Just finding a topic or theme may be enough to start a poem, but not enough to complete one. In the following poem, the writer has discovered a more universal definition for the word "poetry." He links together the composition of music and poetry, intertwining subject and theme, but doesn't arrive at a deeper understanding of his material. He ends the poem on an aside, a throw-away minor comment, which does not contribute to the poem's development.

Notes

I don't know anything about music
 so maybe that explains my surprise.
I was listening to piano pieces
on the stereo just before sleeping.
I heard the notes the chords the tone the tempo
and I knew I was hearing poetry.
Music is like poetry.

It starts with an idea and then it grows
it tries new directions it changes.
I had forever wondered how music
happens. Strangely enough I assumed
a composer set down at once
in finished form his work.
Maybe some do. But I doubt it.

BURIED THEME At some point in the composing process, the conscious or unconscious levels of the mind must come to an understanding of what the poem wants to say. It may not be necessary to make an outright statement of the poem's discoveries—imagery and tropes can carry these embedded as implied statements within themselves—but in one way or another the poet has to control the revealing of theme. The following poem displays a kind of blindness toward its own statement-in-imagery. The poet isn't aware of what his images mean in a larger, literary sense, and so he has lost the opportunity to develop something penetrating and powerful even though he has the means in hand.

Windows

the dryer windows, confronting you, are a crowd of vacant
stares, the clothes roll across their eyes like vague
memories—and you catch yourself gaping
(quickly—look away)
trying to remember what it was you just saw that reminded you of— (this question, hanging)
and as it rolls by again, again you look, trying harder to
grasp, catch a glimpse of this formless mass, tossed over
and over gently, floating past the small window rimmed
with stainless steel.

PROBLEMS OF CONTROL EXERCISE

1. Read through a poem you have written with an objective and critical eye toward deciding whether or not every single part of the poem contributes substantially to the development of the poem's theme. First look for material that presents:
   a. confused messages,
   b. digressions,
   c. overly decorated or impressionistic imagery and rhetoric,

d. distracting details, obscure references, over-intellectualized or idiosyncratic experience,
e. content that "tells" too much instead of "showing,"
f. endings that close by saying what has already been said or that end up saying something not prepared by the poem.

2. Then, as another step in the revision process, assign content that seems potentially problematic as falling under one of the following three levels:
   a. obviously unnecessary, confused, or obscure material
   b. somewhat thematically productive material
   c. marginally thematically related material

WORKSHOP MISSION STATEMENT

The purpose of a poetry workshop is to:

1. nourish the creative spirit;
2. celebrate the uniqueness of our individual differences and common humanity;
3. foster respect and further understanding for the process and products of the imagination and intellect;
4. promote a knowledge of terminology and excellence in craft.

WORKSHOP MODELS

In the 1950s a few universities, such as Stanford and Iowa, instituted the "workshop" class. It was designed as a craft space in which writing students could learn from practicing professionals the inside-out about writing practices, theory, and history. By the mid 1970s, workshops were being established at hundreds of institutions of higher learning and at independent literary and community centers across the country. And the expansion continues today on the secondary-education level.

The model most widely used by far is what has come to be known as "the Iowa workshop model." A teacher/writer heads up a group of up to 15 students who submit their current and/or revised poems to a "worksheet" (a photocopied sheath of student poems) for critique and discussion. The content of the course is composed, in various proportions, of discussion of student work, assigned common and individual readings, directed exercises, and the keeping of literary journals that contain anything from reactions to class discussions, to important personal events, to dream records, to notes and drafts toward poems. Sometimes, students report on selected poets or some aspect of craft or theory.

Typically, in the format of the Iowa model, the student reads his or her work, and then listens, without interruption, to a discussion of the work. The idea behind the student "gag rule" is to insure that the student obtains objective feedback, uncolored or torqued by the author's explanations of context or intentions behind the poem. Aside from the exception of supplying factual information, the student waits until the discussion concludes, and then he or she may offer a reaction to the class comments in the form of defending the piece, referring to what triggered or inspired the work, supplying context for it, offering explanations in terms of meaning, or explaining his or her intentions.

The ethos of the workshop strives to create a situation in which, due to the various perspectives and craft concerns of classmates and teacher, the student might eventually come to be empowered with a fuller array of tools, ideas, and revising methods for when he or she is working alone. Most teachers try to create an atmosphere in which student work is fairly, objectively, and benignly treated, as if the poem under discussion were as anonymous as a painting on a museum wall. But, of course, in actuality it is practically impossible for an author to stand completely aside from his or her work and not feel somewhat defensive. Often, careful attention to the technical aspects of the work, and the use of humor and interesting anecdotes, relax and de-intensify the workshop atmosphere when it becomes too charged or personally difficult. And humor and obvious good intentions go a long way toward finding ways to say difficult things so that the student hears and accepts them.

A few related pitfalls to the Iowa workshop model are "hand holding" and the "bandwagon effect." "Hand holding" typically occurs when students tacitly agree to be overly nice and complimentary to each other's work ("If I'm nice to her, she'll be nice to me."). The "bandwagon effect" usually occurs when a well-made or strongly persuasive point preempts or coopts individual thinking in favor of a unified, full-frontal group response. Teachers and writers have adjusted the Iowa format in various ways to facilitate a more "sharing" and permissive atmosphere, one borrowing aspects from group therapy. Some classes are team-taught by professionals so that a difference of perspectives, tastes, and styles is ensured; some teachers hold back from leading and controlling the initial discussion so as to ensure student participation. (In some cases, students are extemporaneously called upon to offer feedback.) Some classes encourage the poet whose work is under discussion to fully participate. Another model sets up the format of student-moderators whose job it is to initiate a brief overview and evaluation of the work before it is discussed by the full class, a practice that forces the student-moderator to read the work closely, form a critical opinion, access a common critical terminology, and introduce discussion with a "hook," a thematic or craft issue for further consideration.

WORKSHOP PROTOCOL

In terms of the tenor of discussion about student work, be direct, honest, and tactful: follow the Golden Rule and treat others' work as you would like your own work to be treated. The most effective help a poem can receive comes from readers who adopt a sympathetic stance toward the poem and the poet's intentions. Fairness, in terms of the length of a discussion, can be maintained by assigning a classmate as timekeeper to hold the discussion of each poem to, say, 20 minutes apiece. While many teachers prefer students to make detailed, technical remarks, there's no reason why starting out with a comment such as "I like this work," or "There's something confusing here," wouldn't be appropriate if the student then tracks down what it is that makes the work appealing or problematical. The overall arc of comments should begin with the positive aspects of the work, then go into further detailed, constructive criticism in the form of pointing out areas for discussion and offering possible remedies, and then end on a positive note again. Generally, if the student-critic is not sure about some aspect of the work but has a general sense of where the problem lies, it is best to address an open question to the group for it to take up. A very effective, fair, and instructive method for suggesting improvements for the work under discussion is to bring in example poems, passages, or quotations from other writers and critics on the topic being discussed. Obviously, the student whose work is under consideration should take notes to refer to later on; and the same is good advice for the class as a whole, since what applies to one poet's work often has or will have a bearing on other student-poets' work as well. And last, if the work under discussion has been edited on the page by various classmates, it's helpful to offer those tear sheets for the author to peruse during his or her later revision process. As for the student whose work is under discussion, his or her most helpful contribution is, after the poem has been scrutinized, to ask pointed questions about previous remarks, and/or defend or explain what might have seemed unclear.

Don Colburn's comedy-of-errors poem presents from the author's perspective the standard sorts of workshop lingo and feedback.

In the Workshop after I Read My Poem Aloud

All at once everyone in the room says
nothing. They continue doing this and I begin to know
it is not because they are dumb. Finally

the guy from the Bay Area who wears his chapbook
on his sleeve says he likes the poem a lot
but can't really say why and silence

starts all over until someone says she only has
a couple of teeny suggestions such as taking out
the first three stanzas along with

all modifiers except "slippery" and "delicious"
in the remaining four lines. A guy who
hasn't said a word in three days says

he too likes the poem but wonders why
it was written and since I don't know either
and don't even know if I should

I'm grateful there's a rule
I can't say anything now. Somebody
I think it's the shrink from Seattle

says the emotion is not earned and I wonder
when is it ever. The woman on my left
who just had a prose poem in *Green Thumbs & Geoducks*

says the opening stanza is unbelievable
and vindication comes for a sweet moment
until I realize she means unbelievable.

But I have my defenders too and the MFA from Iowa
the one who thinks the you is an I
and the they a we and the then a now

wants to praise the way the essential nihilism
of the poem's occasion serves to undermine
the formality of its diction. Just like your comment

I say to myself. Another admires the zenlike polarity
of the final image despite the mildly bathetic
symbolism of sheep-droppings and he loves how

the three clichés in the penultimate stanza
are rescued by the brazen self-exploiting risk.
The teacher asks what about the last line

and the guy with the chapbook volunteers it suits
the poem's unambitious purpose though he has to admit
it could have been worded somewhat differently.

(Don Colburn, "In the Workshop after I Read My Poem Aloud")

READING ALOUD

Most poetry workshop formats call for the poet to read his or her work aloud so that the audience can get a sense of poem's dramatic and performance-oriented sweep by way of the poet's voice, inflections, body language, and tone. Some workshops vary this format by either having a classmate read the poet's work, which allows the author to hear it more objectively, or by having the poet read the work, followed by a reading from a classmate, a format which offers advantages of both formats. But reading a poem out loud effectively takes practice, belief in the work, and courage. (It's been said that most people fear public speaking over death!) Dylan Thomas, one of the great twentieth-century bards, said, "The page is the place where you study the works of a poem; the platform is the place where you give the poem the works." It doesn't matter what style or model you use as a guide for honing your recitation skills; what matters is that you feel comfortable with your preferred style and that this style is the most effective one for the work.

Some poets, such as Andrei Voznesensky, Antonin Artaud, and Brother Antoninus, recite in a forceful, theatrical style, emphasizing words and phrasing in a very emphatic, dramatic way. Others, such as Theodore Roethke, Seamus Heaney, and Dylan Thomas, focus on laying out the lyrical and musical qualities of their work. Old recordings of T. S. Eliot and Ezra Pound seem monotonous and monochromatic, featuring an impersonal style in which the poet seems to prefer to let the work do the work; or some, such as Louise Glück, work in a limited two-to-three-note range, which produces a kind of mesmerizing and sustained tension. Robert Frost and W. H. Auden tended toward the public, oratorical mode. John Weiners, in his "Magical Evening" readings in Boston apartments, prefers an intimate tonality. Tom Lux likes to megaphonically overplay his reading for humorous effect. Robert Creeley relies heavily upon highlighting line endings and rhetorical stresses. Amiri Baraka's style is in the purposeful propagandistic mode of inflammatory political rhetoric. Master precisionists, such as Donald Justice and Tomas Tranströmer, model their readings after the clean phrasing of classical music, while poets such as Al Young and Michael Harper use improvisational, jazz styles.

But the bulk of the mainstream style of reading stems from the character of the poem's speaker, toward the style of the **dramatic monologue** and **persona poem.** Within this limited aesthetic, there's a great deal of room for variation, from John Ashbery's tickertape-like thinking out loud, to Ralph Angel's modulated, carefully considered, serious introspections, to Charles Bukowski's, over-the-top braggadocio performances. Each poet, in honing the **voice** in their work, usually, as a by-product, hones his or her own reading style.

Reading performances, like acting, aren't just a preset, rehearsed affair. Oftentimes, because there's a very different set of expectations and tensions when the poet is testing the poem in a public arena, the poet hears his or her own poem in a new or different way, and may go back and revise it accordingly. Then there are the considerations of the entertainment factor. While some poets, such as Jack Gilbert, assume the audience is there both to hear the poem being read and to learn, and thus prefer to read the poem bare of any accompanying commentary or context, others will mention the origins and inspiration of the poem, any significant aspects or words, approach its theme from an angle the poem itself doesn't cover, or relate humorous anecdotes before and/or after reading the work. And because of the developing nature of the work, the nature of the audiences, and/or the current cultural scene, poets often change their reading styles. With all of these variations and aesthetics, the fact remains that there's nothing that can substitute for hearing the poet read his or her own work. Anyone who has ever attended a poetry reading has inevitably come away with strong impressions they could not have gotten from the page alone. After all, a primary rule of poetry is that it should be written to be read aloud. And there's nothing that can be substituted for the feedback the poet intuits or explicitly receives from doing a reading.

C H A P T E R

10

Practical Matters

This section offers a brief overview of some practical, professional topics and concerns that poets who are just starting out might have: submission guidelines for journal publication; putting together a chapbook; structuring a first, full-length collection of poetry; and a list of major "Po' Biz" references.

MANUSCRIPT SUBMISSIONS

Unless you have an established name and reputation, even if you are a fine poet, submitting work is really more akin to a lottery than something you might reasonably expect to feature reason and predictability. You would be surprised how often it isn't just a question of how good the work might be; on the editorial end, editors have to contend with space limitations, theme issues, overstock, diversity, stylistic preferences, verbal and contractual obligations, subject matter, and a host of other concerns (not to mention the often numbing effect of the daily forced march of having to read manuscripts). The *New Yorker* receives over 1,000 poems a week, publishes only a few poems per issue, has contracted with a number of established poets, and features only a few unknowns a year. For peace of mind, it would be better to send yourself a lifelong rejection slip from them. On the other hand, highly respected journals such as the *American Poetry Review* and *Poetry* make it a practice to keep their issues fresh with a mix of new and well-known poets. It's best to treat submissions as a minor piece of business you do one morning every month or so. If, and probably when, your work is rejected, quickly turn around pieces that you still like and have faith in, and, above all, persevere. It's common for a journal to take work by poets it has rejected a number of times before publishing, which makes it a matter of educating the screeners and editors to your work.

Philip Dacey's "Form Rejection Letter," composed in the clichéd and obfuscating language of editors, will give heart and laughter to those who have experienced the ignominy of the submission (pun intended) process.

Form Rejection Letter

We are sorry we cannot use the enclosed.
We are returning it to you.
We do not mean to imply anything by this.
We are sorry we cannot use the enclosed.
We are returning it to you.
We do not mean to imply anything by this.
We would prefer not to be pinned down about this matter.
But we are not keeping—cannot, will not keep—
   what you have sent us.
We did receive it, though, and our returning it to you
   is a sign of that.
It was not that we minded your sending it to us
   unasked.
That is happening all the time, they
   come when we least expect them,
   when we forget we have needed or might yet need them,
   and we send them back
It is not that we minded.
At another time, there is no telling.
But this time, it does not suit our present needs.

We wish to make it clear it was not easy receiving it.
It came so encumbered.
And we are busy here.
We did not feel
   we could take it on.
We know it would not have ended there.
It would have led to this, and that.
We know about these things.
It is why we are here.
We wait for it. We recognize it when it comes.
Regretfully, this form letter does not allow us to
   elaborate why we send it back.
It is not that we minded.

We hope this does not discourage you. But we would
not want to encourage you falsely.
It requires delicate handling, at this end.
If we had offered it to you,
   perhaps you would understand.
But, of course, we did not.
You cannot know what your offering it meant to us.

And we cannot tell you:
There is a form we must adhere to.
It is better for everyone that we use this form.

As to what you do in the future,
we hope we have given you signs,
that you have read them,
that you have not misread them.
We wish we could be more helpful.
But we are busy.
We are busy returning so much.
We cannot keep it.
It all comes so encumbered.
And there is no one here to help.
Our enterprise is a small one.
We are thinking of expanding.
We hope you will send something.
(Philip Dacey, "Form Rejection Letter")

There have been numerous editorial panels at conferences and residencies where well-known professionals have taken up the question of content and format of poetry submissions (as book manuscripts and individual poems) to journals and presses. Some editors have rejected the need for an accompanying cover letter, maintaining the work is self-sufficient, while others have said they are interested in the poet's background and credentials. Unless you just want to meet the editors, it would be best to save the money you would pay for the conference and use it for stamps. Since the message as a whole is mixed and highly individualized, here are some standard guidelines and practices for submissions.

Submitting Individual Poems

In sending off a packet of individual poems to journals, send to publications that you have already read or are familiar with, magazines that you would like to have your work appear in. Know their general style, taste, and appearance before submitting. Send three to six clearly legible poems, and make sure your name, address, telephone number, and/or e-mail address are on each poem. Compose a brief cover letter expressing your interest and include a bit about your background, present situation, pertinent references, workshops affiliations, conferences you have attended, and any recent publications you may have had. Be sure to include a self-addressed, stamped envelope (S.A.S.E) for a reply, and keep a record of when, where, and what you sent. If a poem goes over a page or more in length, be sure to include whether there is or there is not a stanza break at the bottom of the page, since the length of the work in typescript and the length of the work in print are usually different: something to the effect of **(new stanza), (stanza continued),** or **(no break).** Typically, literary journal editors do not mind if the poems are simultaneously submitted to other journals ("multiple submissions"), as long as they're notified of that. There's no need to put a copyright notation or symbol at the bottom of the page since there aren't many poetry thieves out there. (That's because there's no money in it—besides, it's a sure sign of being an amateur: editors work off the honor system, and, if and when, the work is published, it'll be copyrighted automatically.) If you still are worried about plagiarism, use the time-honored, poor man's method of copyrighting: mail yourself a copy of the poems (with your name written across the seams of the flap) so that the post office stamps a date on it as proof of when it was mailed, and when it comes back, keep it sealed. That is a legal and inexpensive method.

Generally speaking, there are four tiers of literary journals to which you might consider sending poems (slick, national literary magazines such as the *Atlantic Monthly* and the *New Yorker* aside): (1) highly respected and established journals with comparatively large circulations (such as *Poetry,* the *American Poetry Review,* the *Paris Review,* the *Southern Review*); (2) established private and university-associated publications (the *Georgia Review, Third Coast, Southwest Review,* the *Seneca Review, Quarterly West, Columbia, Poetry East,* the *Harvard Advocate, Willow Springs,* the *Kenyon Review,* the *Pittsburgh Quarterly*); (3) small, mom-and-pop enterprises (*Defined Providence, Salt River Review, 5 a.m.,* the *Contemporary Review,* the *Eleventh Muse*, the *Great River Review*); and (4) the host of new on-line, Internet "zines." There are more places in which to publish than ever, and if a poet is skilled, talented, and persevering he or she can and will succeed.

The Chapbook

A chapbook (the wrenched term for the sixteenth-century English "cheap book") is composed of up to about 25–30 pages, and can range anywhere from an inexpensive pamphlet to a high-end, individually numbered booklet produced on fine, expensive papers with special slip cases. It's often the poet's first step in bookmaking before a first, full-length collection. Established poets commonly publish these small collections that focus on a particular style, theme, or subject matter between major books. There is a plethora of respectable chapbook contests that reward with publication and sometimes prize money. And many small, private presses routinely look for exciting new work by known and unknown poets. Since there's almost never any real monetary profit to be made in publishing chapbooks, it's inevitably a labor of love on the part of both poet and publisher. The rules that apply to submitting a full-length manuscript also apply to the submission of a chapbook manuscript.

Submitting a Full-Length Book Manuscript

Unlike fiction writers, 99.9% of poets don't use or need a literary agent—there's just not enough money involved in poetry publishing for an agent to make a living. Typically, when a book of poems is taken, if it has an advance against future sales at all, it will be $500 to $1,000, and will sell only 500–2,000 copies. No agent can make a living on 10% of that. Before submitting an unsolicited book manuscript, it's best to send a query letter (with an S.A.S.E.) asking whether or not the press is interested and is in a position to look over your work. This will save both you and the editor time and money. On the other hand, if the press is running a contest, a query letter isn't necessary. Just follow the stated guidelines as to submission period, format, number of copies, and whether or not manuscripts are being judged on a disclosed or an anonymous ("blind") basis (in which case your name and address will appear only on the manuscript's cover sheet). Nowadays most presses don't mind if the author multiple-submits (since the over-the-transom editorial process can last anywhere from two to six months or more), as long as the press is notified if and when the book happens to be taken by another press. If you want your manuscript returned, provide the appropriate S.A.S.E; if not, since reproduction is easy and inexpensive, let the press know they can discard the submission if it's not accepted.

STRUCTURING A MANUSCRIPT

While some readers dip into a poetry collection in a peripatetic manner, looking first at poems with interesting titles, or maybe reading a book in a random fashion, poets take the structuring of a manuscript quite seriously, even though their readers may not sense the shape of the book as a whole. (On the other hand, in this era of ubiquitous poetry manuscript contests, some poets try to second-guess how overworked judges might perfunctorily screen hundreds of manuscripts by placing the strongest poems at the beginning, middle, and end of their manuscripts, which is said to be the way some overworked judges review manuscripts.) Generally speaking, organizing a manuscript toward book stature is dictated by the types of poems, their number (most poetry manuscripts are 60–90 pages in length), and an overall strategic plan organically developed from the poems themselves. The following is a list of individual, common types of poetry collection structures (though they aren't necessarily mutually exclusive).

Chronological

This basic type of structure lays out the poems by date of their composition, from early to recent. It is a solid kind of ordering if the incremental run of the poems demonstrates some sort of developing narrative, formal aspect, thematic cycle, or inclusive purpose. The rationale of Bill Knott's *Poems: 1963–1988,* 25 years of work, obviously fall into the last category, but a more complicated example of the chronologically structured book is Sharon Olds' *Gold Cell,* which blocks thematically and topically related poems into four major chronological sections.

Thematic

This is one of the most common poetry book organizations, most probably because cycles of poems, as they're being written, naturally tend to fall into categories of concerns the poet has been wrestling with, such as coming of age, rites of initiation, and rites of passage poems; stages of grief poems; questions of origins and destination poems; and poems about the individual soul's place in the cosmos. A less organically derived version of this was prepared by the editor Daniel Hunter, who ordered William Stafford's *My Name is William Tell* from six previously published limited edition chapbooks into four thematic sections: (1) the poet's ephemeral work of feeling and perceiving; (2) the soul's formation in childhood; (3) the emotional and spiritual aspects of a local place; and (4) the way the soul has learned the world despite its places of schooling. The book as a whole holds together beautifully.

Topical

Often the individual poems for a book of poetry easily fall into topical categories: poems about places and people (Edgar Lee Masters' *Spoon River Anthology;* Carl Sandburg's *Good Morning, America*), nature (Mary Oliver's *American Primitive*), generations (Allen Ginsberg's *Howl*), war (Robert Bly's *The Teeth-Mother Naked at Last*), travel (Elizabeth Bishop's *Questions of Travel*), relationships (Ai's *Killing Floor*). It's not uncommon to come across whole books dedicated to one topic, such as Cincinnati poet Terry Stokes' persona book entitled *Crimes of Passion,* which dons the masks of various sexual felons: the stalker, the slasher, the voyeur, etc. And there's an apocryphal tale about the way in which the prodigious poet William Stafford would decide the content of his books. It seems he kept a kind of pigeonhole case whose individual boxes were labeled according to subject matter. When enough poems for a book had accumulated in a particular box—regardless of their widely disparate dates of composition—he would put a book together from that box's contents. Whether or not this is true, it's another way to create organization for a book.

Stylistic

A less common but nonetheless standard aesthetic that makes a book coherent is that of employing a particular style that suits the subject. Federico García Lorca's *Poet in New York,* a stylistically anomalous volume that exhibits Lorca's shocked and manic reaction at having to live in the hurly-burly imbroglio of the Big Apple, was matched by the impacted, surreal style he created for or from the experience. The French surrealist Francis Ponge wrote a "poetic dictionary," *The Voice of Things,* consisting of a series of definitions of common objects and things (fire, water, wine, horses, etc.) in the wild form of Petrarchan conceits.

Narrative

Another solid and basic book structure borrows the narrative devices from the genre of fiction, although typically the "plot" or storyline has to be inferred from the poems' contents rather than being explicitly expressed. Often this type of book also follows a straight chronological route; but just as contemporary films such as *Pulp Fiction* have fractured the chronology of events, and even structured them backward, some books of poems use the same model. Michael Van Wallgehen's *Blue Tango* recounts in muscularly tight vignette-style a wide array of seminal, autobiographical events in the speaker's life, as is true of Leslie Ullman's meditative and personal poems in her *Natural Histories* and *Slow Work through Sand.* Rita Dove's Pultizer Prize-winning volume, *Thomas and Beulah,* and Garrett Hongo's *River of Heaven* both trace a few generations of ancestry in a foreshortened poetic equivalent of Alex Haley's *Roots.* And, of course, Ovid's *Metamorphosis* and Virgil's *Aeneid* eminently qualify as early narrative epic poems.

Formal

This type of structure uses a formal device of one kind or another to organize and unify its content. C. K. Williams, after having written a series of books using a long narrative line, suddenly put out a book of sonnets, *Flesh and Blood.* The same is true of John Berryman's series, *Dream Songs,* which invents a unifying triple-masked persona to speak from different perspectives. Frank O'Hara's book *Lunch Poems* is held together by their spontaneous style and by virtue of their having been written on lunch breaks from his job as curator at the New York City Modern Museum of Art. Richard Hugo's volume *31 Letters and 13 Dreams* is just that, a series of prosy letter and dream poems, which incidentally helped him bridge an earlier formal style and his later more conversational style. Stephen Berg, who usually writes in a mainstream, conversational mode, recently published a stream-of-consciousness prose-poem volume, *Porno Diva Numero Uno,* whose fast track, surreal style is appropriate to the aesthetic of the ghost presence of painter and poet Marcel Duchamp in the book.

Dramatic

As the term implies, this book's structure is based upon principles of drama, some sort of emotional, dramatic curve in the poems' tenor that might follow classic dramatic structure: from (1) introduction, to (2) rising action, to (3) climax, to (4) falling action, to (5) catastrophe and denouement. Obviously Homer's

Odyssey (it *is* a poem) falls into a hybrid of this and the narrative form. Ariel Dorfman's *Last Waltz in Santiago,* a true dramatic poetic form, is composed of a heart-rending series of dialogues that depict the terror of the Chilean families of *los desaparecidos* ("The Disappeared Ones" who were taken from their homes and presumed killed) under the military dictatorship of the Pinochet *junta.* And Raymond Carver's masterful *A New Path to the Waterfall* has a double dramatic impact as it tracks the shadow-depths of a speaker and author who is dying of cancer.

Interactive

This structure relies more on an interactive, run-of-the-book process, in which contiguous and far-flung poems comment back and forth on each other, sometimes sequentially, sometimes leap-frogging ahead or falling back out of sequence, rather than employing a more obvious external form of organization. My volume *Blindsided* is composed of repeating cycles of poems that are, by turns, lyrical, satirical, dramatic, comedically slapstick, and meditative. The organizing principle for the book came from its title, and the intended effect is to keep the reader constantly off-guard. Tess Gallagher's profoundly moving *Moon Crossing Bridge* is a book of interreflecting poems grieving the loss of her husband, Ray Carver. The poems, tightly focused yet various in imagery and tropes, effectively build off each other.

Rubric

This type of organizational structure depends upon an overarching umbrella term, whether it is in the form of an allusion, a topic, a place, a time, etc. Kate Daniels' book, *The Niobe Poems,* uses the Greek myth of Niobe as the framework for a series of feminist-oriented poems that stretch from Niobe herself to Rosa Parks of civil rights fame. More of a catch-all container, but still well focused, is Albert Goldbarth's volume *Popular Culture,* which takes up serious themes through the milieu of cartoon characters, superheroes, and 1950s period sets, like the Joke Store and vaudeville-strip stage. Robert Hass' *Human Wishes* directly and indirectly takes up the subject of the many and varied forms of human desire and what they lead to. One might also consider Chaucer's *The Canterbury Tales* to be a rubric form since, aside from its thin narrative frame of the pilgrimage, it is basically a collection of tales.

POETRY REFERENCES

The following is a listing of a few respected and established sources for information on the whereabouts and specialties of poets, publishing and job opportunities, and creative writing institutions.

The Associated Writing Programs: Tall House, Mail Stop 1E3, George Mason University, Fairfax, VA 22030, e-mail: awp@gmu.edu

The Writer's Chronicle: bimonthly issues containing essays on craft and teaching, listings of grants, awards, fellowships, and publishing opportunities

The AWP Joblist: semiannual listing of poetry and writing-related university and private positions

The Official Guide to Writing Programs: lists about 300 undergraduate B.A., graduate M.F.A., and Ph.D. requirements and faculty for programs in creative writing, conferences, residencies, and festivals

Poets & Writers, Inc.: 72 Spring Street, New York, NY 10012, e-mail: www.pw.org

A Directory of American Poets and Fiction Writers: annual; addresses of over 7,000 poets, writers, agents, and sponsors of readings and workshops

Poets & Writers Magazine: bimonthly; contains articles on craft and career, listings of current resources, needs, contests, awards, and job opportunities, 200,000 readers

Dustbooks publishes several sourcebooks on literary markets and contacts for writers and writing programs. P.O. Box 100, Paradise, CA 95967, e-mail: dustbooks@dcsi.ne

International Directory of Little Magazine and Small Presses: annual; contains over 5,000 detailed entries of magazine and book publishers

Directory of Poetry Publishers: annual; lists more than 2,000 publishers of poetry

Glossary

actual time Time as it is normally measured outside the illusion of literary, *felt time.*

additive revision A form of revision in which material is added to previous draft.

aesthetic distance (a.k.a. "physical" or "psychic distance") The degree of objectivity, or lack thereof, that a work, speaker, or author maintains toward subject matter or audience.

aesthetics An artistic ordering of ideas, or concept, as to how form relates to beauty.

aesthetic surface A poem's "texture" composed of a combination of imagery, rhythm, sonics, rhetorical tactics and form.

agroikos A classic, stock comic character whose innocence, inexperience, and ineptitude cause him to blunder about (e.g., Lou Costello of Abbott and Costello; Jerry Lewis of Martin and Lewis).

alazon A classic, stock comic character of the braggart type (e.g., Jackie Gleason as Ralph in *The Honeymooners,* Homer Simpson of *The Simpsons*).

alliteration The repetition of proximate consonants, vowels and/or syllables in a line; usually the term is used for beginning letters of words.

amplification See elaboration.

anagogical writing Writing that contains multiple levels of meaning (literal, metaphorical, spiritual, etc.).

anaphora The repetition of the same word, phrase, or clause at the beginning of lines.

anchor Grounding an abstract reference to a concrete image or circumstance.

angle The camera angle or physical position from which something is being viewed.

apperception The process in which the mind observes and tracks its own thoughts.

arbitrary image An image or trope that does work only for a local, limited purpose; as opposed to a *functional image* that contributes meaning throughout a work.

associational logic An intuitive form of reasoning based upon the similarities, dissimilarities, parallels, figurative characteristics, or proximity in time or space between one thing and another.

associational structure Organization of a poem based upon *associational logic.*

assonance The repetition of similar vowels of words in close proximity.

autologue The self talking to itself, as opposed to the *monologue* which is meant to be overheard by another.

automatic writing A process of spontaneous, unpremeditated writing meant to tap into the unconscious level of thought.

bird's-eye view A perspective or camera angle taken from above.

breath units The length of a line, as determined by what poet Allen Ginsberg termed a "mind-breath." Typically it is one-and-a-half to two normal line lengths.

caesura A rhythmic or metrical pause in a line in initial, medial, or terminal position.

catachretic metaphor A strained or logically wrenched metaphor.
centrifugal thematic shape The outward-directed development of a poem from its central thesis.
centripetal-centrifugal thematic shape The simultaneously inward- and outward-directed development of a poem from and to its central thesis.
centripetal thematic shape The inward-directed development of a poem toward its central thesis.
characterization The representation of real or fictional characters via physical, psychological, attitudinal, or anecdotal description.
circular closure The *closure* of a poem that ends back where the poem began.
circular thematic shape The circular shape of a poem's thematic development.
classic syndrome An action or event that is a cultural, moral, or social norm.
closed couplet Two lines linked by end-rhyme.
close-up shot A camera angle or physical perspective that is close to its subject.
closure The conclusion of a poem.
clustering A five-part grouping of qualities and images derived from associating a thing through taste, touch, hearing, smell, and sight.
collage The overall design of a work whose materials are from widely disparate sources.
commentary An editorial or authorial reflection upon the narrative, descriptive, argumentative, lyric, or dramatic surface of the poem.
committing word A word or phrase that triggers a line of associative images or thoughts.
conceit An elaborated trope that forms a parallel understanding to another point of reference.
concision The principle and practice of succinctness in modern poetics.
conclusive statement A statement that sums up a condition, situation, narrative, argument, or feeling and gives a sense of final meaning to the poem.
connotation The associations of a word that are beyond its lexical, denotative meaning.
consonance Repetition of consonants in words of close proximity without regard to the vowels they may contain.
contrast cut A cinematic editing technique that employs a segue from one image, scene, or character to something of an opposite nature.
controlling gesture A gesture that acts as a symbol or trope of some kind and that directs and unifies the development of the poem.
controlling image An image that directs and unifies the content of a poem and that may have been its catalyst.
controlling metaphor A metaphor that acts as the contextual frame of reference for the rest of the poem.
conversational mode Informal style of writing that is modeled upon the rhythm, topical give-and-take, and segues of conversation.
conversational phrasing Phrasing that mimics or evokes the flavor and informal intimacy of conversation.
correlatives Any device in a poem that acts as a parallel instance to another action, trope, or reference.

correspondences Elements that echo or in some way correspond to other elements in a poem.
couplet Two unrhymed lines that form a stanza, or two rhymed lines in any size stanza.
crosscut The depiction of two simultaneous scenes, actions, or images with little or no transition between them.
cut A cinematic editing term for a change in scene, action, references, or imagery.
cut-and-shuffle poem A structure that sequentially alternates two or more scenes or actions.
cutting-to-continuity The efficient editing of a series of action shots that create the illusion of continuous motion in real time.

Dada A World War I precursor to Surrealism that based its poetics on chance operations, absurdity, and chaos.
deductive-inductive thematic shape An argumentative hourglass shape that begins with the general, develops toward the particular, and then opens up again to end with the general.
deductive thematic shape An argumentative or narrative shape that begins with the general and narrows toward the particular.
deep focus shot A cinematic term for a physical perspective in which foreground, middleground, and background can all be seen in focus.
Deep Image A school of poetry that employed images and tropes with multiple dimensions and levels of consciousness (archetypal, cultural, personal, spiritual, etc.).
definition poem A poem written in the form of a dictionary definition.
diction The arrangements and level of language style (informal, formal) or word choice in a poem.
digressions As a device, content that leads away from the thematic focus, logic, plot, or thrust of a poem in order to arrive at a new understanding.
digressive mode As a device, content that leads away from the thematic focus, logic, plot, or thrust of a poem in order to arrive at a new understanding.
dinggedicht A German school of poetics that sought to create and imbue objects with a numinous sense of life.
discovery mode A method of organic composition in which content and form arise without preset ideas.
double entendre Words or phrasing that have two or more levels of meaning.
dramatic irony Meanings that the speaker or characters in a poem are not aware of.
dramatic lyric A form of soliloquy in the lyric genre in which a speaker or character reveals his nature, situation, and feelings to a silent listener.
dramatic monologue A form of soliloquy in which a speaker or character reveals his nature, situation, or feelings to a silent listener.
dramatic situation A situation in which forces of tension and conflict are present in an explicit or implied manner.

Eastern ending A type of closure that is subtle and implied.
elaboration A form of detailing that extends or embellishes.

emblem A complex of images that symbolize qualities or characteristics of its subject.
end-rhyme Rhyme that appears at the end of lines in a poem (as opposed to internal rhyme).
end-stopped line A line ending whose syntax stops at the end of the line.
enjambment A line ending whose syntax carries over to the next line.
epiphany A moment of revelation or insight in a poem.
episodic structure The structuring of a poem according to individual scenes, action sequences, or anecdotes.
erotic poem A poem, usually a lyric love poem, that focuses on the sensual and sexual aspects of the human body.
establishing shot A cinematic term for a long-range point of view.
exposition An explanation that defines, explains a process, or shows how the parts are related to one another and other things.
exquisite corpse (*Cadavre Exquis*) A French Surrealist poetry game, in which a group "poem" is fashioned by each participant blindly filling in a prescribed grammatical unit or sentence.
extended metaphor A poem created from the content and parameters of an established metaphor.
extension The extending of a detail, trope, action, or characteristic.

fable An allegorical story in which animals represent human qualities.
felt-thought Synchronic combination of fused thought and feeling.
felt time The illusion of real time passing in a work of art.
fevered enjambment Enjambed lines ending with incomplete syntactical units (also called *rhetorical stress*).
figurative The connotative, as opposed to the denotative, level of meaning.
figure of speech Words or phrases that depart from their normal usage, syntax, semantics, effects, or associations and aspire toward metaphor in order to arrive at a new form of expression.
figure of thought An explicit or implicit idea, often in the form of a symbol, that acts as a controlling presence in the poem.
fill-in-the-blanks poem A poetic structure whose content is developed from and created by an opening image, action, situation, or definition.
fixed form Any traditional type of regularly rhymed and metered form of poetry.
fixed form ghosting Semi-free verse that is based upon the influence of a fixed form.
fixed image A specific, as opposed to a general or abstractly evoked, image.
flashback A cinematic term for presenting scenes, actions, or characters from the past.
flashforward A cinematic term for presenting scenes, actions, or characters in the future.
flat statement A non-figurative, abstract, and unadorned statement.
flow The overall pacing and development of a poem.
folktale A narrative celebrating an event, character, or system of values or behavior among a homogeneous culture.
form dissolve A cinematic editing technique that uses the physical qualities of one object to segue to another object with similar charactersitics.

found poem A poem made from or perceived in what are not normally poetic materials.

fractured narrative A structure composed of juxtaposed actions, plot elements, and characters that are not related in linear, chronological order.

free image An image that is evocative and general, rather than specific or fixed.

free verse Poetry freed from the conventions (rhyme, meter, and formal rules) of externally controlled fixed forms.

free verse analogue The explicit or implicit form of communication upon which a poem is based.

free verse fixed image A specific, as opposed to a general or abstractly evoked, image.

functional image An image whose meaning contributes not only to its local context but also to other aspects of the poem.

genre A main category of a type of literary writing.

gestalt A psychological term indicating an intuitive, holistic, overall sense of something.

ghost form A fixed form exerting a controlling formal presence behind a poem.

haiku A Japanese lyric form composed of three lines totaling 17 syllables: 5, 7 5, respectively.

heroic couplet A two-lined, rhymed verse in iambic pentameter.

homolochos A classic, stock physical-comedy character of the buffoon type (e.g., roles that Chevy Chase, Buster Keaton, Woody Allen play).

horizontal content Content of a poem that extends, widens, or elaborates upon non-thematic material.

hyper-figure A controlling thought, gesture, action, or trope that helps direct the development of a poem, usually from a conscious level of awareness.

hypo-figure A controlling thought, gesture, action, or trope that helps direct the development of a poem, usually from an unconscious level of awareness.

hypotaxis Transitional words or phrases that connect and often show a change in the direction of a thought, argument, narrative, or description.

idée fixe An obsessive image or *leitmotif.*

identity An equivalency; one of the main functions of a metaphor.

image narrative The thematic "story," by way of composed visual tensions, that the seminal images in a poem tell.

imagery Any image, sensation, or apprehension of one of the five senses.

imitation The exercise of modeling a poem based upon a previous poem.

immediacy A quality of aliveness, presence, and freshness.

incremental line units Lines built and arranged upon individual units of thought, sense, figure, image, or plot.

inductive-deductive thematic shape A diamond-shaped argument that begins with the particular, develops toward the general, and then narrows again to end with the particular.

inductive thematic shape An argumentative shape that begins with the particular and develops toward the general.
in medias res A dramatic term for a work that begins in the middle of things.
inscape The interior landscape of an experience.
instress The forces of tension and pressure inherent in any experience.
irony Generally, a trope that says one thing but intends another.

jump cut A cinematic term describing the splicing together of linear narrative events so the sequence has the illusion of the way the actual event would occur.
juxtaposition The placing of one thing next to another without an express transition or connection.

laddering The step-by-step ascent or descent of imagery from the concrete to the abstract or vice versa.
lateral move The sideways development of content (via description, narration, argument, elaboration of tropes, or characterization), as opposed to vertical thematic development.
leap The jump from one level of consciousness to another (via image or trope or logic) without any intervening transition or commentary.
leaping poetry Poetry that relies upon the associative and unconscious logical operations with no explicit transitions.
leitmotif A recurring image, phrase, statement, trope, or theme in a work.
letter poem A poem that uses the form of a letter, usually to an intimate or friend.
light verse Forms of poetry, often in metrics and rhyme, that are witty, playful, and entertaining.
limited point of view The limited perspective of a speaker or character who does not know all that is occurring in the situation and in the minds of the characters around him or her.
lineation The composition, length, type of lines, and line breaks used in a poem.
line break The word with which a line ends.
list poem A poem whose content is composed of a list of attributes, characteristics, actions, or qualities of its subject.
litany A series of repetitive lines, often beginning with the same phrasing.
location The perspective of consciousness or mental stance a poet assumes in the initial stages of a work.
logic of the metaphor Hart Crane's term for the logic of the associative mode of thinking.
logopoetics Ezra Pound's term for the poem's "dance of ideas"; that is, all the logical relationships among parts of a poem.
low-angle shot A cinematic term for a camera angle that looks upward toward a scene or image.

Magical Realism A South American school of literature that transforms and telescopes the literal and real into the fantastical.
masked pronoun A pronoun ostensibly referring to one person's point of view when in reality it refers to another's.

meditative moment A place in a poem where the speaker or character muses on the implication of what has been or will be.

melopoetics Ezra Pound's term for the category of effects that sound and rhythm make in a poem.

memory narrative A poem whose subject is something from the memory of its speaker.

metaphor A trope that works directly through a comparison of similarities, dissimilarities, substitution, or identity.

metaphorical dissolve A cinematic term for an editing technique whereby the metaphorical meaning of one image is segued into a different image with similar meaning.

metonymy A trope of division in which a part associated with something is named for the whole.

mixed message A poem that unintentionally communicates ambivalent, contradictory, or confusing ideas.

mnenomic Devices, techniques, and forms employed in a poem to facilitate memorization.

Modernism A movement of the first half of the twentieth century that called for reliance upon distillation, compression, and the image.

monologue A form of discourse in which a single speaker's speech is overheard.

monostich A one-line stanza.

montage A pattern whereby disparate but associated images, scenes, or actions are composed into a unified whole.

moves The equivalent in poetry to tactical moves employed in chess or sports.

moving image An image that is processed so that it moves, as opposed to being static.

moving shot A cinematic term for a camera view taken moving toward or away from a scene.

myth A supernatural narrative that seeks to pass on explanations of natural phenomena or a culture's origins, values, or beliefs.

narrative A non-dramatic form that tells a story.

narrative summary Summation of a plot.

narrator agent Any poetic device that substitutes for and acts on behalf of what would normally be a narrator's commentary. Highly selected images and tropes often perform this function.

natural thematic shapes Shapes that occur naturally in nature.

negative capability John Keats' term for the ability of the poet to remain in "uncertainties" while composing.

New Criticism A modern mid-twentieth-century school of poetics that proposed close reading of the text alone as a source for critical interpretation and a systematic and balanced architecture upon which a poem should be built.

nuance Subtle touches of detailing, description, gesture, dialogue, etc., that shade and deepen meaning.

objective correlative A literal image, action, setting, or other device that contains figurative levels of meaning.

object poem A poem that focuses upon an object for its subject and theme.

occasional poem Poems written for a specific occasion, person, or event.

off-rhyme Nearly full harmonic values in the sound of consonants and vowels.

omniscient point of view A perspective from which virtually anything can be known about a character, situation, or event.

open field composition Robert Duncan's term for a method of composition in the associative mode that allows anything germane into its field of consideration.

organic composition Composition that is derived from and relies upon the inner forces and impulses of an experience.

organic metaphor (a.k.a. ***functional metaphor***) A metaphor that is created from and contributes back to the context of a poem (as opposed to an arbitrary metaphor that has merely a local effect).

organizing principle A principle of order that directs and arranges how a poem assumes its development and form.

pacing The speed and flow of rhythms and lines in a poem.

packing the poem Salting a poem with imagery, sonics, rhetoric, syntax, plot points, and meditative moments that all correspond to one another in some way.

pan A cinematic term for a camera angle that sweeps across a scene or image.

parable A short story whose allegorical content parallels certain values or beliefs the author is trying to get across.

paradox A logical phrasing of balance and tension that contains ideas that are simultaneously equal and opposite.

paraphrase A concise summary statement that captures the essence of a poem's message and theme.

parataxis (a.k.a. ***juxtaposition***) The placing of one thing against another without transition, comment, or connectives.

parsing Refers to lines composed of full syntactical units.

pathetic fallacy A poetic form of logic and a metaphorical device that so closely connects how we feel to something outside of us that it seems to mirror our feelings.

perfect rhyme (a.k.a. ***full rhyme***) The repetition of stressed vowels and their subsequent consonants.

persona The speaker of a poem other than one recognized as the poet.

persona poem Technically, a poem spoken in the voice of an animal or inanimate object, although the term has come to be popularly used to denote the voice of another human speaker (properly termed "mask").

personification A poetic device by which human traits are displayed by inanimate or abstract entities.

phanopetics Ezra Pound's term for visual aspect of poetry.

plot The actions or events of a narrative.

plot point One of a series of dramatic junctures in a plot.

poetic fallacy Refers to the associative logic of poetic devices.

poetics Various forms of the theory, aesthetics, and criticism of poetry.

poetization The adaptation of a non-poetic text into a poetic form.

point of view The physical, mental, or personal perspective of a speaker or character in a work.

political poem A poem whose theme has political meaning.

Postmodern Post-World War II neonarrative, self-referential movement that generally relaxed the strictures of Modernism.

processed image An image that is changed into something different from what it was (as opposed to a static image).

process poem A poem whose subject is instruction on how to make something.

proposition poem A poem whose rhetorical frame relies on the stating of a proposition.

prose poem A poem containing poetic devices, but with no line endings.

prosody The principles and conventions of the logical, musical, structural, and figurative devices of poetry.

pun A witty play on the sound or form of a word that is similar to another word.

quatrain A four-line stanza or poem, usually rhymed.

range A cinematic term referring to the camera distance from which a shot is taken.

real time The equivalency between the literary time it takes to report an event and the time it actually takes for an event to occur.

recombinant syntax The process of reordering, fusing, or separating elements in a poem so that a new order of meaning is achieved.

reductive revision A major form of the revision process that subtracts material from previous drafts.

reflexive line ending A line ending that refers back to previous content in that line.

refrain A phrase or line(s) repeated at intervals in a poem.

repetend A variation of the *refrain,* in which a phrase or line is partially repeated.

resonance The quality of richness and reverberation, through repetition and variation, of meaning in a poem.

restraint A rhetorical and tonal form of understatement that employs implication and subtlety.

retake A scene or event that is repeated in a variety of ways from various perspectives.

rhetoric Any form of persuasive speech or effective wording that organizes an argument or set of ideas.

rhetorical emphasis The reliance on a preponderance of devices of persuasive speech.

rhetorical question The posing of a question not meant to be answered but meant to make a point or create an effect.

rhetorical stress A line ending that stresses the meaning of a word in an incomplete syntactical unit, or, metrically, stresses a normally unstressed syllable.

rhyme scheme The pattern of end-rhymes of a poem.

riff An improvisational takeoff on a word, phrase, or image, resulting in a series of associations.

rite of initiation poem A poem that portrays one's honorific or harrowing joining of a new group or order of experience.

rite of passage poem A type of poem whose subject is that of passing through a major life experience.

scooter technique Lines following an image or phrase composed of a series of telescoping, appositional variations on the original line.

sectioning A poem that is divided into sections by numbers, letters, or symbols such as asterisks.

segue The transition from one thing to another.

selected detail A specific image, gesture, or action especially chosen for its telling or figurative implications.

selective perception The experiencing of an event through an already established subjective, emotional, or intellectual stance.

semantics The levels of meaning or study of the origins of words.

semantic springboard A word or phrase whose meaning triggers new content in a poem.

sense units Words that stem from sensations from any of the five senses and are the basic units of measurement for a line.

sensory line units The use of imagery (taste, touch, smell, hearing, or sight) to form the basic unit of measurement for a line.

sentence sounds The intellectual, emotional, and musical import of the syntax and inflections—not the words—of a sentence.

sentencing The types and qualities of flow of sentences in a poem.

sequence A cinematic term for a series of shots or images cohering in some logical order.

sestina A fixed form composed of six stanzas of six unrhymed lines.

simile A poetic device that indirectly compares the characteristics of one thing with those of another.

simultaneity The literary illusion of two or more events occurring at once.

slant imagery Images that visually rhyme with each other.

slant rhyme A form of rhyming that uses approximate musical harmonies of assonance and consonance.

sonics The aspect and quality of sound and sound systems employed in a poem.

sonnet A 14-line lyrical fixed form, in iambic pentameter, characteristically using one of several specific rhyme schemes and expressing a single theme or emotion. The two basic types of sonnets are the Petrachan or Italian (14 lines divided into an octave rhyming abbaabba and a sestet rhyming cdecde, cdcdcd, or cdedce), and the Shakespearean or English (three quatrains rhyming ababcdcdefef and a concluding closed couplet (gg).

sound dissolve An aural segue or transition that juxtaposes sounds of equal or very similar values.

sound system A musically coherent set of words with harmonic consonant and vowel values.

speakerless poem A poem that does not contain a mediating personality or character who filters experience through his or her perspective.

specificity The particularity and detailing of an image or trope.

sprung rhythm Gerard Manley Hopkins' term for a unit of rhythm that measures only the accented syllables in a line.

squinting William Stafford's term for the aesthetic double-seeing of the literal and figurative in an image, phrase, or event.

stanza A discrete unit of lines in a poem.

sticchic (a.k.a. block poem) A poem composed of lines without stanza breaks.

stock response The predictable and common reaction a reader has to what and how something is being said.

straight cut A cinematic term for the selective cutting of sequential action to form a coherent flow.

strategy The overall plan or major device employed in moving a poem from its opening to its *closure.*

stream of consciousness The unbroken recording of images, ideas, and action from the unconscious level of thought.

strophic A poem composed of stanzas.

substitute image An image that stands as a substitute for an implied, predictable image the reader can easily surmise.

substitution One of the equivalency operations of metaphor; a form of syncopation in meter; also the replacement of a predictable image, action, characteristic, or plot element with another.

Surrealism A revolutionary, early twentieth-century movement that sought to displace traditional realism with a change in consciousness brought about by dreamlike, odd juxtapositions, changes in the context and size of things, and the use of automatic writing, poetry games, and the absurd.

syllogism A formulaic type of logic that adds a major premise to a minor premise in order to arrive at its conclusion.

symbol A poetic device in which a literal image or a phrase stands as a sign that takes its meaning and order of ideas from its surrounding context.

Symbolist A nineteenth-century French movement that reacted against Realism by using concrete phenomena as symbols to represent unconscious, primordial ideas.

synchronicity Narrative points of view that offer two simultaneous events or versions of an event.

syncopation A rhythmic pattern that substitutes unaccented syllables for accented ones, and vice versa.

synecdoche A trope of division in which a part of something stands for the whole of it.

synesthesia The transformation of one physical sensation or perception into another of the body's senses.

syntax The conventional ordering and arrangement of words in a sentence.

tactics Small technical maneuvers or "moves" within the larger strategy of a poem.

telescoped metaphor A metaphor that leads directly into a series of other metaphors.

tension The action of the cohesive forces that unify a work of art and that result from contrasting or contrary elements, such as meter against propositional sense, rhythm against counter-rhythm (*see* syncopation), diction against action, abstract statement against concrete image, general against specific, what is said against what is meant (*see* irony), and appearance against reality.

tercet A three-line stanza having external rhyme, usually aaa, bbb, etc.

texture The surface effects of rhythm. sound, imagery, and rhetoric in a poem.

thematic montage A pattern of ideas and images that contribute to building the theme.

thematic shape The argumentative or narrative, logical shape and structure of a work.

theme The main idea(s) of a poem; what it is about.

thought line units The use of a thought as a basic unit of measurement for a line.
time frame The frame of time (past, present, future) in which an event in a poem takes place.
tone The speaker's or writer's attitude toward his or her subject or audience.
tone color The emotional *texture* of a poem created by its *sonics*.
transformational line ending A type of line ending in which the last word or phrase in a line changes its meaning in the context of the subsequent line.
transition The movement from one subject, image, action, or thought to another.
transparent lyric A poem in which there is no discernible character-as-speaker, just the experience interfacing with the reader.
triggering town A setting that acts as a metaphor or symbol for another dimension of reference.
triggering word A word, image, or scene that catalyzes and generates the succeeding content of the poem.
triplet An unrhymed stanza of three lines.
trope Language whose interpretation goes beyond the literal to the figurative.

verbal gesture Loose, lazy, vague, and generalized phrasing.
vertical content The content of a poem that contributes to creating theme.
villanelle A French fixed form consisting of 19 lines of five 3-line stanzas and a closing quatrain with two rhymes and two refrain lines.
virgule A symbol in prosody (/ and //) used to mark metrical feet, a line break, midline pause (/), or new stanza (//).
voice The quality of character in a speaker's speech.
voiceless poem *See* transparent lyric.

Western ending General term for poetic closure that has the quality of a dramatic finality to it.
white space The space between stanzas or section of a poem.
writer's block A psychological block to creativity.

Index

Credits

Betty Adcock
"Word-Game" by Betty Adcock. Reprinted by permission of Louisiana State University Press from *Walking Out,* by Betty Adcock. Copyright © 1975 by Betty Adcock.

W. H. Auden
"Musee des Beaux Arts" copyright 1940 and renewed 1968 by W. H. Auden, from *W. H. Auden: The Collected Poems* by W. H. Auden. Used by permission of Random House, Inc.

Jimmy Santiago Baca
"I Am Here" by Jimmy Santiago Baca from *Black Mesa Poems* copyright © 1989 by Jimmy Santiago Baca. Reprinted by permission of New Directions Publishing Corp.

Amiri Baraka
"A Poem for Black Hearts" from *Selected Poetry* by Amiri Baraka. Reprinted by permission of Sterling Lord Literistic, Inc. Copyright © 1979 by Amiri Baraka.

Coleman Barks
"The Reed Flute" and "Some souls flow like clear water. . ." by Jelaluddin Rumi from *The Hand of Poetry.* Copyright © Coleman Barks. Reprinted by permission.

Robin Behn
"Station" by Robin Behn. Reprinted by permission of the author.

Marvin Bell
Excerpt from the poem "Against Stuff," from the book *Drawn by Stones, by Earth, by Things that Have Been in the Fires,* Atheneum Publishers, copyright © 1984 by Marvin Bell; and excerpt from the essay "The Technique of Re-reading," from the book *A Marvin Bell Reader: Selected Poetry and Prose,* Middlebury College Press/ University Press of New England, copyright © 1994 by Marvin Bell. Reprinted by permission of Marvin Bell.

Robert Bly
"Snowbanks North of the House" from *The Man in the Black Coat Turns* by Robert Bly, copyright © 1981 by Robert Bly. Used by permission of Doubleday, a division of Random House, Inc.

Bertolt Brecht
"Buddha" from *Poems: 1913–1956* by Bertolt Brecht, translated by Michael Hamburger, John Willett & Ralph Manheim. Reprinted by permission of Methuen Publishing Limited and Suhrkamp Verlag.

John Brehm
"When My Car Broke Down" by John Brehm from *Poetry,* August 1997. "When My Car Broke Down" by John Brehm first appeared in *Poetry* and subsequently in the book *The Way Water Moves* (Flume Press, 2002) by John Brehm Reprinted by permission of The Modern Poetry Association and John Brehm.

William Bronk
"Against Biography" by William Bronk from *Life Supports.* Reprinted by permission of The Trustees of Columbia University.

Michael Dennis Browne
Reprinted from *Selected Poems 1965–1995*, "Paranoia" by Michael Dennis Browne by permission of Carnegie Mellon University Press. Copyright © 1997 Michael Dennis Browne.

Charles Bukowski
"Space Creatures" and "No Charge" from *Burning in Water, Drowning in Flame: Selected Poems 1955–1973* by Charles Bukowski. Copyright © 1963, 1964, 1965, 1966, 1967, 1968, 1974 by Charles Bukowski. Reprinted by permission of HarperCollins Publishers Inc.

Lorna Dee Cervantes
"Colorado Blvd." by Lorna Dee Cervantes is reprinted with permission from the publisher of *From the Cables of Genocide: Poems on Love and Hunger* (Houston: Arte Publico Press—University of Houston, 1991).

Brian Clements
"Who You Are" by Brian Clements from *Essays against Ruin.* Reprinted courtesy of Texas Review Press.

David Clewell
"We Never Close" from *Blessings in Disguise* by David Clewell, copyright © 1991 by David Clewell. Used by permission of Viking Penguin, a division of Penguin Putnam Inc.

Don Colburn
"In the Workshop After I Read My Poem Aloud" by Don Colburn. First published in *The Iowa Review,* Vol. 19, No. 2, Spring–Summer 1989. Reprinted by permission of the author.

Gregory Corso
"Poets Hitchhiking on the Highway" by Gregory Corso from *The Happy Birthday of Death* copyright © 1960 by New Directions Publishing Corp. Reprinted by permission of New Directions Publishing Corp.

Mark Cox
"In His Suit," "The Word" and "Donald" from *Smoulder* by Mark Cox. Reprinted by permission of David R. Godine, Publisher, Inc. Copyright © 1989 by Mark Cox.

Robert Creeley
"For My Mother: Genevieve Jules Creeley" by Robert Creeley from *Collected Poems 1945–1975.* Reprinted by permission of University of California Press. Essay on "For My Mother. . ." from *45 Contemporary Poems* by Robert Creeley. Reprinted by permission of the author.

Victor Hernandez Cruz
Victor Hernandez Cruz, "dot" from *By Lingual Wholes* (San Francisco: Momo's Press, 1982). Copyright © 1982 by Victor Hernandez Cruz. Reprinted with permission of the author.

Philip Dacey
"Skating" from *The Man with Red Suspenders* (Minneapolis, Milkweed Editions, 1986). Copyright © 1986 by Philip Dacey. Reprinted with permission from Milkweed Editions. Reprinted from *How I Escaped from the Labyrinth and Other Poems,* "The Birthday" and "Form Rejection Letter" by Philip Dacey by permission of Carnegie Mellon University Press. Copyright © 1977 by Philip Dacey.

Kate Daniels
"Bathing" by Kate Daniels from *The Niobe Poems.* Reprinted by permission of the University of Pittsburgh Press.

Michael Decker
"The Tour Guide" by Michael Decker. Reprinted by permission of the author.

Robert Desnos
"The Day It Was Night" by Robert Desnos from *Corps et Biens,* translated by John F. Nimis. Reprinted by permission of Editions Gallimard.

Emily Dickinson
"I Heard a Fly Buzz—When I Died" reprinted by permission of the publishers and the Trustees of Amherst College from *The Poems of Emily Dickinson,* Thomas H. Johnson, ed., Cambridge, Mass.: The Belknap Press of Harvard University Press, Copyright © 1951, 1955, 1979 by the President and Fellows of Harvard College.

Stephen Dobyns
"Tomatoes" copyright © 1986 by Stephen Dobyns, from *Cemetery Nights* by Stephen Dobyns. Used by permission of Viking Penguin, a division of Penguin Putnam Inc.

Mark Doty
"The Pink Palace" from *Turtle Swan* by Mark Doty. Reprinted by permission of David R. Godine, Publisher, Inc. Copyright © 1987 by Mark Doty.

Rita Dove
"Elevator Man" © 1988 by Rita Dove. Originally published in *The Black Scholar.* Reprinted by permission of the author.

Jack Driscoll
"Memories of My Deaf Mother" from *Fishing the Backwash* by Jack Driscoll. Reprinted by permission of the author.

Alan Dugan
"On a Seven-Day Diary" and "Love Song: I and Thou" from *Collected Poems* by Alan Dugan. Reprinted by permission of Seven Stories Press.

Robert Duncan
"Food for Fire, Food for Thought" by Robert Duncan from *The Opening of the Field* copyright © 1960 by Robert Duncan. Reprinted by permission of New Directions Publishing Corp. Reprinted from *Full of Lust and Good Usage,* "The Routine Things Around the House" and "The Dark Angel Travels With Us to Canada and Blesses Our Vacation" by Stephen Dunn by permission of Carnegie Mellon University Press. Copyright © 1976 by Stephen Dunn.

Russell Edson
"The Nostril Affair" by Russell Edson from *The Clam Theatre.* Reprinted by permission of Wesleyan University Press.

Lynn Emanuel
"In praise of Malice" by Lynn Emanuel from *The Practice of Poetry.* Copyright © 1992. Reprinted by permission of the author. "The Politics of Narrative—Why I Am A Poet" from *Then, Suddenly—,* by Lynn Emanuel, © 1999. Reprinted by permission of the University of Pittsburgh Press.

John Engman
"Mushroom Clouds" from *Keeping Still, Mountain* by John Engman. Reprinted by permission of Galileo Press.

D. J. Enright
"The Typewriter Revolution" by D. J. Enright from *Daughters of the Earth.* Rerpinted by permission of Open Court Publishing Company, a division of Carus Publishing Company, Peru, IL.

Constantine FitzGibbon
From *The Life of Dylan Thomas* by Constantine FitzGibbon. Copyright © 1965 by Constantine FitzGibbon. By permission of Little, Brown and Company (Inc.).

Maya Flamm
"display" by Maya Flamm. Reprinted by permission of the author.

Robert Francis
"Yes, What?" and "Silent Poem" by Robert Francis from *Like Ghosts of Eagles.* Reprinted by permission of University of Massachusetts Press.

Robert Frost
Excerpt from letter dated February 22, 1914 from Robert Frost to John T. Barlett from *Selected Letters of Robert Frost* edited by Lawrance Thompson, © 1964 by Lawrance Thompson. Reprinted by permission of Henry Holt and Company, LLC. "Stopping by Woods on a Snowy Evening" by Robert Frost from *The Poetry of Robert Frost* edited by Edward Connery Lathem, © 1923, 1969 by Henry Holt and Co., © 1951 by Robert Frost. Reprinted by permission of Henry Holt and Company, LLC.

Tess Gallagher
"Black Silk," "The Hug," and excerpt from "Each Bird Walking" by Tess Gallagher. Copyright © 1987 by Tess Gallagher. Reprinted from *Amplitude: New and Selected Poems* with the permission of Graywolf Press, Saint Paul, Minnesota. "Now That I Am Never Alone" by Tess Gallagher. Copyright © 1992 by Tess Gallagher. Reprinted from *Moon Crossing Bridge* with the permission of Graywolf Press, Saint Paul, Minnesota.

George Gibian
"Symphony #2" from *The Man with the Black Coat: Russia's Literature of the Absurd* by Daniil Kharms. Copyright © 1987 by George Gibian. Translation by George Gibian. Reprinted by permission of the Estate of George Gibian. All rights reserved.

Gary Gildner
"First Practice" by Gary Gildner from *First Practice.* Reprinted by permission of University of Pittsburgh Press.

Beckian Fritz Goldberg
From "Monsoon" and "The Possibilities" by Beckian Fritz Goldberg from *In the Badlands of Desire,* Cleveland State University Poetry Center, 1993. Reprinted by permission.

Barry Goldensohn
"Post Morten as Angels" from *The Maranno* by Barry Goldensohn. Reprinted by permission of the author.

Linda Gregg
"What They Ate What They Wore" and excerpt from "The Copperhead" by Linda Gregg. Copyright © 2002 by Linda Gregg. Reprinted from *Too Bright to See* and *Alma* with the permission of Graywolf Press, Saint Paul, Minnesota.

Kimiko Hahn
"When You Leave" by Kimiko Hahn from *Columbia: A Magazine of Poetry and Prose,* Issue #3. Reprinted by permission of the author.

Donald Hall
"Ox Cart Man" from *Old and New Poems* by Donald Hall. Copyright © 1990 by Donald Hall. Reprinted by permission of Houghton Mifflin Co. All rights reserved.

Mark Halliday
"Seventh Avenue" by Mark Halliday from *Tasker Street.* Reprinted by permission of University of Massachusetts Press. "Reality USA" from *Little Star* by Mark Halliday. Copyright © 1987 by Mark Halliday. Reprinted by permission of HarperCollins Publishers Inc.

William Hathaway
"Oh, Oh" from *Looking Into the Heart of Light* by William Hathaway. Reprinted by permission of Cincinnati Poetry Review.

Samual Hazo
"Silence Spoken Here" from *Silence Spoken Here.* Evanston: Northwestern University Press, 1988, pp. 3–4. Reprinted by permission.

Seamus Heaney
"An Artis" from *Opened Ground: Selected Poems 1966–1996* by Seamus Heaney. Copyright © 1998 by Seamus Heaney. Reprinted by permission of Farrar, Straus and Giroux, LLC.

Bob Hicok
"Prodigal" by Bob Hicok from *The Legend of Light.* Winner of the 1995 Felix Pollak Prize in Poetry. © 1995. Reprinted by permission of The University of Wisconsin Press.

Tony Hoagland
"One Season" by Tony Hoagland from *Sweet Ruin.* Winner of the 1992 Brittingham prize in poetry. © 1992. Reprinted by permission of The University of Wisconsin Press.

Jonathan Holden
Reprinted from *Style and Authenticity in Postmodern Poetry* by Jonathan Holden, by permission of the University of Missouri Press. Copyright © 1986 by the Curators of the University of Missouri.

Lynda Hull
"Shore Leave" and "Love Song During Riot With Many Voices" by Lynda Hull from *Star Ledge.* Reprinted by permission of the University of Iowa Press.

Allison Hunter
"Trophy" by Allison Hunter. Reprinted by permission of the author.

Cynthia Huntington
Excerpt from "Breaking" by Cynthia Huntington from *We Have Gone to the Beach.* Copyright © 1996 by Cynthia Huntington. Reprinted with the permission of Alice James Books.

Richard Jackson
From "The Image Narrative" by Richard Jackson (lecture given at Vermont College). Reprinted by permission of Richard Jackson. From "A Violation" by Richard Jackson from *Alive All Day,* Cleveland State University Poetry Center, 1992. Reprinted by permission.

Donald Justice
"Anniversaries" by Donald Justice from *The Summer Anniversaries.* Reprinted by permission of Wesleyan University Press.

Richard Katrovas
"A Dog and A Boy" from *Snug Harbor* by Richard Katrovas. Reprinted by permission of Wesleyan University Press.

Yusef Komunyakaa
"Temples of Smoke" by Yusef Komunyakaa from *Neon Vernacular.* Reprinted by permission of Wesleyan University Press.

Michael Lally
"Things to Do Around Newark" from *Rocky Dies Yellow* by Michael Lally. Reprinted by permission of the author.

Philip Larkin
"Poetry of Departures" by Philip Larkin is reprinted from *The Less Deceived* by permission of The Marvell Press, England and Australia.

Robert Lax
"Novel" by Robert Lax from *Retort.* Reprinted by permission of Robert Lax Papers, Rare Book and Manuscript Library, Columbia University.

David Lehman
"Fear" and "Perfidia" from *Operation Memory* by David Lehman. Reprinted with the permission of Writers' Representatives Inc.

Philip Levine
"Animals are Passing from Our Lives" and "To A Child Trapped in a Barber Shop" by Philip Levine from *Not This Pig*. Reprinted by permission of Wesleyan University Press.

Larry Levis
"The Poet at Seventeen" by Larry Levis from *The Selected Poems.* Reprinted by permission of University of Pittsburgh Press. "Winter Stars" by Larry Levis from *Winter Stars.* Reprinted by permission of University of Pittsburgh Press.

Robert Long
"Saying One Thing," "Time and its Double," "Chelsea," and "Have a Nice Day" from *What Happens* by Robert Long. Reprinted by permission of Galileo Press.

Adrian Louis
"The First of the Month" by Adrian Louis from *Fire Water World.* Reprinted by permission of West End Press.

Thomas Lux
"The Midnight Tennis Match" by Thomas Lux from *Memory's Handgrenade*. Reprinted by permission of the author.

Heather McHugh
"Inflation" and "Earthmoving Malediction" by Heather McHugh from *Shades.* Reprinted by permission of Wesleyan University Press.

Stephen McNally
"Mysteries" by Stephen McNally from *Child in Amber.* Reprinted by permission of University of Massachusetts Press.

Morton Marcus
"Tuba" and "The Moment for Which There Is No Name" by Morton Marcus from *Origins.* Reprinted with permission of the author and Story Line Press (www.storylinepress.com).

Thomas Merton
"There Has to Be a Jail for Ladies" by Thomas Merton from *The Collected Poems of Thomas Merton,* copyright © 1963 by The Abbey of Gethsemani, Inc. Reprinted by permission of New Directions Publishing Corp.

W.S. Merwin
"The Lice," "The Room," and "Fly" by W.S. Merwin from *The Second Four Books of Poems.* Copyright © 1993 by W.S. Merwin. Rerpinted by permission of The Wylie Agency, Inc.

Robert Mezey
"White Blossoms" and "My Mother" by Robert Mezey from *The Collected Poems.* Reprinted by permission of the University of Arkansas Press. Copyright © 2000 by Robert Mezey.

Stanley Moss
"The Lace Makers" by Stanley Moss from *Asleep in the Garden.* Reprinted by permission of Seven Stories Press.

Jack Myers
"Something Important" by Jack Myers from *Oneonone.* Copyright © Jack Myers, reprinted by permission of the author and Autumn House Press.

Catherine Minor-Neuhardt
"My Favorite Maple" by Catherine Minor-Neuhardt. Reprinted by permission of the author.

Naomi Shihab Nye
"With the Greeks" and "Rain" from *Words under the Words: Selected Poems* by Naomi Shihab Nye. Reprinted by permission of the author. "Ropes" from *Yellow Glove* by Naomi Shihab Nye. Reprinted by permission of the author.

William Olsen
"Tomorrow" by William Olsen from *The Hand of God and a Few Bright Flowers.* Reprinted by permission of the author.

Frankie Paino
"The Truth" by Frankie Paino from *Out of Eden,* Cleveland State University Poetry Center, 1997. Reprinted by permission.

Kenneth Patchen
"O My Love the Pretty Towns" by Kenneth Patchen from *The Collected Poems of Kenneth Patchen* copyright © 1942 by New Directions Publishing Corp. Reprinted by permission of New Directions Publishing Corp.

Cesare Pavese
"Summer" from *Hard Labor* by Cesare Pavese, translated by William Arrowsmith, copyright © 1976 by William Arrowsmith. *Lavorare Staca* Copyright 1943 by Giulio Einaudi editore, Torino. Used by permission of Viking Penguin, a division of Penguin Putnam Inc.

Felix Pollack
"The Dream" by Felix Pollack from *Subject to Change.* Reprinted by permission.

Mary Anne Redmond
"Thematic Shapes from Nature" by Mary Anne Redmond. Reprinted by permission of Mary Anne Redmond, author of the *Spirit of Abundance Daily Reminders.*

Alberto Rios
"Madre Sofia," "The Inquietude of a Particular Matter," and "In the Woman Arms of the Ground" by Alberto Rios. Copyright © 1985 by Alberto Rios. First published in *Five Indiscretions* (Sheep Meadow Press). Reprinted by permission of the author.

David Rivard
Excerpt from "Earth to Tell of the Beasts" by David Rivard. Copyright © 1996 by David Rivard. Reprinted from *Wise Poison* with the permission of Graywolf Press, Saint Paul, Minnesota.

Pattiann Rogers
"The Hummingbird: A Seduction" by Pattiann Rogers from *The Tattooed Lady in the Garden.* Reprinted by permission of Wesleyan University Press.

Michael Ryan
"TV Room at the Children's Hospice" from *God Hunger* by Michael Ryan, copyright © 1989 by Michael Ryan. Used by permission of Viking Penguin, a division of Penguin Putnam Inc.

Sherod Santos
"The Evening Light Along the Sound" from *Accidental Weather* by Sherod Santos. Used by permission of Doubleday, a division of Random House, Inc.

Philip Schultz
"A Letter Found on a January Night in Front of the Public Theatre" from *Deep Within the Ravine* by Philip Schultz, copyright © 1984 by Philip Schultz. Used by permission of Viking Penguin, a division of Penguin Putnam Inc.

Tim Seibles
"Trying for Fire" by Tim Seibles from *Hurdy Gurdy,* Cleveland State University Poetry Center, 1992. Reprinted by permission.

Anne Sexton
Excerpt from "And One For My Dame" from *Live or Die* by Anne Sexton. Copyright © 1966 by Anne Sexton. Reprinted by permission of Houghton Mifflin Company. All rights reserved.

Charles Simic
"True History" and "Tragic Architecture" from *Hotel Insomnia,* copyright © 1992 by Charles Simic, reprinted by permission of Harcourt, Inc.

Jim Simmerman
"Moon Go Away, I Don't Love You No More" from *Moon Go Away, I Don't Love You No More* by Jim Simmerman (Miam University Press). Copyright © 1994 by Jim Simmerman. Used by permission of the author.

Louis Simpson
"The Ice Cube Maker," "The Beaded Pear," and "American Classic" from *Caviar at the Funer* by Louis Simpson. Copyright © 1980. Reprinted by permission of Louis Simpson. "American Poetry" from *At the End of the Open Road* by Louis Simpson. Copyright © 1963. Reprinted by permission of Louis Simpson.

John Skoyles
A list of questions from teaching handout by John Skoyles. Reprinted by permission. Reprinted from *A Little Faith,* "Burlesque," "Conviction," "Once or Twice," and "No Thank You" by John Skoyles by permission of Carnegie Mellon University Press. Copyright © 1981 by John Skoyles.

Dave Smith
"In the House of the Judge" by Dave Smith. Reprinted by permission of Louisiana State University Press from *The Wick of Memory: New and Selected Poems 1970–2000* by Dave Smith. Copyright © 2000 by Dave Smith.

Holly Smith
"Traffic" by Holly Smith. Reprinted by permission of the author.

Gary Snyder
"Hitch Haiku" by Gary Snyder from *The Back Country* copyright © 1968 by Gary Snyder. Reprinted by permission of New Directions Publishing Corp.

Marcia Southwick
Reprinted from *Why the River Disappears,* "The Rain's Marriage" by Marcia Southwick by permission of Carnegie Mellon University Press. Copyright © 1990 by Marcia Southwick.

Mark Spencer
"Detenshun" by Mark Spencer. Reprinted by permission of the author.

William Stafford
"The Animal That Drank Up Sound" and "Passing Remark" by William Stafford. Copyright © 1966, 1998 by the Estate of William Stafford. Reprinted from *The Way It Is: New & Selected Poems* with the permission of Graywolf Press, Saint Paul, Minnesota.

Maura Stanton
"The Conjurer" by Maura Stanton from *Snow on Snow.* Reprinted by permission of Yale University Press. From "The Grocery Store" by Maura Stanton in *Tales of the Supernatural.* Reprinted by permission of David R. Godine, Publisher, Inc.

Gerald Stern
Excerpt from "I Remember Galileo" and "The Angel Poem" from *The Red Coal.* Copyright © 1981 by Gerald Stern. Reprinted by permission of Houghton Mifflin Co. All rights reserved. "What It Is Like" from *This Time: New and Selected Poems* by Gerald Stern. Copyright © 1998 by Gerald Stern. Used by permission of W. W. Norton & Company, Inc.

Ruth Stone
From "Turn Your Eyes Away" and "Curtains" by Ruth Cohen from *New American Poets of the '90s.* Reprinted by permission of David R. Godine, Publisher, Inc.

James Tate
"Deaf Girl Playing" by James Tate from *James Tate: Selected Poems.* Reprinted by permission of Wesleyan University Press.

Thea Temple
"Modern Love" by Thea Temple from *Yellow Silk: Journal of Erotic Arts.* Reprinted by permission.

Dylan Thomas
"After the Funeral" by Dylan Thomas, from *The Poems of Dylan Thomas,* copyright 1938 by New Directions Publishing Corp. Reprinted by permission of New Directions Publishing Corp.

Leslie Ullman
"Desire" by Leslie Ullman from *Slow Work through Sand.* Reprinted by permission of the University of Iowa Press.

Jean Valentine
"The Second Dream" by Jean Valentine from *The Dream Barker.* Reprinted by permission of Yale University Press.

Belle Waring
"Baby Random" by Belle Waring from *Refuge.* Reprinted by permission of University of Pittsburgh Press.

Michael Waters
Quotation from an essay by Michael Waters from *The Practice of Poetry: Writing Exercises from Poets Who Teach,* edited by Robin Behn and Chase Twichell. Copyright © 1992 by Robin Behn and Chase Twichell. Reprinted by permission of HarperCollins Publishers Inc.

Bruce Weigl
"A Romance" by Bruce Weigle from *A Romance.* Reprinted by permission of University of Pittsburgh Press. "The Black Hose" by Bruce Weigl from *Archaeology of the Circle.* Copyright © 1992 by Bruce Weigl. Used by permission of Grove/Atlantic, Inc. "The Confusion of Planes We Must Wander in Sleep" by Bruce Weigl from *New American Poets of the '90s.* Edited by Jack Myers and Roger Weingarten. Reprinted by permission of David R. Godine, Publisher, Inc. Copyright © 1991 Edited by Jack Myers and Roger Weingarten.

Roger Weingarten
"From the Temple of Longing" from *Infant Bonds of Joy* by Roger Weingarten. Reprinted by permission of David R. Godine, Publisher, Inc. Copyright © 1990 by Roger Weingarten. From "Jungle Gliders" in *Ghost Wrestling* by Roger Weingarten. Reprinted by permission of David R. Godine, Publisher, Inc.

James L. White
Excerpt from "Naming" by James L. White. Copyright © 1982 by the Estate of James L. White. Reprinted form *The Salt Ecstasies* with the permission of Graywolf Press, Saint Paul, Minnesota.

William Carlos Williams
"A Negro Woman" by William Carlos Williams, from *Collected Poems 1939: 1962, Volume II,* copyright 1944, 1948 by William Carlos Williams. Reprinted by permission of New Directions Publishing Corp.

David Wojahn
"White lanterns" by David Wojahn from *Late Empire.* Reprinted by permission of University of Pittsburgh Press.

Charles Wright
"Yellow" and "Nightdream" from *Hard Freigh* by Charles Wright. Reprinted by permission of Wesleyan University Press.

Franz Wright
Franz Wright, "Certain Tall Buildings" from *Ill Lit: New and Selected Poems,* Oberlin College. Copyright © 1998 by Oberlin College. Reprinted by permission of Oberlin College Press.

James Wright
"Lying in a Hammock at William Duffy's Farm in Pine Island, Minnesota" by James Wright from *Above the River.* Reprinted by permission of Wesleyan University Press.

Dean Young
"Lace" from *Design with X* by Dean Young. Reprinted by permission of Wesleyan University Press.